THE CHARITABLE
NONPROFITS

William G. Bowen
Thomas I. Nygren
Sarah E. Turner
Elizabeth A. Duffy

THE CHARITABLE NONPROFITS

An Analysis of Institutional
Dynamics and Characteristics

Jossey-Bass Publishers • San Francisco

Substantial discounts on bulk quantities of Jossey-Bass books
are available to corporations, professional associations, and other
organizations. For details and discount information, contact the
special sales department at Jossey-Bass Inc., Publishers.
(415)433-1740; Fax (415)433-0499.

For international orders, please contact your local Paramount Publishing
International office.

Manufactured in the United States of America. Nearly all Jossey-Bass
books and jackets are printed on recycled paper that contains at least
50 percent recycled waste, including 10 percent postconsumer waste.
Many of our materials are also printed with vegetable-based inks;
during the printing process these inks emit fewer volatile organic
compounds (VOCs) than petroleum-based inks. VOCs contribute to
the formation of smog.

Library of Congress Cataloging-in-Publication Data

The charitable nonprofits : an analysis of institutional dynamics and
   characteristics / William G. Bowen . . . [et al.]. — 1st ed.
      p.   cm. — (The Jossey-Bass nonprofit sector series)
   Includes bibliographical references and index.
   ISBN 0-7879-0024-9.
   1. Charities—United States. 2. Nonprofit organizations—United
States. I. Bowen, William G. II. Series.
HV91.C454 1994
361.7'63'0973—dc20   94–21301
                                                 CIP

FIRST EDITION
HB Printing   10 9 8 7 6 5 4 3 2 1   *Code 94105*

The Jossey-Bass
Nonprofit Sector Series

CONTENTS

**Part Three: Institutional Characteristics:
Comparisons of Selected Fields**

Appendixes

FIGURES AND TABLES

Figures

Tables

PREFACE

B y any measure (and any definition), the nonprofit sector is of great importance in the United States. As the Prologue indicates, the existence of a large, influential set of nonprofit institutions has been one of the distinguishing features of our society from its beginnings. No other country in the world has anything comparable to it in the present day. Ironically, one of the surest signs of the current status of the nonprofit sector is that it now attracts the same kind of public scrutiny that is given to business and government. It is judged secure enough, and consequential enough, to warrant critical appraisal.

Still, the universe of nonprofits remains a puzzling domain, and not just to the ordinary citizen. Press accounts often fail to distinguish among different types of entities ("charitable" nonprofits versus "mutual benefit" nonprofits, for example). Also, while much more scholarly attention is now being given to this sector, it is far from a mature field of study. The herculean efforts of some scholars and some research centers notwithstanding,[1] there has been relatively little sustained empirical analysis of phenomena as basic as trends in rates of institutional formation and differences in funding patterns among types of nonprofits.

The Charitable Nonprofits is an effort to fill part of this gap. While it does not purport to be either comprehensive or definitive, it is intended to provide one kind of frame for the nonprofit field. We are persuaded that *institutions* matter greatly in this sector—even more than they do in the business sector—and that conviction is our point of departure. We seek to frame the nonprofit landscape by examining what might be called its institutional demographics: the number of existing entities and their distribution by field and geographic region; trends in organizational births and deaths; the ages and sizes of organizations. We also analyze characteristic revenue profiles of different sets of institutions, rates of increase in expenditures, and trends in funding patterns.

The institutional demographics of the nonprofit sector is a surprisingly complex territory, and the learning curve is a long one, with few steep trajectories along the way. At least, that has been our experience. We would like to help others ascend this learning curve faster, and this book is meant to be one kind of primer.[2] More specifically, it is intended to serve those interested in doing research in the field and those interested in reviewing, assessing, and using research results obtained by others. Our intent is to identify key issues, raise questions, and suggest hypotheses and ways of testing them. There is much important work of this kind to be done, and we hope to encourage others to dig deeper in areas of special interest to them.

The Importance of an Institutional Perspective

There is much to be said for aggregating data and studying broad trends in employment, expenditures, and services provided in the nonprofit sector. Fruitful comparisons can be made with corresponding trends in business and government. The changing interactions and interdependencies among the sectors can be examined and described. This type of work is no substitute, however, for detailed study of the sets of institutions that generate the aggregative data. In the nonprofit sector, in particular, the sizes and shapes of institutional populations make a great difference. An institutional perspective is especially important in studying the nonprofit sector for one principal reason: external, market-driven forces play a *relatively* weaker role in determining outcomes. Thus, there is more "room" for institutionally driven factors to operate.[3]

The best-known for-profit companies operate in public markets, and ownership interests in them are continually bought and sold. Share prices are quoted constantly, and movements in market valuations represent more or less instantaneous votes of confidence (or of no confidence) in corporate actions or inactions. Moreover, large-scale transactions, perhaps involving the purchase or sale of a subsidiary and sometimes even an entire entity, can occur quite suddenly in response to changed circumstances or new opportunities. Thus, for-profit organizations may have their futures altered dramatically by external buyers or sellers, as observers of corporate mergers will attest. More generally and less dramatically, capital markets are constantly regulating the behavior of for-profit companies.

We emphasize the word *relatively* in describing the weaker role played by external forces in the nonprofit world because we certainly do not want to suggest that any nonprofit entities are free of either incentives or constraints (often tough ones) imposed by the realities of what are, in effect, their own markets. These markets contain pools of potential volunteers, donors, and consumers and purchasers of services; nonprofit entities of every stripe compete vigorously, and sometimes even voraciously, for their allegiance. Performing arts organizations need to sell tickets, service providers must find clients, and nonprofit entities of all kinds have to recruit volunteers and, year after year, persuade potential donors of their virtues. Life in many parts of the nonprofit world is demanding and difficult for those with oversight responsibilities—often more demanding and difficult, for managers at least, than life in many parts of the for-profit world, conventional images and assumptions notwithstanding.

In this book, we pay considerable attention to the effects of external, market-driven forces on nonprofits, precisely because they are so consequential. Shifts in the demand by the public for classes of goods and services (such as education) affect the fortunes of nonprofit entities quite directly. Trends in the rate of institutional formation in a field are affected by changes in the tax code, in the inclinations of governmental entities to contract with nonprofit entities for the provision of services, and in the behavior of financial markets, among other variables.

Nonetheless, managements and boards of nonprofit entities generally retain more degrees of freedom from external forces than do their counterparts in the for-profit world. This is true, first, because nonprofit entities can choose among a wider variety of objectives, and can assign a wider variety of weights to different objectives, than can for-profit entities, which are presumed to have earnings and profits always in mind. In the nonprofit world, outputs and outcomes are more difficult to measure, and constituencies are more difficult to define. There is no single measure of success, or even of progress, that is analogous to the proverbial "bottom line" for a business.

There is another key difference. Fundamental choices can be made by nonprofit institutions without anyone worrying that these decisions may be subject to abrupt reversal by market forces—or, for that matter, by outside forces of any kind. After all, nonprofit entities are not routinely for sale, and mergers and closings tend to occur only when nonprofit institutions are in deep trouble. While some watchdog entities exist (such as the National Charities Information Bureau), there is, in many situations, no body of watchful critics. Moreover, there are few publicly available indicators for critics to watch, even if there were observers inclined to look for them.

A worrisome corollary is that at least some nonprofits may lead lives which are simultaneously undistinguished and largely unnoticed. As the recent experience of the United Way illustrates so well, outrages generate bad publicity.[4] In general, however, it is fair to say that nonprofits as a group are far less closely monitored externally than are for-profit organizations. Nonprofits have no owners ready to sell their stock or to complain loudly about performance, and there are only rather poor substitutes for them. The Internal Revenue Service (IRS) devotes far less time to scrutinizing the returns of nonprofits than to examining the returns of profit-making entities, for the simple reason that there is so little tax revenue to be claimed. *In extremis*, the attorney general of the state in which the nonprofit entity operates (or is chartered), or the courts in that state, will become involved—but only *in extremis*. These representatives of the public interest are, ultimately, the owners in the nonprofit world of the underlying assets, but they exercise a far different degree of oversight than do owners and their surrogates in the for-profit world.

Since they lack most of the mechanisms for radical transformation that markets represent, some nonprofits may well survive too long. The questions of when—and how—to transform, or even to dissolve, a nonprofit entity are of great significance as issues of public policy, but they attract attention only when some combination of the press and political interests alerts the general public to the travails of an organization such as the New-York Historical Society. Generally speaking, by the time this kind of alert has been sounded, a number of perhaps promising options will have been closed off altogether or made much more expensive. More thought needs to be given, in our view, to ways of achieving "death with dignity" when it is appropriate.

For these and other reasons, we are strongly in favor of efforts now being made at research centers, business schools, and schools of public affairs to improve management practices and institutional performance in the nonprofit sector. Program officers at foundations are confronted regularly with situations in which nonprofit entities are in serious difficulty, and it is clearly important to understand better how such problems arise and how they can be addressed at earlier stages in the life cycles of organizations. It is equally clear that much better external benchmarks are needed to calibrate the condition of a particular organization operating in a particular field. Have its expenditures been rising more or less rapidly than expenditures of similarly situated entities? Is it more or less dependent on earned income than comparable organizations are? Is it managing its financial resources as effectively as others are managing theirs? Are its fundraising efforts effective (or ineffective)?

In an effort to address such issues, The Andrew W. Mellon Foundation has been supporting research and carrying out studies on its own, focused on such specific questions as the extent to which the nonprofit sector has been commercialized, the roles played by state attorneys general and courts in overseeing the activities of nonprofits, ways of improving the presentation of financial data, and the relationships among portfolio management, spending rules, and strategic planning.

Scope and Organization of This Book

The Charitable Nonprofits is much less focused on individual institutions than the above comments might imply. It is intended to provide a broad context and framework within which more particularistic studies can be placed. It is also intended to serve as one kind of guide to national data, and especially to the IRS files, which can be of invaluable assistance in studying both broad sectors and specific groups of organizations.

We should also note that we have been far from evenhanded in discussing various parts of the nonprofit universe. As the title of the book indicates, and as we explain in Chapter One, we focus on the so-called charitable nonprofits, as contrasted with mutual benefit associations and other kinds of entities which do not fall under section 501(c)(3) of the tax code. In certain parts of our work, we also emphasize those types of charitable nonprofits which are most familiar to us. In particular, we pay attention to organizations in the broad fields of the arts and culture (including performing arts entities, museums, and historical societies) and education (including colleges and universities).

One consequence of this emphasis is that we say less about governmental sources of support for nonprofits than would be appropriate if we had chosen to focus on, for example, nonprofits providing social services, many of which depend heavily on governmental agencies for funding. Conversely, we pay relatively more attention to the role of the private sector—to individual contributions, investment income, and grants from corporations and foundations—because these sources of revenue are especially significant in the sectors which we emphasize. We also concentrate most heavily on the circumstances of the larger and better-established organizations, in part because they can be studied over longer periods of time and often have better records. There are a great many small organizations in the nonprofit sector, and they deserve more attention than we have been able to give them in this book.

The organization of the book is straightforward. It begins with a Prologue (by Kellum Smith), which provides a general historical perspective on the nonprofit sector. The body of the study is then divided into three relatively distinct parts: The Nonprofit Sector Today, Institutional Dynamics: Patterns of Births and Deaths, and Institutional Characteristics: Comparisons of Selected Fields. The content of each part is explained most readily by describing the various chapters.

- Chapter One lays the foundation for Part One (and the rest of the book) by providing a road map through the nonprofit sector. Its purpose is to help readers understand the often confusing definitions and terminology that are found in the nonprofit world (such as the distinction between "charitable" and "noncharitable" nonprofits and the difference between public charities and private foundations). The chapter also describes the broad dimensions of the nonprofit sector.
- Chapter Two describes the universe of charitable nonprofits as it existed in the fall of 1991. We discuss the size distribution of grantmaking foun-

dations, the numbers of public charities in major fields (arts/culture, education, health, and so on), the size range of institutions in many of these fields, and, finally, the geographic distribution of both private foundations and public charities.

- Chapter Three begins Part Two (the discussion of trends in institutional births and deaths) by exploring the overall dynamics of the sector. We define a proxy for institutional births and then chart the establishment of new entities since the mid-1960s. We distinguish public charities from private foundations and examine, in particular, the differing effects of tax-reform legislation on their respective rates of institutional formation.
- Chapter Four extends this discussion by comparing rates of institutional formation within twelve selected fields, ranging from arts/culture to employment. We contrast entry rates in the last fifteen years with entry rates during the late 1960s and early 1970s and distinguish "old enthusiasms" from "new enthusiasms."
- Chapter Five contains a more detailed discussion of trends in the creation of new entities within three sectors: higher education, civil rights, and performing arts. This chapter includes discussions of waves of institutional formation in higher education, the effects of specialization on institutional formation in the civil rights sector, and the variety of patterns of institutional formation found within the performing arts.
- Chapter Six complements the discussion of trends in entrants by analyzing—really for the first time, we believe—exit rates among varied types of charitable nonprofits. We find that there are systematic differences in the probability of institutional demise across fields, and that these differences may be related to the costs of closing, among other factors.
- Chapter Seven begins Part Three of the book. After outlining the conceptual framework that underlies this final part, we analyze the relationship between field of activity and institutional size, emphasizing the importance of fixed costs.
- Chapter Eight focuses on differences in revenue profiles. The relative importance of earned income is seen to depend fundamentally on the nature of the product offered by various types of nonprofits. In this chapter we also consider the diversification of revenue sources.
- Chapter Nine is concerned with the complex interrelationships between the age of an organization and its size, its field of activity, and its access to various sources of revenue, particularly investment income.
- Chapter Ten presents newly collected data for thirty-two arts and culture organizations. These data, which extend over two decades, allow us to examine changes over time in the major relationships identified in Chapters Seven, Eight, and Nine.
- The Conclusion summarizes major findings and suggests areas for future research.
- The Appendixes contain technical commentary on sources of data and

methods, as well as tables of detailed data, which we believe will be of interest to other students of the nonprofit sector.

Old and New Raw Material

To achieve our purposes, we have both reworked raw material already available, sometimes extensively, and developed new materials of our own. To illustrate, the road map through the nonprofit sector presented in Chapter One is basically a description of concepts and a reorganization of data familiar to students of the nonprofit sector. It also contains one new element of importance: the results of a test-case analysis, which convince us that many of the smaller organizations in the IRS files no longer exist, and therefore that the population of the nonprofit sector may be *much* smaller than presumed.

The analysis of trends in institutional births, or entrants, is based on an extensive reworking of basic IRS files. The analysis of rates of institutional demise (exits), on the other hand, required a rather elaborate coding by our staff of the organizations listed in the inactive portion of the IRS's Business Master File, a resource of potentially great value which is rarely used.

The effort made in Part Three to understand relationships among institutional characteristics (field, age, size, revenue profiles) draws on both old and new materials. For the cross-sectional part of the analysis, we used standard IRS data, including the financial information for special samples of institutions assembled by the Statistics of Income Division of the IRS. In order to gain even a rudimentary understanding of trends, on the other hand, we had to build an entirely new data set by obtaining and laboriously reviewing audited financial statements provided by individual organizations.

Acknowledgments

Any empirical study of this kind and scope requires many hands, and the four of us listed as the authors realize full well that we are, as it were, but the visible tip of a large iceberg.

Among the many organizations and individuals who played key roles in this study, we want to mention particularly:

- The Internal Revenue Service, and especially Theodore Bozovich, senior exempt organizations program analyst; his associate, Robert Gardiner; and Cecelia Hilgert and Margaret Riley of the Statistics of Income Division. Mr. Bozovich and his colleagues were invaluable guides to the Business Master File and were unfailing sources of good advice and encouragement.
- The National Center for Charitable Statistics at Independent Sector; its director, Virginia Hodgkinson; and Stephen Noga, associate director of research. As many others will attest, Virginia Hodgkinson deserves spe-

cial recognition for her leadership over many years in stimulating work on the nonprofit sector.

- The Foundation Center; its president, Sara Engelhardt; and its vice president for research, Loren Renz, who answered many questions about private foundations and helped us make full use of the data assembled with such care by the center.

The Andrew W. Mellon Foundation has supported this study, and we are especially grateful for the steady encouragement of the trustees—who bear no responsibility, however, for the methods of analysis chosen or the conclusions reached. The chairman, John C. Whitehead, has been a particularly strong advocate of research and education intended to strengthen performance in the nonprofit sector. Our colleagues on the staff of the foundation have helped in innumerable ways:

- Kellum Smith, now senior adviser to the foundation, wrote the Prologue and contributed valuable insights while simultaneously attempting to improve our use of language.
- Kamla Motihar, the foundation's librarian, demonstrated yet again that she can find anything, more or less instantly.
- Martha Sullivan took special responsibility for the preparation of the figures, a daunting task which she performed admirably.
- Jed Bergman and Kevin Guthrie, while working hard on their own studies of the nonprofit sector, were always ready to exchange ideas, answer technical questions, and insist that they could create better graphs.
- Rachel Bellow and Elizabeth Breyer made major contributions to our understanding of the performing arts and assisted in both the collection and interpretation of data for these fields.
- Alice Emerson waged unceasing war on our inappropriate choices of metaphors.
- Joan Gilbert, research coordinator in the foundation's Princeton office, did her best to control the flow of paper and to resist our tendencies toward disorganization.
- T. Dennis Sullivan, financial vice president, and Harriet Zuckerman, vice president, provided encouragement, support, and useful comment throughout.
- Dorothy Westgate and Ulrica Konvalin, along with other members of the support staff, helped in countless indirect ways.
- Brenna Smith, a Princeton undergraduate who worked for us part-time, extracted data from the financial reports of organizations and prepared tables and graphs.
- Jackson Lee, an undergraduate at the City University of New York who also worked part-time, tracked down small performing arts organizations in New York in an effort to determine if they exist and, if so, what they are doing.

- Nick DiFonzo, a graduate student at Temple University who worked as a consultant, was responsible for coding organizations in the inactive file and assisting with other computer tabulations.

We were also fortunate to find a publisher, Jossey-Bass, and an editor, Alan Shrader, who identified strongly with what we were trying to accomplish and who were eager to assist us in every possible way.

Joint authors sometimes end prefaces by identifying their separate contributions. This is impossible in the present instance because of the thoroughgoing nature of our collaboration. We can note, however, that one of us, Sarah Turner, who has been a keen contributor of analytical propositions from the very start of the project, has now gone on to doctoral study in economics at the University of Michigan. Another of our group, Elizabeth Duffy, joined us later but has more than made up for her tardiness by doing much of the late-stage writing and editing. The remaining authors, William Bowen and Thomas Nygren, have been involved throughout and have fewer excuses than their colleagues do for any errors of omission or commission that have remained undetected.

August 1994

William G. Bowen
Princeton, New Jersey

Thomas I. Nygren
Princeton, New Jersey

Sarah E. Turner
Ann Arbor, Michigan

Elizabeth A. Duffy
New York, New York

Notes

1. Today there are almost forty nonprofit academic centers in the United States, involving over two hundred full- and part-time faculty members (Crowder and Hodgkinson, 1993). This number represents an exponential increase from 1988, when Independent Sector first started tracking programs. There are also ninety-two journals published in the United States, devoted in whole or in part to the field.

2. A more basic primer, intended primarily for public officials, is Lester M. Salamon's *America's Nonprofit Sector: A Primer* (1992). Salamon's primer is a most useful compilation of definitions, data, and interpretive comment.

3. The ideas presented in this section are developed at greater length in a recent book which examines principles and practices of governance by boards in both the nonprofit and for-profit sectors (see Bowen, 1994, especially Chapter One).

4. Appendix B of Bowen (1994) gives a capsule summary of the United Way case.

THE AUTHORS

WILLIAM G. BOWEN is president of The Andrew W. Mellon Foundation and president emeritus of Princeton University, where he was also professor of economics from 1965 to 1988. He is the author of numerous books and articles, most recently *Inside the Boardroom: Governance by Directors and Trustees* (1994) and (with Neil Rudenstine) *In Pursuit of the PhD* (1992). Mr. Bowen earned his undergraduate degree at Denison University and his Ph.D. in economics at Princeton. He has been actively involved with many kinds of nonprofit organizations throughout his career, having served on the boards of the Center for Advanced Study in the Behavioral Sciences, Denison University, the Public Broadcast Laboratory of National Educational Television, the Sloan Foundation, the Smithsonian Institution, and the Wallace–Reader's Digest Funds.

THOMAS I. NYGREN is a research associate at The Andrew W. Mellon Foundation, where he is now at work on a study of waves of institutional formation and adaptation in higher education. He has coauthored an article on the NTEE Classification System, with William G. Bowen and Sarah E. Turner (*Voluntas* 4[1]). Mr. Nygren graduated with distinction from Stanford University, where he majored in political science. After serving as an administrator for Mercy Corps International in Pakistan from 1987 to 1989, he earned a master's degree from the Woodrow Wilson School of Public and International Affairs at Princeton University.

SARAH E. TURNER is studying for a doctorate in economics at the University of Michigan. After graduating from Princeton University magna cum laude in economics, she worked in the research division of J. P. Morgan and then on the research staff of the Mellon Foundation. She has coauthored several articles on the nonprofit sector and higher education, including "The Flight from the Arts and Sciences: Trends in Degrees Conferred". (*Science*, October 1990).

ELIZABETH A. DUFFY is on the research and program staff of The Andrew W. Mellon Foundation, where she concentrates on liberal arts colleges. Ms. Duffy earned master's degrees from the Graduate School of Business and the School of Education at Stanford University. Earlier, she graduated magna cum laude from Princeton University, having majored in molecular biology, and then served as administrator of the Student Volunteers Council at Princeton from 1988 to 1991.

PROLOGUE

J. Kellum Smith, Jr.

A book analyzing the contemporary condition of organized charitable activity in the United States deserves to be introduced by an outline, at least, of the history of such activity.[1] At the individual, family, and village levels, charity is presumably as old as mankind, representing simply the impulse to assist the less fortunate. Organized charity, however, has less remote origins, largely because until the nineteenth century there were few entities other than the church to receive and administer funds given for charitable purposes. Living as we do in an institutional age, we can easily forget that the nonprofit corporation and the formally established unincorporated association are latecomers in human affairs. Through most of history there have been few "institutions" other than the sovereign state, agencies created by and responsible to the state, feudal lords, guilds, municipalities, and the established church. Much of what we would now consider charity was in earlier days provided by the sovereign or by feudal lords, in recognition of a customary obligation. Poverty and even starvation have been so pervasive until recent times that the exercise of sovereignty has characteristically entailed large responsibilities for "alimentation" of the poor.

If the United States today is said by some to be a welfare state, consider the case of ancient Rome. Most of the population of that great city in the classical period ate at the public trough. The clamorous plebs demanded and were given a weekly grain ration, and a succession of emperors considered it their duty to supply "bread and circuses" for the sake of peace in the streets. They did so by using the spoils of foreign conquest, or by taxing any class of citizens able to pay and suitably compliant. Nor did the sense that the sovereign was obliged to feed his people die with the Roman Empire—although sovereigns usually found ways to meet that responsibility indirectly, or to shed it entirely. The history of Europe during and after the Middle Ages is replete with "poor laws" and other arrangements under which exactions from landholders and municipalities were codified and responsibilities for the care of the poor assigned.

The role of the Church in this process, both before and after the Reformation, can hardly be exaggerated. In most periods, the Church has been able to persuade the sovereign that its activities are intrinsically charitable; indeed, the literature of the Church used to be where charity chiefly found its definition. St. Thomas Aquinas classified the spiritual acts of charity as to counsel, to sustain, to teach, to console, to save, to pardon, and to pray; the corporal acts of charity as to clothe, to give drink to, to feed, to free from prison, to shelter, to assist in sickness, and to bury. It is notable that what we now call education and medical care are on Thomas's list. Perhaps it should also be pointed out that "to free from prison" did not mean to accomplish the prisoner's escape. It meant to obtain his release by meeting, on his behalf, whatever unmet obligations had brought about his confinement.

Because the Church was so obvious a beneficiary of charitable gifts and bequests—the making of which might be supposed to better the donor's chances in the afterlife—it received large volumes of them, in both money and land. Operating its landholdings (especially those of its Benedictine and Cistercian orders) with an efficiency unprecedented at the time, it became rich and powerful. Ultimately, the Church was accused of using its charitable benefactions less for their intended purposes than for its own aggrandizement, and most of its landholdings were expropriated by temporal sovereigns. It remained, however, and is today (although today there is no single established church in most nations) a favored beneficiary of charitable gifts and a major executant of charitable activity.

An important later definition of charitable activity appears in the 1601 Statute of Charitable Uses, enacted during the reign of Queen Elizabeth I in an effort to rationalize and improve not only provision for the poor of the realm but the public good more generally. That statute enumerates as objects of charitable activity relief of the poor; maintenance of sick and maimed soldiers and mariners, poor chiefly by reason of war; schools of learning, free schools, and scholars in universities; repair of bridges, ports, havens, causeways, churches, seabanks, and highways; preferment of orphans; relief, stock, or maintenance of houses of correction; marriages of poor maids; assistance to young tradesmen, handicraftsmen, and persons decayed; relief or redemption of prisoners or captives; and aid to the poor in meeting their property-tax obligations.

This law and subsequent parliamentary enactments of the seventeenth and eighteenth centuries validated charitable gifts and bequests in general, provided for their administration by individual trustees or by eleemosynary corporations, including endowed hospitals and colleges, assigned oversight of trustees and eleemosynary corporations to the Court of Chancery and a charity commission, conferred upon charitable institutions exemption from certain forms of taxation, and established the doctrine of *cy pres* (as near as possible), under which the purpose of a charitable gift or bequest could be formally altered if the original purpose became impracticable or the recipient institution ceased to function.

Charity in the American colonies operated, of course, under English law. After independence, it operated under the laws of the several states, which addressed themselves to it in various ways but generally in conformity with English principle and practice (although some state legislatures, wishing to limit tax exemption, and perhaps suspicious of the motives of charitable organizations, passed laws making the Statute of Charitable Uses inapplicable within their jurisdictions).

Many uncertainties had to be resolved under the new constitution. The Dartmouth College case of 1819 reached the Supreme Court on appeal from the highest court of New Hampshire, which had upheld an effort by the legislature to convert Dartmouth College, a privately endowed educational corporation, into a public institution. The college's trustees had sued the state on the ground that the charter awarded to the college constituted a contract, which the legislature could not constitutionally undo. Before the Supreme Court, Daniel Webster argued successfully not only for the inviolability of the contract created by the charter but also for the validity of the concept of the private charitable corporation under the constitution.

The case is regarded as having set the stage for the efflorescence of private charitable activity in the United States that so impressed European observers—impressed them not least because of the relative absence of such activity on the Continent. In *Democracy in America*, published in 1835, Alexis de Tocqueville described the situation in the following wonderful (and often quoted) words:

> The political associations that exist in the United States are only a single feature in the midst of the immense assemblage of associations in that country. Americans of all ages, all conditions, and all dispositions constantly form associations. They have not only commercial and manufacturing companies, in which all take part, but associations of a thousand other kinds, religious, moral, serious, futile, general or restricted, enormous or diminutive. The Americans make associations to give entertainments, to found seminaries, to build inns, to construct churches, to diffuse books, to send missionaries to the antipodes; in this manner they found hospitals, prisons, and schools. If it is proposed to inculcate some truth or to foster some feeling by the encouragement of a great example, they form a society. Wherever at the head of some new undertaking

you see the government in France, or a man of rank in England,
in the United States you will be sure to find an association.

Although that passage was written more than a century and a half ago, it remains essentially accurate today. Organized private charitable activity continues to be more at home in the United States than anywhere else.

The major practical effect of incorporation as a charity, apart from
commitment to charitable enterprise, was and remains exemption from various forms of taxation. Until the second quarter of this century, exemption
for U.S. charities was chiefly from real-estate taxes, although certain other
minor exactions (such as occupancy or doing-business taxes) might also be
at issue. The importance of exemption grew greatly with the onset of income
and estate taxes. Income-tax exemption was doubly valuable to charities. The
deductibility (from taxable income) of gifts to them encouraged the generosity of donors, and the exemption of income on their endowments and
incidental income earned from their charitable activities greatly enhanced
their capacity to do their charitable jobs. As tax rates rose during the second
and third quarters of the century, these exemptions and deductions became
ever more significant. Not surprisingly, the Internal Revenue Code and its attendant regulations became the principal front on which the legal development of charity proceeded.

Here, it is necessary to distinguish between "charitable" activities, on
the one hand, and, on the other hand, "noncharitable" activities defined by
the Internal Revenue Code as "nonprofit" and therefore tax-exempt. The latter are of many sorts, with varied purposes that are related to mutuality, self-
help, and cooperation or to activities which for special political reasons have
been deemed to deserve nonprofit status. These nonprofit (but not charitable) organizations, including civic leagues, labor unions, and social or recreational clubs, share with their charitable counterparts the benefit of
exemption from taxes that would otherwise be levied on them—chiefly real-
estate and income taxes. But, with few exceptions, they do not share with
their charitable counterparts the benefit of deductibility from taxable income of donors' gifts to them.

The most visible threads in the elaborate fabric of nonprofit exemption are cooperative endeavor and promotion of community welfare. The exemptions can almost be seen as a codification of Tocqueville's observations.
It is notable that many of the functions performed by these exempt organizations either are or could be performed by governmental entities or for-
profit corporations, with which the exempt organizations compete in fact or
in principle. The view of Congress appears to have been that government
and business cannot be relied upon to meet all needs, and that (chiefly) local
efforts to fill the gaps, if these efforts are mutual and nonprofit, deserve the
reward of tax exemption.

To turn back to the charitable organizations that are grouped together principally under section 501(c)(3) of the tax code (the subject of this book), we should note that this set of fully tax-exempt entities, originally limited to religious, educational, charitable, and scientific organizations, has continually added classes to its ranks, including organizations that seek to prevent cruelty to children or animals (1918), serve literary purposes (1921), test for public safety (1954), or foster international amateur sports competitions (1976). As is well known, the provisions of the Internal Revenue Code are fleshed out by regulations which, when approved by Congress, have the force of law. The current (1991) regulation explicating section 501(c)(3) is interesting for its specificity with respect to current societal concerns:

> Charitable includes: Relief of the poor and distressed or of the underprivileged; advancement of religion; advancement of education or science; erection or maintenance of public buildings, monuments, or works; lessening of the burdens of Government; and promotion of social welfare by organizations designed to accomplish any of the above purposes, or (i) to lessen neighborhood tensions; (ii) to eliminate prejudice and discrimination; (iii) to defend human and civil rights secured by law; or (iv) to combat community deterioration and juvenile delinquency.

As the law of the charitable tax exemption has developed in the United States, perhaps its most surprising feature is the concession of charitable character to activities either engaged in or primarily of interest to the intellectual or economic elite. Although educational activities have been deemed charitable from ancient times (when not conducted for profit, as they have frequently been), and the Statute of Charitable Uses included scholars in universities, *research* came to be a specific area of charitable activity—partly, perhaps, because the university was its most natural (although not exclusive) home, but surely also because of a general confidence that the results of research would benefit everyone. Thousands of research workers, conducting inquiries opaque to most people, are now supported by funds designated as charitable. Another relatively new charitable field is "the arts," broadly perceived. Although museums and symphonies had long been considered charitable if they elected a charitable mode of operation (which not all did), the concept has been extended to virtually all forms of artistic expression or display, including public television, whose audience is far better educated and richer than that of commercial television.

These developments, however, were and remain consistent with what is probably the best general definition of the term *charity*: activity that tends toward human betterment. And that brings us to one of the more remarkable charitable developments of this century—the endowed general-purpose foundation, whose charter may commit it to nothing more confining than the well-being of mankind. Such foundations, usually arising through the generosity of an individual donor out of a major industrial or commercial fortune, have been a conspicuous feature of recent charitable history in the United States (much less so abroad). With portfolio values as high as $6.5 billion and annual philanthropic budgets up to $265 million, they have been extremely important sources of support for the charitable activities of the organizations they support, which by law, with few exceptions, must themselves be charitable.

The body politic has always been nervous about foundations, chiefly because of their capacity to go their own way (select their beneficiaries) without having to be fettered (guided?) by an electorate, stockholders, contributors and members, or customers—that is, without the constraints that bind government, business, and most other charitable and nonprofit organizations. But it is precisely the absence of those constraints that has enabled the best of the foundations to pursue important but unpopular goals, support research that will show results only after decades of work, and foster categories of intellectual activity for which there is little if any public support. The fact that they are not the government, General Motors, the Red Cross, or the American Cancer Society is what enables them to be useful in ways very different from the ways in which those important instrumentalities are useful.

Since the onset of the Great Society programs of the 1960s, and the consequent increase in governmental provision of a wide range of social services, government agencies have found it opportune to contract many of those services out to nonprofit organizations. The result has been a growing partnership between the nonprofit sector and government in these areas, and a concomitant increase in the number of nonprofit organizations adapted to the provision of such services. Indeed, many have been formed explicitly because of the availability of governmental support, and such support now composes a sizable fraction (if not in fact all) of the revenues of many nonprofits. At the same time, both new and previously existing nonprofits have turned to fees, service charges, and other forms of quasi-commercial income to supplement the individual and corporate contributions that have been their traditional resources. Lines of demarcation among the business, governmental, and nonprofit sectors have blurred, to some extent.

During the recent phase of these developments, the relative capacity of federal, state, and local governments to meet perceived public needs has visibly diminished, which is another way of saying that the capacity (or willingness) of the private business sector and the individual citizen to supply tax revenues appears to have fallen behind the rising costs of providing services through government. This, together with the evident growth in the number and size of nonprofit organizations, has led to increasing scrutiny of the charitable sector from several points of view, but always on the background of evidence that ever-larger amounts of capital, income, and real estate "escape" what seems to some their fair share of the tax burden. To be balanced against that "escape" is the undeniable fact that much charitable activity substitutes for or supplements governmental expenditure and thereby "saves the government money." (And, as noted above, much charitable activity is in effect sponsored by government, which suggests that some charities, from this point of view, would be analogous to governmental agencies.) But, of course, much charitable activity neither substitutes for nor supplements governmental expenditure. Indeed, many charitable dollars go to projects and programs that have been explicitly rejected for governmental support, or which at least could never muster enough public enthusiasm to engender a congressional appropriation.

During the 1970s, Stanley S. Surrey, who had been a Treasury Department official in the 1960s, developed the "tax-expenditure principle," which viewed every tax exemption or deduction as being, in effect, a governmental expenditure benefiting the "favored" activity or group. The deduction of home mortgage interest was seen as a governmental disbursement in favor of homeowners; the charitable exemption was seen as a disbursement to charitable institutions. Conservatives bridled because the principle came fairly close to a declaration that all money is government's, and that if government lets you keep any, it is doing you a special kindness. But if the rhetoric of the principle was rejected in some quarters, at least it framed the question of expenditure efficiency. If it is true (as it is) that Congress could do away with charitable exemptions and deductions, thus presumably raising a good deal more money in taxes, is it credible that government would spend that money more effectively than it is now spent by charitable organizations? To most people, this proposition is not credible. But what of the many millions in tax-exempt funds that go for purposes which, though clearly charitable and even commendable, rank low on any legislator's list of priorities? On basic democratic principles, should those funds not be taken instead by government and applied to needs that it considers paramount?

The difficulty is that since very early days—those of the Statute of Charitable Uses, if not of St. Thomas—the guiding principle has been that certain kinds of private action are intrinsically so admirable and beneficial that they deserve unique recognition and, at the very least, the encouragement represented by exemption from the tax rolls. Thus for centuries the private charitable sector, especially in England and the United States, has proceeded on a course roughly parallel to but distinctly separate from that of government, occasionally intersecting with governmental activity but often diverging from it quite widely. On the whole, the results achieved have seemed well worth the sacrifice of tax revenues. Besides, as members of the charitable community point out, if the exemption were removed, many charitable organizations would rather quickly cease to exist, leaving little to be taxed; that is, the amplitude of the exempt funds, if not the value of the real estate, depends precisely on the exemption whose withdrawal is proposed.

Debates continue on the effectiveness of charitable organizations, and there have been widely publicized examples of apparent incompetence or worse (note the cases of the United Way and Empire Blue Cross–Blue Shield). Still, the charitable nonprofits continue to increase in number and in significance, as this study illustrates. Even as we seek to improve their current and future performance, it behooves all of us to appreciate the roles they have played in this country since its earliest days. They are, without question, a distinctly American phenomenon of growing importance, and it is necessary that they be better understood.

Note

1. The material presented in this Prologue has been drawn from such a wide variety of sources that the usual methods of citing references do not work. Readers interested in more detailed histories of the nonprofit sector and its constituent parts may consult the fine essay by Hall (1987) and the bibliography in it.

THE CHARITABLE
NONPROFITS

PART ONE

The Nonprofit Sector Today

ONE

A Road Map Through the Nonprofit Sector

T he nonprofit sector can be delimited in a dazzling variety of ways. Simply arriving at a definition of the term *nonprofit* turns out to be a daunting task. In addition, wherever the boundaries are set, the sector can be examined from many vantage points (contributions to the gross national product, employment share, number of institutions, and so on). It is all too easy to become lost in a maze of legal constructs, odd terminology, and seemingly disconnected statistics. The purpose of this chapter is to present, in as clear a fashion as we can, a road map through this terrain. Investing time in understanding the main features of this map is the dues that one must pay in order to work with the principal sets of IRS data and to interpret much of the literature properly.

Broad Dimensions

The most important generic characteristic of a nonprofit organization is its adherence to what Henry Hansmann has called the "nondistribution constraint," which prohibits the distribution of profits or residual earnings to individuals who control the entity.[1] Contrary to what some people think, nonprofit organizations *are* permitted to have revenues in excess of expenses, but they cannot make distributions to (nonexistent) "owners" by paying dividends or repurchasing shares of stock. This constraint is what most clearly distinguishes nonprofit organizations from for-profit entities: nonprofits can make "profits," but they cannot distribute them.

Nonprofit organizations may apply to the Internal Revenue Service to qualify for tax-exempt status, which, if approved, exempts them from the

3

obligation to pay federal income taxes. In addition, contributions to certain nonprofit organizations are tax-deductible for donors (however, tax-exempt status does not in and of itself confer this benefit). As described in the Prologue, Congress has determined, through a series of acts (the first of them in 1894), the various types of organizations that are eligible to receive tax-exempt status. These acts have been codified in twenty-nine subsections of Sections 501 and 521 of the Internal Revenue Code, each one defining a particular type of eligible organization.

If one defines the nonprofit sector as all organizations recognized as tax-exempt by the IRS, then in 1991 there were over 1 million organizations in the nonprofit universe. These organizations accounted for about 6 percent of GNP and 10 percent of total employment.[2] The full universe of nonprofit entities is even larger in some respects. Very small nonprofit organizations with less than $5,000 in annual revenues, churches of any size, and charities that are incorporated by governmental bodies (such as state universities) do not have to apply for tax exemption, although they may choose to make application. It is difficult to estimate the number of entities that fall into these categories. The consensus seems to be that there are about 350,000 churches all told,[3] but we have been unable to find any estimate of the number of very small organizations or governmentally sponsored public charities. Thus the total universe of nonprofit organizations, defined most broadly, would appear to be on the order of 1.5 million entities—or conceivably even larger.[4] This total can be compared with the total number of incorporated business establishments, which is estimated to exceed 6 million.[5]

For some purposes, it would be desirable to analyze this full universe of nonprofits. For practical reasons, however, we are forced to make our starting point the list of organizations recognized as tax-exempt by the IRS. In particular, we focus on those nonprofits which have qualified for exemption under Section 501(c)(3). These organizations are often referred to simply as *501(c)(3)s*, or as the "charitable" nonprofits. It is mainly these entities—private foundations, as well as educational, religious, scientific, literary, social welfare, and other charitable organizations—which are entitled to receive tax-deductible contributions. (There are also small pockets of deductibility within the other 501(c) subsection codes. For example, war veterans' associations, cemetery organizations, and fire companies are eligible to receive tax-deductible contributions.) The rationale for permitting donors to enjoy the benefits of tax-deductibility is that these organizations are thought to serve broad public purposes which transcend the personal interests of their members and benefactors.[6]

When most people speak of nonprofits, the 501(c)(3)s are the organizations which they have in mind. Section 501(c)(3) may match the common meaning of the term *nonprofit*, but it most certainly does not capture the full range of nonprofit entities granted tax-exempt status by the IRS. Indeed, Section 501(c)(3) includes *less than half* of all tax-exempt organizations.

The general characteristics of the twenty-nine tax-exempt subsections of the tax code are shown in Table 1.1, along with the number of entities in each category in 1991.[7] Of the over 1 million tax-exempt organizations, 516,554 were 501(c)(3)s. Over 140,000 were civic leagues and social welfare organizations; nearly 100,000 were fraternal societies and associations; more than 70,000 were labor, agricultural, and horticultural organizations; more than 68,000 were business leagues and chambers of commerce; and an additional 64,000 were granted exemption as social and recreational clubs. There were also cemetery companies and credit unions, as well as such a highly specialized category as "black lung trusts."

Table 1.1. Number of Tax-Exempt Entities by Section of the Tax Code, 1991.

Section of Tax Code	Type of Organization	Number of Entities	Percent of Total
501(c)(1)	Corporation organized under act of Congress	9	0.0
501(c)(2)	Title-holding corporation	6,408	0.6
501(c)(3)	Religious, educational, charitable, scientific, etc.	516,554	48.9
501(c)(4)	Civic league, social welfare organization	142,811	13.5
501(c)(5)	Labor, agricultural, or horticultural organization	72,009	6.8
501(c)(6)	Business league, chamber of commerce	68,442	6.5
501(c)(7)	Social or recreational club	63,922	6.1
501(c)(8)	Fraternal beneficiary society or association	98,840	9.4
501(c)(9)	Voluntary employees' beneficiary association	14,708	1.4
501(c)(10)	Domestic fraternal beneficiary society	18,360	1.7
501(c)(11)	Teachers' retirement fund	10	0.0
501(c)(12)	Benevolent life insurance association	5,984	0.6
501(c)(13)	Cemetery company	8,781	0.8
501(c)(14)	State-chartered credit union, mutual reserve fund	6,219	0.6
501(c)(15)	Mutual insurance company or association	1,147	0.1
501(c)(16)	Cooperative organization to finance crop operations	20	0.0
501(c)(17)	Supplemental unemployment benefit trust	644	0.1
501(c)(18)	Employee-funded pension trust	8	0.0
501(c)(19)	War veterans' organization	27,962	2.6
501(c)(20)	Legal service organization	206	0.0
501(c)(21)	Black lung trust	23	0.0
501(c)(22)	Multiemployer pension plan	0	0.0
501(c)(23)	Veterans' association founded prior to 1880	2	0.0
501(c)(24)	Trust described in Section 4049 of ERISA	0	0.0
501(c)(25)	Holding company for pension, etc.	181	0.0
501(d)	Religious or apostolic association	93	0.0
501(e)	Cooperative hospital service organization	72	0.0
501(f)	Cooperative service organization of operating educational organization	1	0.0
521(a)	Farmers' cooperative association	2,129	0.2
	Total	1,055,545	100.0

Source: Internal Revenue Service, 1991 *Annual Report,* Table 25. Data are for the fiscal year ending September 30, 1991.

The various categories of "noncharitable" nonprofits, most of which are ineligible to receive tax-deductible contributions, are thought to have more of a "mutual benefit" character than the charitable nonprofits because they provide goods or services that benefit their members, rather than the public more generally. They differ from for-profits in that they provide services collectively, rather than on a transactional basis.[8] Mutual benefit nonprofits raise quite different questions of public policy and should be distinguished carefully from both charitable nonprofits and for-profit organizations.

The Mysterious World of the Business Master File

The IRS maintains its records of tax-exempt organizations in a computerized database known as the Exempt Organizations/Business Master File (established in 1963), which we hereafter refer to simply as the BMF. Computer runs of the BMF are available to researchers for a modest fee; however, we must warn the casual purchaser: *caveat emptor.* To tackle the BMF is to enter a complex maze that will test the persistence of even the most stout-hearted soul. We have attempted to clarify the structure of the BMF classification system by constructing a "tree" (Figure 1.1) which shows the various branches of the database. The dedicated reader may be helped by referring back to this figure as the discussion of the BMF proceeds. (Those readers with no interest in working with the BMF database, and who are content to take on faith our decisions about which sets of entities to include and exclude from the rest of this analysis, may turn directly to the concluding section of this chapter for a description of our core group of public charities.)

The first thing to understand about the BMF is that it is an administrative file, updated regularly. The data included in this study were obtained from this file as it existed in October 1991. In this study, we are concerned only with the charitable, 501(c)(3) portion of the tax-exempt universe. The tapes we obtained from the BMF in October 1991 included 481,788 charitable nonprofits which were deemed "active" at that time (see the center box just below the dotted line in Figure 1.1).

We call attention to the modifier "active" to emphasize an important distinction. There are both active and inactive parts of the BMF. All entities granted exempt status are placed in the active part of the BMF, and there they stay unless they are moved to the inactive part of the file. Transfer to inactive status occurs primarily when an organization notifies the IRS that it has ceased its activities, or if one of the IRS's periodic letters of inquiry to an organization is returned unopened. This distinction between organizations that are "alive" and those that have "died" is useful—critical, in fact, to our subsequent analysis of exits—but no one should invest it with specious precision. The assignment of organizations to the inactive file is in part a function of available resources and administrative zeal. As we suggest at the end of this chapter, comatose organizations may exist within the active file for a very long time.

Figure 1.1. A Typology of the Charitable Nonprofits by Filing Characteristics, 1991.

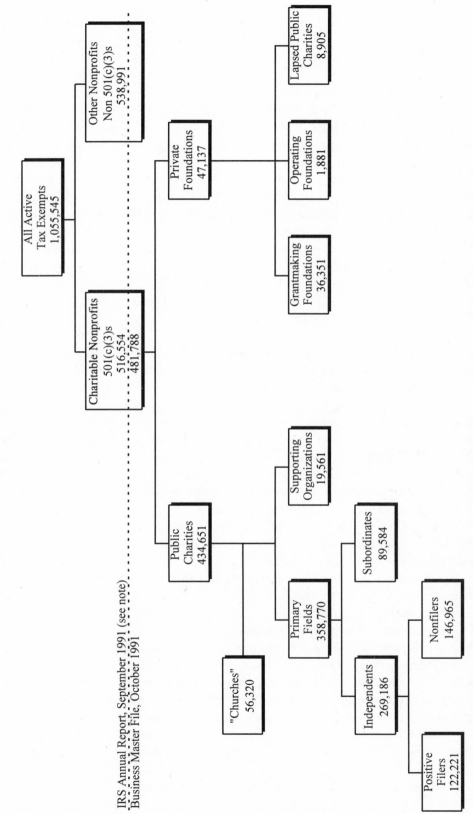

IRS Annual Report, September 1991 (see note)
Business Master File, October 1991

Sources: Business Master File, October 1991, active only, and IRS 1991 *Annual Report.* See also Appendix G, Table G.1-1.
Note: The 516,554 organizations in the IRS count of charitable nonprofits include 34,916 organizations that the IRS is unable to locate.

All the data below the dotted line in Figure 1.1 are from our October 1991 computer run. The figures shown above the dotted line are from the IRS's September 1991 annual report. The published figures differ from the corresponding BMF figures primarily because the IRS's annual report includes organizations that the IRS is unable to locate. For most other purposes, the IRS considers such organizations to be inactive. When the 34,916 501(c)(3)s that fall into this unable-to-locate category are removed, the resulting total is almost identical to the number obtained from our computer run (481,638 versus 481,788).[9] In addition to demonstrating the rough consistency of the published data and the data from our BMF computer run, the other function of the above-the-line part of Figure 1.1 is to remind us again of the large number of tax-exempt entities that exist outside the 501(c)(3) category—approximately 539,000. The rest of our discussion will focus on the below-the-line data taken directly from the BMF file.

Private Foundations

The first branching of the tree below the dotted line shows the statutory dichotomy between "public charities" and "private foundations." In general, public charities provide services, whereas private foundations fund charitable activities. According to Section 509(a) of the tax code, all 501(c)(3) organizations are classified as private foundations unless they are able to meet the criteria of one of its subsections—that is, the category of private foundation is the default category.[10] To obtain public-charity status, an organization must (1) be classified as a "favored" activity under the tax code (for example, be classified as a church, a school, or a hospital), or (2) meet one of two public-support tests, or (3) be classified as a supporting organization (see below). Since the universe of private foundations is defined as all those 501(c)(3) entities that could not qualify as public charities in a given year, it follows that entities once classified as public charities can lapse into private foundation status if they fail to continue qualifying as public charities (usually by failing to meet the public-support tests; see Appendix A for a fuller discussion of these classifications).

Organizations want to be classified as public charities, if at all possible, because it is substantially less advantageous to be classified as a private foundation. Private foundations are subject to an excise tax on net investment income that is not levied on public charities. Many other restrictions and requirements also apply to private foundations. For example, private grant-making foundations are required to meet a total annual payout requirement of approximately 5 percent of their assets. In addition, private foundations may be subject to more state and local taxation and regulation than public charities are.[11]

All told, 47,137 private foundations were included in the October 1991 computer run. This total includes both operating and nonoperating (or grantmaking) foundations, as well as the somewhat anomalous group of institutions which have lapsed into private foundation status (see Figure 1.1). Roughly 36,000 of these entities were regular grantmaking foundations.[12]

The relatively few operating foundations (fewer than 2,000) are best thought of as hybrids, since they share some of the programmatic characteristics of public charities while operating under the organizational and financial structure of private foundations. Operating foundations devote most (at least 85 percent) of their income to the active conduct of their programmatic activities, where "active conduct" means direct expenditure of the funds by the organization, rather than disbursements to grantees.[13]

The foundation world has been described by Elizabeth Boris as a "collage of disparate elements." As she explains, "The few largest foundations hold most of the assets, employ most of the staff and dispense most of the grants. Small foundations rarely have full-time staff and are usually run by family and friends, or by bankers and lawyers."[14] It has been estimated that fewer than 3,500 independent foundations (less than 10 percent of the total number) have endowments in excess of $1 million.[15]

Most of the small foundations are known only to individuals in the localities in which they operate. In their interests and modes of activity, they bear almost no resemblance to the large national foundations, such as Ford, Kellogg, MacArthur, Rockefeller, and Carnegie. A large number are family foundations (such as the Gould Family Foundation, in Ojai, California, and the Brenner Family Foundation, in Weston, Connecticut). Others are corporate-sponsored (such as the Dun and Bradstreet Foundation, Inc., in New York City, and the Nashua Trust Company Foundation, in New Hampshire). Still others are named after real or even imaginary people (for example, the Little Red Riding Hood Charitable Foundation, in Illinois).

The large foundations have a disproportionate impact, simply because of their size and the programming which substantial resources permit. It would be a great mistake, however, to undervalue the importance of their smaller cousins, which often serve complementary functions. Some of the smaller entities may also grow into the large foundations of another generation.

One set of foundations not included under the category of private foundations in the BMF is community foundations. These institutions are classified as public charities, rather than as private foundations. They are required by federal law to raise a certain fraction of their total revenues from the broader public; therefore, they meet one of the two public-support tests.[16] In 1990, there were about 250 active community foundations.[17]

Public Charities

Public charities are far more numerous than private foundations. Indeed, nine out of every ten 501(c)(3) entities have satisfied the criteria for classification as a public charity. Altogether, we found 434,651 public charities in the BMF in October 1991 (see Figure 1.1).

The total must be divided between the 56,320 "churches" and the 378,331 "nonchurches." This branching of the tree is important because filing requirements for churches are so different from filing requirements for all other public charities. Under the law, churches of any size do not need to file for tax exemption, although some do file. In any case, it is clear that the churches in the BMF are a subset of a vastly larger universe (estimated at around 350,000) which cannot be studied by reference to IRS records.

Another complication with the church category is that it includes church-affiliated organizations, as well as actual congregations. Some of the "churches" which appeared in the BMF when we made our computer run are schools or social welfare organizations administered by religious denominations and qualifying for 501(c)(3) status under a church's exemption. Unfortunately, we have no way of knowing how many fit such descriptions, or what other characteristics unite those "churches" that chose to file for tax exemption. Given all these uncertainties and anomalies, it seemed best simply to exclude the entire group of churches in the BMF from the body of our study.

Primary Fields Versus Supporting Organizations

Moving along the "public charity" trunk of the organizational tree depicted in Figure 1.1, we see that all nonchurch public charities can next be divided into two categories: "supporting organizations" and organizations which operate on their own in various broad "primary fields" (arts/culture, education, human services, and so on). The "supporting organization" branch of the tree contains 19,561 entities, or just over 5 percent of all nonchurch public charities. By far the larger branch consists of the remaining 358,770 public charities, to which we assign the collective label *primary fields*. These are the universities, museums, day-care centers, and social welfare organizations that one usually envisions when thinking of the nonprofit sector.

What exactly is a supporting organization? This category is reserved for organizations operated solely for the benefit of and in conjunction with other public charities.[18] In many instances, these organizations are fundraising arms of the larger organizations being supported, or they are "pass-through organizations." Examples of supporting organizations include the Lila A. Wallace Fund for the Metropolitan Museum of Art, the Quincy Humane Society Endowment Fund, and the Iowa Dental Association Relief Foundation.

We exclude supporting organizations from our subsequent analyses, both because of their ancillary nature and because of the difficulty of interpreting their IRS filings. As mentioned above, some supporting organizations raise or receive funds which they then pass on to another public charity, rather than expend themselves for the provision of charitable services. One consequence is that double counting of income often occurs. A supporting organization will record as revenue all gifts it receives. The same funds may then be recorded again as revenues by the organizations it is assisting. A further complication is that the IRS coding system does not permit us to link supporting organizations to the public charities which are the recipients of their support. Therefore, we are left with an incomplete picture of the structure of organizational families.

Independents Versus Subordinates

Moving down the primary-field branch of our tree, the next distinction which needs to be drawn is between "subordinate" organizations and entities that are classified as either "independents" or "parents." Some nonprofits have multiple branches that perform similar functions—the Boy Scouts of America is one example of an organization with such a structure. IRS regulations permit the entire family of organizations to obtain tax-exempt status as a group under a provision known as "group exemption." The branch organizations are called "subordinates" (or sometimes affiliates), and the central organization is known as the "parent." For the IRS, group exemption alleviates the need for separate recognition of many related entities. For the charities, group exemption saves processing costs by permitting the parent to file a single return for all associated subordinates (plus a separate return for the parent).

There is no limit to the number of subordinates that can be associated with any parent, and subordinate organizations are far from a trivial component of the overall population of public charities. As can be seen from Figure 1.1 (immediately below the "primary fields" box), there were 89,584 subordinate organizations within the 501(c)(3) universe as of October 1991. Together, they accounted for about one-quarter of all entities in the primary fields.

Subordinates are highly concentrated within certain sectors, however, and they are most often the progeny of particular organizational parents. It is striking that just over 3 percent of all parents—33 organizations—account for more than half of all subordinate organizations (Table 1.2). The Future Homemakers of America, Ducks Unlimited, Toastmasters International, the California PTA, the Daughters of the American Revolution, and Little League Baseball together account for over one-quarter of the total number of subordinate organizations. The list of subordinate organizations in Table 1.2 is fascinating in its own way and provides an unusual insight into the popularity of certain kinds of volunteer activities. We find organizations with religious missions or affiliations (Full Gospel Business Men's Fellowship International, B'Nai B'Rith Women, and Child Evangelism Fellowship are examples), support organizations (Parents Without Partners, and Compassionate Friends), and singing groups (Society for Preservation and Encouragement of Barbershop Quartet Singing, and Sweet Adelines International).

Table 1.2. Parent 501(c)(3) Organizations with More Than 500 Subordinates, 1991.

Parent Organization	Number of Subordinates
Future Homemakers of America	6,463
Ducks Unlimited	4,122
Toastmasters International	3,373
PTA California Congress of Parents, Teachers and Students	3,503
National Society of the Daughters of the American Revolution	2,947
Little League Baseball	2,344
PTA Texas Congress Parent Teacher Association	1,968
PTA New York Congress	1,570
Civil Air Patrol National Headquarters	1,167
Boy Scouts of America National Council	1,136
Illinois Congress of Parents and Teachers	1,121
International Reading Association	1,085
4-H Clubs & Affiliated 4-H Organizations	1,063
PTA Ohio Congress	985
Full Gospel Business Men's Fellowship International	972
PTA North Carolina Congress	863
The Questers	854
PTA Florida Congress State Headquarters	801
Society for Preservation and Encouragement of Barbershop Quartet Singing	762
PTA Maryland Congress of Parents and Teachers	675
Parents Without Partners International Office	674
Future Farmers of America and Its State Associations and Local Chapters	668
Texas Extension Homemakers Association	645
PTA Pennsylvania Congress	622
B'Nai B'Rith Women	604
United Federation of Doll Clubs	599
Child Evangelism Fellowship	569
Citizens' Scholarship Foundation of America	569
Phi Theta Kappa Fraternity	566
Sweet Adelines International	535
Compassionate Friends	527
PTA Alabama Congress State Headquarters	512
B'Nai B'Rith Youth Commission	501
Total	45,365

Source: Business Master File, October 1991, active only.

The existence of subordinate organizations, like the existence of supporting organizations, complicates efforts to measure the number of institutions which comprise the nonprofit sector. Some subordinates are of substantial size and file independently with the IRS. Some do not file returns because their gross receipts are below the minimum filing requirement. Others that are very small file with their parent organizations. The lines between the categories are hazy; simply adding them all together to arrive at a grand total can lead to overall counts that are significantly affected by myriad arbitrary decisions concerning the structure of organizations and modes of reporting. In addition, the data for subordinates can be misleading. For example, the year when tax-exempt status was granted is often recorded as the year when the parent became tax-exempt, rather than as the year when the subordinate was established. Similarly, financial data are hard to interpret when group returns are filed. Because of these difficulties, we focus our subsequent analysis primarily on parents and on the other independent organizations, which total 269,186 (see Figure 1.1). For the sake of simplicity, we refer to this combined group as *independents*, even though about 1,000 of these organizations are parents.

For the sake of completeness, it should be noted that there are also "subsidiary" organizations, which are for-profit organizations legally controlled by tax-exempt entities. Tax law encourages the establishment of for-profit subsidiaries and transfer of commercial activities to them if the commercial activities of a tax-exempt organization become substantial. Because subsidiaries are for-profit entities, they do not appear in the "exempt organizations" part of the BMF.

Positive Filers Versus Nonfilers

We have now come (at last) to the lowest branch of the tree portrayed in Figure 1.1, a branch which makes a critically important distinction between two strange-sounding categories: "positive filers" and "nonfilers." Depending on their size (as defined by their average annual gross receipts in the preceding three years, including the current year), tax-exempt organizations face different requirements for filing annual reports with the IRS (the equivalent of a tax return for a taxpayer).

Organizations with annual gross receipts that are normally greater than $25,000 are required to file Form 990 (Return of Organization Exempt from Income Tax) or Form 990EZ (Short Form Return of Organization Exempt from Income Tax). We refer to these entities as *positive filers*. Organizations with annual gross receipts normally less than $25,000 are not required to file Form 990. We designate these organizations *nonfilers*. In our nonfiler category we include organizations that technically should be called "zero filers." Many organizations that fall below the $25,000 threshold send in a Form 990, even though they are not required to do so. When these very small organizations file, providing actual figures for their gross receipts and assets, the IRS replaces their entries with zeroes in the BMF. (For a further explanation of zero filers, see Appendix A.)

Of the nearly 270,000 independent public charities in 1991, more than half (55 percent) were nonfilers. We initially believed that the large percentage of nonfilers implied a population of public charities that was highly stratified by size, with the majority of organizations apparently falling below the level of $25,000 gross receipts that triggers the Form 990 requirement. At the same time, we were puzzled. The $25,000 threshold is a very modest one indeed, and it is not easy to imagine how so many independent public charities (more than 140,000) could function with such tiny budgets. More recently we discovered, in the course of trying to determine exactly what a performing arts organization in New York City with less than $25,000 in gross receipts could accomplish, that the activities of some nonfilers are very modest and, more important, most nonfilers no longer give evidence of existing at all.

These conclusions are based on a painstaking effort to locate 290 performing arts organizations with Manhattan zip codes which fall into the nonfiler category. We first tried to call these organizations, but only 23 of them are listed in the phone book, and we were able to reach only 16 of those that are listed. We then employed a determined student intern, Jackson Lee, to visit all the organizations for which we have street addresses (for 13 organizations we have only post office boxes). Lee consulted directories, doormen, and even neighbors, all in an effort to find these organizations. His best efforts notwithstanding, Lee actually found only about 20 percent of the organizations he investigated. Some of these organizations may have been reclassified as inactive after October 1991, when we accessed the BMF, but anecdotal evidence from doormen, neighbors, and even the founders themselves suggests that many were defunct even then, if not earlier. (See Appendix B for a full description of Lee's efforts.)

Our presumption that the overwhelming number of nonfilers simply do not exist is supported by other evidence. For example, Kirsten A. Grønbjerg and colleagues tried to locate 1,452 targeted organizations from an IRS list of Illinois nonprofits. Despite the fact that their list included positive filers as well as nonfilers, they were able to locate only 60 percent of the organizations.[19] It is likely that a high percentage of the organizations that Grønbjerg and her colleagues were unable to locate were nonfilers. A mail survey conducted by Independent Sector in 1992 is also revealing. Survey instruments were sent to 8,075 nonprofit organizations, including 1,450 pure nonfilers (Independent Sector did not include zero filers in this category). Only 3 percent of the nonfilers returned the surveys, as compared with 11 percent of the filers.[20]

When we first called attention to the distinction between the active and inactive portion of the BMF, we noted that the Exempt Organizations Division of the IRS has simply not had the resources needed to purge the active file of comatose entities. Our own efforts in New York, as well as the studies conducted by Grønbjerg and Independent Sector, illustrate how extremely difficult it is to find many of these organizations.

Our conclusion is that the active portion of the BMF contains a large number of organizations which are in fact inactive. This conclusion has implications for the overall size of the institutional population of nonprofits generally and more particularly for our choice of organizations to study. If our findings are representative of the general status of nonfilers, then the overall number of active, nonchurch, 501(c)(3)s is closer to 230,000 than to the reported figure of 425,000.[21] Whatever the exact number, the unreliability of the information on nonfilers argues strongly in favor of concentrating on the positive filers in describing the universe of charitable nonprofits at any point in time.

The nonfilers are of greater interest for studying trends in institutional births, since the very act of obtaining tax-exempt status tells us something about the impulse to found an organization. Many very small organizations, including those that operate without any formal organizational structure, are important components of the social fabric. The fact that they are hard to find and analyze certainly does not mean that they are inconsequential.

The dimensions of the main categories which we have been discussing are summarized schematically in Figure 1.2. The complex map that was needed to reach this destination demonstrates how important it is, in working with

Figure 1.2. Components of the Nonprofit Universe, 1991.

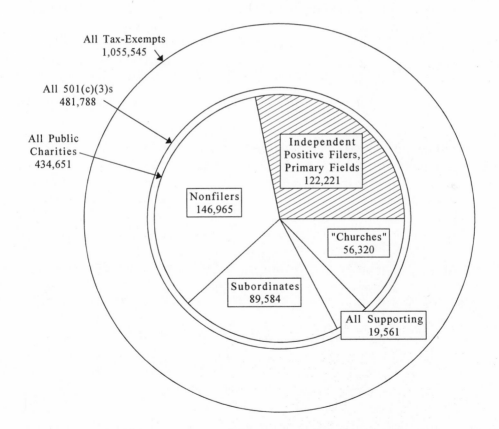

Source: Business Master File, October 1991, active only, and IRS 1991 *Annual Report.* See also Appendix G, Table G. 1-1.

such large databases as the BMF, to select relevant subsets with great care. We are also reminded again of how difficult it can be to answer a seemingly simple question: How many active charitable nonprofits are there?

We began this chapter by considering a universe of over 1 million tax-exempt organizations. From here on, we will focus predominantly on the 122,221 independent public charities, operating in primary fields, which have gross receipts of at least $25,000 per year (and are thus classified as positive filers). We concentrate our subsequent analyses on this group because we are confident that these organizations exist and that we can interpret their IRS filings in a meaningful way. Although this subset constitutes just 12 percent of the entire BMF universe, it is an extremely important component of the nonprofit sector. Indeed, it approximates the universe of institutions which many people have in mind when they use the term *nonprofits*.

We do, however, include other parts of the nonprofit universe on occasion. As explained above, we include nonfilers in our analyses of trends in Part Two of this volume because the formation of these small organizations helps us trace changing patterns of interest in various fields. In addition, where comparisons are useful, we refer to grantmaking foundations, selected types of public institutions, and for-profit organizations. In the next chapter, for example, we describe both public charities and grantmaking foundations because the contrasts between these two types of charitable nonprofits are helpful in understanding the overall shape of the nonprofit sector today.

Notes

1. Hansmann (1980). Salamon (1992, pp. 6–7) lists five other defining characteristics of nonprofits. They must also be (1) formally constituted, (2) private as opposed to governmental, (3) self-governing, (4) voluntary, and (5) designed to serve some public purpose.
2. General data on the size of the nonprofit sector are reported in a variety of sources, including Salamon (1992, especially Chapter 2), Hodgkinson, Weitzman, Toppe, and Noga (1992, Chapter 1, especially Tables 1.1 through 1.5), Rudney (1987b), and Weisbrod (1988, especially Chapter 4).
3. Salamon (1992, p. 13) and Hodgkinson, Weitzman, Toppe, and Noga (1992, p. 16).
4. The complexity of institutional "head counts" in the nonprofit area is illustrated by a 1992 survey by the Nonprofit Coordinating Committee of New York (NPCC), titled *The Nonprofit Sector in New York City* (Haycock, 1992). NPCC abandons the IRS listing of nonprofits entirely, citing both data errors and the failure to account fully for religious organizations, organizations incorporated in other jurisdictions, and organizations operating under the fiscal sponsorship of other entities. The universe specified by NPCC was compiled from a variety of field-

specific and organizational listings. The initial NPCC universe contained 24,211 organizations, more than 10,000 of which were not in the IRS listing, and the IRS listing included 19,721 organizations, 9,000 of which were not in the NPCC listing (p. 4).

5. Table 838 in U.S. Bureau of the Census (1992, p. 526).

6. Weisbrod (1988, pp. 59–79). Weisbrod puts particular emphasis (appropriately, we believe) on the provision of collective goods by the "charitable" nonprofit organizations.

7. For further descriptions of tax-exempt categories, see Figure 1 in Sullivan and Coleman (1991, pp. 46–47).

8. Douglas (1987, pp. 51–52).

9. The remaining difference between the two figures (150 organizations) is the product of two offsetting considerations. On the one hand, we eliminated 1,659 organizations that were not registered in one of the fifty states or that were missing codes integral to our analysis. On the other hand, our numbers are for a later month (October 1991) than the published figures (September 1991).

10. IRC Section 509(a) was adopted as part of the Tax Reform Act of 1969 and was a response to concerns raised in the 1965 Treasury Department report on private foundations (Hopkins, 1987, pp. 436–437).

11. For a much more detailed discussion of the tax benefits of public-charity status, see Simon (1987).

12. The most carefully maintained records of the foundation universe are those kept by the Foundation Center, an institution in New York that is primarily concerned with tracking the activities of grantmaking institutions in order to locate potential funding sources for public charities. There are a number of differences between the Foundation Center's data and the tallies derived from the BMF. The Foundation Center counted 28,743 independent grantmaking foundations in 1990 (Renz and Lawrence, 1992, p. 19). The BMF total of 36,351 grantmaking foundations is higher than the Foundation Center's total because, in addition to those foundations counted by the Foundation Center, the BMF data set also includes 3,592 private foundations that either have not filed a first return or are not in compliance with the law, plus another 653 foundations established in 1991. Some part of the remaining discrepancy (3,363) is probably due to time lags. The Foundation Center adds a foundation to its directory only after receiving a microfiche copy of the grantmaking organization's tax return (personal communication with Loren Renz, vice president for research at the Foundation Center). See Appendix A of Renz and Lawrence (1992) for a more complete exposition of the Foundation Center's methodology.

13. See Renz (1990, pp. 7–9) for a more detailed comparison of different types of foundations. See also Hopkins (1987, pp. 478–486) for a full discussion of the legal requirements necessary for qualifying as an op-

erating foundation. Like grantmaking foundations, an operating foundation may receive its funds from a single source, and it often has a substantial endowment. Approximately one-third of operating foundations are not required to pay the excise tax for which private foundations are generally liable.

14. Boris (1987, p. 66). Odendahl (1987a) also contains extensive discussions about the evolution of foundations in America, foundation profiles today, motives for forming foundations, and the relationships between charitable giving and foundations.

15. Odendahl (1987b, p. 1).

16. Ylvisaker (1987, p. 362).

17. Renz (1991, p. 293).

18. Note 4 in Simon (1987, p. 69).

19. Grønbjerg (1992, p. 9).

20. Personal communication with Stephen Noga, associate director of research at the National Center for Charitable Statistics, Independent Sector.

21. The total number of nonchurch 501(c)(3)s in 1991 was 425,468, but 246,764 of those organizations (including 83,635 of the 91,106 subordinates) were nonfilers (see Appendix G, Table G.1-1). Assuming only 20 percent of the nonfilers actually exist, we are left with 228,057 organizations. If in fact a larger fraction of subordinate nonfilers exists, the true size of the universe is greater but still fewer than 300,000.

TWO

A Snapshot
of the Public Charities

The purpose of this chapter is to provide a statistical snapshot of major parts of the universe of 501(c)(3) entities as it existed at a single point in time (October 1991). As explained in the previous chapter, we focus primarily on the 122,221 public charities which are active in substantive fields of activity (not supporting organizations), which are independent entities (not subordinates), and which have gross receipts of at least $25,000 (positive filers).

We are interested in the relative number of public charities in different primary fields; the median size and number of "small" and "large" organizations in these fields; and the geographic distribution of public charities, seen in relation to the geographic distribution of foundations and the population at large. Surprising as it may seem, information about these three areas is uncommon (if not unknown) in the literature. Nevertheless, a clear understanding of the "institutional demographics" of the nonprofit sector is a prerequisite to exploring issues of a more behavioral sort, such as the factors responsible for the evolution of the sector and relationships among institutional characteristics.

Primary Fields of Activity

The definition of *public charity* provides a large tent under which organizations with a wide range of programmatic missions and organizational structures operate. Until recently, it was impossible to look systematically at sets of organizations with common (or related) purposes because there was no satisfactory classification system. The IRS maintains foundation codes, corresponding to the 509 statutory classifications of entities, but these codes provide insufficient detail. The main categories are church, school, hospital, governmental unit, and other public charities (lumped together). The IRS also maintains three-digit activity codes, which allow for primary, secondary, and tertiary self-reporting of institutional function.[1] Unfortunately, these codes have not been applied consistently over the years and are not considered reliable (see Appendix A).

The National Taxonomy of Exempt Entities (NTEE), developed jointly by the National Center for Charitable Statistics (NCCS) at Independent Sector and the Foundation Center, is potentially a much more informative classification system. With the NTEE, the universe of public charities can be disaggregated into twenty-six broad primary fields (such as arts/culture, education, and community improvement) and then into more specific subfields (for example, arts/culture contains dance, theater, opera, art and science museums, historical societies, and so on).[2]

Unfortunately, during the initial attempt by NCCS to assign entities in the Business Master File (BMF) to categories, a combination of limited resources and an understandable desire to produce results quickly led to a large number of misclassifications. We stumbled onto this problem when we began research for this book, and then we made a systematic effort to estimate the frequency of misclassifications in one field which lent itself to such analysis: higher education. Of the nearly four thousand entities coded within the area of higher education, we found that approximately 60 percent were incorrectly included (these were type II errors, in the language of statisticians). We also discovered that other institutions, equal in number to 10 percent of the institutions in the field of higher education, were incorrectly excluded (type I errors).[3]

These errors resulted primarily from the assignment of codes on the basis of computer scans of the names of organizations. For example, College Park Towers was classified as a college when it is in fact a housing complex for senior citizens. Similar errors, some of them quite startling, occur in fields other than higher education. Our favorite example is the Southern California–Southern Nevada End-Stage Renal Disease Network, which was classified as a theater on the basis of the word *stage*.[4]

Those responsible for the initial coding were of course aware that it was imperfect, but they did not appreciate the magnitude of the problems created by the methods used. In any event, ways have now been found to improve the coding substantially, and a revised coding process is well under way. There is reason to hope that much more reliable data will be available before too long.

Meanwhile, we must work with the available data.[5] The wisest approach seems to be to concentrate on the primary fields (the letter codes, not the secondary and tertiary classifications), since we believe the primary codes are more reliable than the finer breakdowns. The type I and type II error rates mentioned for higher education reflect the coding of entities at the secondary level, as well as at the primary level. Thus that count of errors includes instances in which alumni associations and other ancillary organizations were misclassified as colleges or universities. But these "misclassified" organizations did belong within the NTEE B category (for education) and so were not misclassified at the primary level. In any case, attention should be paid to general patterns, not to small differences.

We begin by examining the distribution of entities by twenty-three primary fields (Table 2.1). [As already explained, the NTEE actually divides nonprofit activities into twenty-six primary codes, with one letter of the alphabet for each category. We combined the four health- and medicine-related codes (E, F, G, and H) into one primary field.[6]] The fields with the largest total number of independent organizations are health (18,316), human services (18,192), education (13,985) and arts/culture (12,442). Together, these "big four" account for over 50 percent of all independent positive filers with assigned primary field codes.

Table 2.1. Number of Public Charities by Primary Field, 1991.

Primary Field	Number of Independent Positive Filers
Health (E,F,G,H)[a]	18,316
Human services (P)	18,192
Education (B)	13,985
Arts/culture (A)	12,442
Community improvement (S)	7,619
Recreation/leisure (N)	5,762
Housing (L)	5,129
Religion (X)	4,222
Youth development (O)	2,514
Philanthropy (T)	2,109
Employment (J)	1,960
Public protection (I)	1,857
Animal services (D)	1,677
Conservation/environment (C)	1,618
Food/agriculture (K)	1,262
Disaster relief (M)	1,209
Public affairs (W)	1,011
Science/technology (U)	1,007
International affairs (Q)	913
Civil rights (R)	641
Social science (V)	473
Mutual benefit (Y)	175
Unknown (Z)	18,128
All public charities	122,221

Source: Business Master File, October 1991, active, independent, positive filers only.
[a] Letters following each field refer to NTEE primary codes.

It should be noted that over 18,000 entities fall into the category "unknown." A significant portion of this group is composed of organizations for which it was impossible to accumulate sufficient information to assign an NTEE code. It is unlikely that these organizations are randomly distributed by field. In addition, organizations recently added to the BMF have not been coded, a situation creating a disproportionate number of new organizations under the "unknown" heading. We expect that the recoding process now under way will significantly reduce the number of "unknowns."

Only three other primary fields contain more than 5,000 positive filers (community improvement, with 7,619; recreation/leisure, with 5,762; and housing, with 5,129). Most of the other primary fields included in the NTEE are relatively small. Indeed, twelve fields contain fewer than 2,000 positive filers, and four of these small fields contain fewer than 1,000 entities (international affairs, civil rights, social science, and mutual benefit).

The number of independent organizations varies by primary field, and so too does the number of subordinate organizations—and thus the ratio of all subordinate organizations to independent positive filers (Table

Table 2.2. Ratio of All Subordinates to Independent
Positive Filers, by Primary Field, 1991.

Primary Field	Ratio
Public affairs (W)[a]	4.27
Youth development (O)	4.19
Animal services (D)	2.81
Science/technology (U)	2.01
Education (B)	1.83
Disaster relief (M)	1.35
Recreation/leisure (N)	0.96
Mutual benefit (Y)	0.86
International affairs (Q)	0.79
Conservation/environment (C)	0.69
Civil rights (R)	0.66
Arts/culture (A)	0.62
Community improvement (S)	0.50
Religion (X)	0.49
Unknown (Z)	0.47
Health (E,F,G,H)	0.26
Human services (P)	0.25
Employment (J)	0.19
Food/agriculture (K)	0.15
Housing (L)	0.10
Social science (V)	0.09
Philanthropy (T)	0.04
Public protection (I)	0.03
All public charities	0.73

Source: Business Master File, October 1991, active only. See also Appendix G, Table G.2-1.

[a] Letters following each field refer to NTEE primary codes.

2.2). In six primary fields—public affairs, youth development, animal services, science/technology, education, and disaster relief—the ratio of subordinates to independent positive filers exceeds 1.00 (that is, there are more subordinates than there are independents). As we saw in Chapter One (Table 1.2), a single parent often accounts for a great many subordinate organizations in a field. For example, there are 6,463 Future Homemakers of America chapters in the youth development category. Subordinate organizations enable a single programmatic mission to be replicated many times in different communities or geographic localities. Perhaps the closest analogue to this type of organizational configuration in the for-profit sector is the franchise system which is used by such companies as McDonald's to ensure that local organizations are operated with similar designs and standards.[7]

The Scale of Public Charities

The typical size of nonprofits also varies considerably by primary field. We use gross receipts to measure size. Gross receipts are defined by the IRS as "the total amount [an organization] received from all sources during its annual accounting period, *without subtracting any costs or expenses.*" Among the costs and expenses that are excluded from this calculation are rental expenses, cost of goods sold, fundraising expenses, and the cost of securities that have been sold. Since the exclusion of all costs and expenses can significantly exaggerate an organization's total receipts, especially if it has a large endowment which is actively managed, we consider median gross receipts to be a better measure of typical size than mean gross receipts.

In investigating the scale of public charities, we concentrate on twelve of the twenty-three primary fields. These fields include all of the largest ones except housing (which as we were warned by NCCS is unreliably coded) and religion (which is difficult to interpret because churches are exempt from filing requirements). Our later analysis of trends in institutional births focuses on the same twelve fields. We also confine our analysis to positive filers because we have no financial data for the nonfilers. In addition, as explained in Chapter One, the nonfilers are an amorphous group of institutions.

Median Receipts

When we rank the twelve primary fields by the dollar values of their median gross receipts (Table 2.3), we find that the field of health has by far the highest median ($496,000). It is joined in the over-$200,000 range by five other fields characterized by direct provision of services (employment, human services, youth development, education, and community improvement) as well as by science/technology. At the bottom of the ranking is recreation/leisure, with median receipts of just $86,000.

Table 2.3. Measures of Organizational Size, Twelve Primary Fields, 1991.

Primary Field	Median Receipts ($)	Percent of Organizations with Receipts of $1 Million or More	Percent of Organizations with Receipts of $25,000–$50,000
Median Over $300,000			
Health (E,F,G,H)[a]	496,000	38.8	9.1
Employment (J)	330,000	28.1	8.5
Median of $200,000–$299,000			
Human services (P)	257,000	19.9	9.9
Science/technology (U)	254,000	26.1	14.0
Youth development (O)	230,000	16.3	10.3
Education (B)	218,000	24.9	14.8
Community improvement (S)	206,000	20.6	14.4
Median of $100,000–$199,000			
International affairs (Q)	167,000	18.3	15.1
Conservation/environment(C)	150,000	12.4	18.3
Animal services (D)	136,000	12.1	17.4
Arts/culture (A)	120,000	11.0	20.7
Median Under $100,000			
Recreation/leisure (N)	86,000	5.7	24.6

Source: Business Master File, October 1991, active, independent, positive filers only.
See also Appendix G, Table G.2-2.
[a] Letters following each field refer to NTEE primary codes.

This distribution is consistent with the capital requirements of the various primary fields. A field such as health, which includes many hospitals and other health care facilities, is much more capital-intensive and has much greater median gross receipts than a field such as recreation/leisure, which comprises mostly local sports leagues and clubs (for example, the Boca Raton Little League, in Florida, and the Andover Soccer Association, in Massachusetts). Chapter Seven explores in more detail relationships among field, fixed costs, and typical size.

The Prevalence of Small and Large Entities

It is also revealing to calculate the relative number of large and small organizations in each primary field. We define large organizations as those having gross receipts of $1 million or more, and small entities as those with gross receipts of between $25,000 and $50,000.

All told, about 20 percent of positive filers, or nearly 20,000 entities in the twelve primary fields, are large. Over one-third of these large organizations are in the health field, and almost 75 percent of the large entities are in just three of the twelve fields: health, human services, and education.

Three other fields have a significant representation of large entities (with the threshold set at 20 percent): employment, science/technology, and community improvement (see Table 2.3).

At the other extreme, almost 15 percent of the positive filers in our twelve fields have gross receipts of less than $50,000. The small organizations are not nearly so unevenly distributed across the twelve primary fields as the large organizations are, but the representation of small organizations still differs substantially, ranging from a high of 24.6 percent in recreation/leisure to a low of 8.5 percent in employment (see the last column of Table 2.3).

Although none of the primary fields has more than 20 percent large organizations *and* more than 15 percent small organizations, all the fields encompass a wide array of organizational sizes. For this reason, no careful study of the typical size of various types of entities (and of the relation between size and other variables, such as age and funding patterns) can be based on such heterogeneous groupings. Rather, it is necessary to look at much finer classifications and even at individual organizations, as we do in Chapters Five and Ten.

Geographic Distribution

We have chosen geography as the final lens through which to describe the universe of charitable nonprofit organizations. It proves to be an unusually revealing perspective, especially because of what it enables us to learn about the power of historical patterns.[8]

The geographic distributions of grantmaking foundations and public charities are of independent interest, but they are also of interest in relation to each other, since they form a kind of "supply-demand" nexus as far as the funding of activities is concerned. The overwhelming majority of the private foundations are grant makers, whereas the public charities are almost all grant seekers; there is clearly a symbiotic relationship between these two sets of nonprofit institutions. (We do not mean to imply, however, that foundations are the only or even the major source of support for public charities.)

In order to measure geographic distribution, we use population as the scalar and calculate an index, I, which has the value of 1.00 if a region's share of the nation's foundations or public charities is exactly equal to the region's share of the national population. A value of 1.50 for foundations, for example, means that the region's share of foundations is one and a half times greater than its share of the population—and that foundations are therefore disproportionately represented in the region.

The geographic distribution of public charities in relation to population is much less skewed than the distribution of private grantmaking foundations. The foundations are heavily concentrated in the Northeast, with both New England ($I=1.77$) and the Middle Atlantic region ($I=1.65$) having far more than their proportionate share of grantmaking foundations. The

Table 2.4. Geographic Distribution of Grantmaking
Foundations and Public Charities, 1991.

	Population Index (I)[a]	
	Grantmaking Foundations	Public Charities
United States	1.00	1.00
Regions		
Northeast	1.68	1.24
New England	1.77	1.59
Middle Atlantic	1.65	1.11
Midwest	1.11	1.00
East North Central	1.12	0.94
West North Central	1.07	1.14
South	0.71	0.84
Atlantic	0.81	0.93
East South Central	0.51	0.73
West South Central	0.67	0.75
West	0.69	1.04
Mountain	0.63	0.96
Pacific	0.71	1.07
Five States		
Massachusetts	2.07	1.66
New Jersey	0.99	0.89
New York	2.31	1.24
Illinois	1.47	0.91
California	0.69	1.02

Source: Business Master File, October 1991, active, independent, positive filers only.
See also Appendix G, Table G.2-3. Population figures for 1990 from *Statistical Abstract of the
United States* (1991).

[a] Population index (I) is the fraction of total organizations in a region divided by the
fraction of the U.S. population in the region. We use U.S. Census definitions of regions.

South and the West are the regions in which foundations are most underrepresented in relation to population (I=0.71 and 0.69, respectively). Table
2.4 presents comparable data for all regions and for five individual states.
Both Massachusetts and New York have indices for foundations of over 2.00,
meaning that they have more than twice as many foundations as would be
predicted on the basis of population alone.

The analogous calculations for public charities (see the right-hand
side of Table 2.4) reveal a general pattern which is a muted image of the one
for private foundations, with a few interesting exceptions. For instance, while
New England again has the highest index of any geographic region (I=1.59
for public charities), the West now has an index greater than unity (1.04).
The South again has a very low index (I=0.84). Among the five individual
states for which we assembled data, Massachusetts ranks first, with an index

of 1.66. Interestingly, Illinois, which has a 1.47 index for foundations, has fewer public charities than would be expected on the basis of population alone (I=0.91). California, however, has many fewer foundations than would have been expected (I=0.69) but slightly more public charities (I=1.02).

Figure 2.1 shows the relationship between the two sets of indices (private foundations and public charities) for the four major geographic regions. We see that foundations are more prevalent than public charities in the Northeast, although both are present in above-average numbers. The West represents the other extreme, with public charities relatively far more numerous than private foundations, which are clearly underrepresented in that region. The South is similar to the West in terms of this relationship. The relative numbers of foundations and public charities are in closest balance in the Midwest.

**Figure 2.1. Geographic Distribution of
Grantmaking Foundations and Public Charities, 1991.**

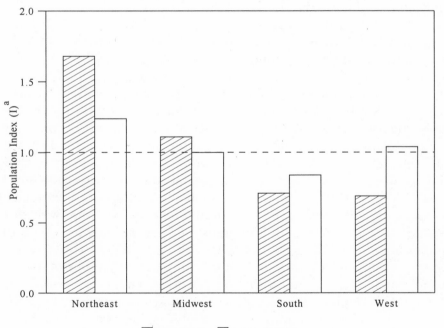

Source: Business Master File, October 1991, active, independent, positive filers only. See also Appendix G, Table G.2-3. Population figures for 1990 from *Statistical Abstract of the United States* (1991).

[a] Population index (I) is the fraction of total organizations in a region divided by the fraction of the U.S. population in the region. We use U.S. Census definitions of regions.

These rough relationships are consistent with the often noted tendency of foundations in the South and in the West to concentrate their giving there. Plainly, their support is needed in their regions. In the Northeast, by contrast, the large number of foundations, relative to public charities, may help explain why they can more comfortably take a national perspective in designing their grantmaking programs. These apparent relationships are at best suggestive, however, since they do not take into account the size of assets (in the case of foundations) or financial need (in the case of public charities).

Differences among regions in income and wealth may well account for some of the differences evident in Table 2.4 and Figure 2.1. In 1991, personal income per capita was $22,111 in the Northeast, $19,598 in the West, $18,586 in the Midwest, and $17,329 in the South.[9] Similarly, 12.5 percent of households in the Northeast and 11.5 percent of households in the West had incomes of $75,000 or more in 1991, whereas only 8.6 percent of households in the Midwest and 7.9 percent of households in the South reported such levels.[10]

The presence of larger numbers of private fortunes in the Northeast is plainly consequential, especially for private foundations. The implications for public charities are less clear, since greater wealth, while increasing the donor pool, could also reduce the need for certain kinds of public services provided by nonprofits. Thus we would expect to find, and we do find, more pronounced differences among the regions in the index for private foundations than in the index for public charities (see Figure 2.1).

Although differences in wealth are clearly consequential, we believe that an even more powerful explanation for regional differences is the long reach of history. It is surely relevant that it was in New England, and especially in Massachusetts, that so many types of nonprofit organizations were born. In providing an historical overview of the nonprofit sector, Hall argues convincingly that in the period from 1780 to 1860, a combination of religious and business elements (the Congregational and Presbyterian churches, joined with Federalist merchants, professionals, and magistrates) created a "culture of organization" that had profound effects. When individuals representing these evangelical and federalist perspectives migrated, new organizations tended to spring up in new locales. As Hall puts it, "Wherever an orphanage, a library, a college, a hospital, an academy, or a professional society operated, it was almost invariably the work of a migrant New Englander with evangelical connections. . . . These two groups [merchants and evangelicals] were distinctive in their willingness to devote their wealth to public purposes and to do so through private nonprofit corporations."[11]

The experiences of New York and Pennsylvania offer a revealing contrast. Their wealth notwithstanding,

> efforts to obtain corporate charters [in these states] became entangled not only in jealousies among Anglicans, Quakers, Dutch Reformed, and Presbyterians but also in conflicting interests be-

tween commercial and agrarian sectors. Thus, as of 1800, the middle states had granted only sixty-seven charters (to New England's two hundred).... New York, moreover, had repealed the Elizabethan Statute of Charitable Uses.... This hostility to private eleemosynary corporations was elaborated during the next three decades.... [New York's] philanthropic resources were scattered among a host of competing institutions, none of them the equal of Harvard, the Boston Athenaeum, [or] Massachusetts General Hospital.... Not until the 1890s, after a major set of legal reforms, would New York City's charitable and cultural organizations match its commercial eminence.[12]

Today's sharp contrast between New England and the Middle Atlantic region in the prevalence of public charities (I = 1.59 and 1.11, respectively) can be seen as a long-lasting consequence of these powerful historical forces.

The other aspect of the geographic distribution of private foundations and public charities which has clear historical roots is the low ranking of the South. According to Hall,

the South ... was the fountainhead of anticorporate legal doctrines.... Thomas Jefferson was hostile to corporations of any kind, regarding them as unwarranted grants of public privilege and property to private persons. Having repealed the Statute of Charitable Uses in 1792, the Virginia legislature in 1801 seized all the properties owned by the recently disestablished Episcopal Church.... By 1806, the legislature had enacted a statute that provided that all property given for charitable purposes was to be turned over to the management of county overseers of the poor.[13]

The overall conclusion which we draw from this blend of empirical evidence and historical commentary is that in the nonprofit sector, perhaps more than elsewhere, patterns established as a result of deep-seated religious, political, and social convictions persist. One part of the explanation is that nonprofit organizations have a capacity to live on. But the more fundamental lesson is that attitudes and assumptions concerning such matters as stewardship and the public responsibility of private citizens are not easily disarranged once firmly in place.

This broad conclusion is reinforced when we perform the same kind of analysis for individual fields of activity within the universe of public charities. Table G.2-3 (Appendix G) contains myriad data for the same twelve fields we used in our discussion of scale. We have summarized some particularly interesting findings in Table 2.5, which compares indices of public charities to population, by field, in four geographic areas: New England, the

Table 2.5. **Geographic Distribution of Public Charities,**
Twelve Primary Fields and Selected Regions, 1991.

Primary Field	Population Index (I)[a]			
	New England	West	Middle Atlantic	South
Arts/culture (A)[b]	1.64	1.07	1.30	0.80
Education (B)	1.99	1.09	1.21	0.82
Conservation/environment (C)	2.32	1.21	0.91	0.85
Animal services (D)	1.18	1.13	0.93	0.94
Health (E,F,G,H)	1.66	0.94	1.21	0.82
Employment (J)	1.33	1.06	0.97	0.81
Recreation/leisure (N)	1.44	1.28	0.84	0.75
Youth development (O)	1.44	1.07	0.95	0.84
Human services (P)	1.55	1.03	1.02	0.83
International affairs (Q)	1.82	1.20	1.40	0.83
Community improvement (S)	1.50	0.75	1.19	0.89
Science/technology (U)	1.56	1.37	1.02	0.85
All public charities	1.59	1.04	1.11	0.84

Source: Business Master File, October 1991, active, independent, positive filers only.
See also Appendix G, Table G.2-3. Population figures for 1990 from *Statistical Abstract of the United States* (1991).

[a] Population index (I) is the fraction of total organizations in a region divided by the fraction of the U.S. population in the region. We use U.S. Census definitions of regions.

[b] Letters following each field refer to NTEE primary codes.

Middle Atlantic, the South, and the West. (We split the Northeast into its two component parts because the differences between these components are so instructive.)

The basic rank-ordering is astonishingly consistent across fields. New England has the highest index of public charities to population in all twelve primary fields. At the other extreme, the South has the lowest index in ten of the twelve fields, and in the remaining two fields (animal services and community improvement) it ranks next-to-last. The Middle Atlantic region and the West are about tied, overall, for second and third place. The West is in second place in seven of the twelve fields, and the Middle Atlantic is in second place in the remaining five fields. Arts/culture, education, health, international affairs, and community improvement have considerably higher indices in the Middle Atlantic; conservation/environment, animal services, recreation/leisure, and science/technology have much higher indices in the West. This division between the Middle Atlantic and the West is generally consistent with what we might have expected, given the usual assumptions about interests specific to one region or another. The fields of conservation/environment and recreation/leisure are more closely identified in most people's minds with the West than with the Middle Atlantic; conversely, such fields as education and philanthropy are understood to have deeper roots in the Middle Atlantic.

From our perspective, the most fundamental point is the nearly relentless consistency of these patterns. Differences in regional interests and specializations do matter (as illustrated by the interesting differences between those public charities most prevalent in the West and in the Middle Atlantic regions), but they are usually overwhelmed by what might be called organizational predilections. For a long time, New England has been so predisposed to the creation of nonprofit entities that it always has a very high index, whatever the field in question. Conversely, the South, dating back to Jefferson's time, has been much less predisposed to this organizational mode, and that predilection is also reflected clearly in these findings. Historical patterns and assumptions matter greatly, much more than we would have guessed.

In many respects, the comments made in this section are only surface impressions. Much more work needs to be done to understand the observed differences in the geographic distributions of charitable nonprofits. Previous studies of nonprofits in various geographic locations provide useful perspectives. For example, a 1993 survey conducted by Independent Sector reports that religious congregations are most heavily represented in the South. Does the South's above-average concentration of congregations (many of which provide a wide range of social services) help explain the area's below-average number of other nonprofit organizations? Similarly, in the early 1980s, the Urban Institute, as part of its landmark study of human service nonprofits in sixteen communities across the United States, found that the South and the West relied more heavily on federal funds than other communities did.[14] Is this phenomenon related to the geographic patterns we found?

There are surely other compelling explanations, such as differences in population density, for the observed geographic differences. Heavy concentrations of population can be expected to generate needs for many of the kinds of services provided by nonprofits, as well as to permit the establishment of organizations of a sufficient scale to be able to meet such needs. One of the broad objectives of this study is to stimulate interest and inquiry, and we believe that there is great opportunity for further research on geographic patterns of activity by various types of nonprofits. Readers with different disciplinary training or particular knowledge of individual fields and regions will peruse the BMF data more perceptively than we can, and they will no doubt see other relationships.

This discussion of geographic patterns completes our portrayal of the universe of public charities as it existed in October 1991. We turn now to an analysis of trends in the establishment of new nonprofits, and then to the intriguing question of why different fields appear to have grown more or less rapidly in various subperiods.

Notes

1. See Figure 4.3 in Weisbrod (1988, p. 68) for a complete list of the activity codes and a discussion of them.
2. For a more elaborate description of the NTEE, including a discussion of its limitations and its history, see Hodgkinson, Weitzman, Toppe, and Noga (1992), especially Chapter 5 and Appendix B. The National Center for Charitable Statistics (NCCS), which is a part of Independent Sector, has assumed primary responsibility for the NTEE. The Foundation Center in New York also uses the taxonomy extensively, but it follows its own coding procedures. See Garonzik (1991) for a more detailed description of the features of this system as it is used by the Foundation Center. The data that we use in this chapter are based on coding done by NCCS.

   Other scholars have proposed alternative classification systems, and there is clearly much to be said for linking the activities of nonprofits to the Standard Industrial Codes used more generally in classifying business activities. For a good discussion of this approach, see Smith (1992). Salamon and Anheier (n.d.) have also worked on this problem, employing an international and comparative perspective.
3. Turner, Nygren, and Bowen (1993).
4. Grønbjerg, who encountered the same problem, found the largest number of misassigned organizations in the residential/custodial care subfield. All organizations whose names contained the word *home* were placed there, including Frank Lloyd Wright Home and Studio, Ronald Reagan Home Preservation Foundation, Homes for Endangered and Lost Pets, and Homeopathic Association (Grønbjerg, 1992, p. 5).
5. As one reviewer of this chapter put it, we are dealing here with a "chicken and egg" problem. Postponing studies until the data are perfect is unlikely to move research along in the field at the optimal pace. Even tentative findings are useful in suggesting new hypotheses and identifying issues that merit further study. They may also stimulate further efforts to improve the underlying data.
6. For a detailed description of the NTEE's twenty-six primary codes, see Appendix B in Hodgkinson, Weitzman, Toppe, and Noga (1992, pp. 593–613).
7. See Oster (1992) for a discussion of the ways in which the franchise system responds to many of the key characteristics of nonprofits, and Young (1989) for an analysis of the factors which have favored the formation of franchiselike systems among national voluntary associations.
8. We use an organization's mailing address, as reported in the BMF, to determine its location. Two limitations to this approach need to be mentioned. First, some nonprofits file under the addresses of their fiscal agents, rather than under their own addresses. Second, subordinate organizations are typically assigned the locations of their parent orga-

nizations (Grønbjerg, 1992, p. 6). The first limitation is probably not serious, given the broad geographic regions we analyze. Although the headquarters problem is more problematic, it is mitigated substantially by our exclusion of subordinate organizations.

9. Table 688 in U.S. Bureau of the Census (1992, p. 439).
10. Table 697 in U.S. Bureau of the Census (1992, p. 446).
11. Hall (1987, pp. 7–8). Hall's essay cites many works by other students of the history of philanthropy and nonprofit organizations, including the influential article by Karl and Katz (1982).
12. Hall (1987, pp. 4–5).
13. Hall (1987, p. 5) and the references cited therein.
14. Results of the Urban Institute's Nonprofit Sector Project are reported in a variety of publications. For a summary of the project and a list of project publications through January 1986, see Salamon, Musselwhite, and DeVita (1986). Wolpert and Reiner (1985) have also found major contrasts in funding patterns and certain structural features of the regional nonprofit sectors that they investigated. Hodgkinson and Weitzman (1992) observe many regional differences in the numbers and activities of congregations.

PART TWO

Institutional Dynamics: Patterns of Births and Deaths

THREE

Institutional Births: Grantmaking Foundations and Public Charities

The existing literature on the growth of the nonprofit sector is generally either discursive (and nonquantitative) or highly aggregative.[1] While considerable attention has been paid to the overall size of the sector—measured, for example, in terms of shares of employment or gross national product originating in it—there has been surprisingly little analysis focused on numbers of organizations and patterns of organizational births and deaths.[2]

Yet analysis of institutional populations is of critical importance if we are to understand the dynamics of the nonprofit sector. Highly aggregative data, such as those derived from national income accounts, do not tell us, for example, whether the hospital output in a given region was provided by one giant entity or by twenty-five smaller ones. Studies of increasing college enrollments do not explain whether existing colleges and universities expanded or whether entirely new institutions were established to accommodate the new students. Examination of data on overall trade-union membership tells us essentially nothing about major changes within the labor movement. Clearly, there is no escaping the need for institutional analysis.

In this part of our study, we examine institutional populations at many levels. In the remainder of this chapter, we compare trends in institutional births among grantmaking foundations and public charities. Then, in Chapter Four, we look more closely at various types of public charities by examining patterns of institutional formation in twelve primary fields. In Chapter Five, we consider trends in entrants within three more narrowly defined sectors: higher education, civil rights, and the performing arts. Finally, in Chapter Six, we complete our analysis of institutional populations by examining exits, or institutional deaths.

Data, Concepts, and Terminology

A major reason for the dearth of studies of institutional births and deaths within the nonprofit world is the lack of readily available data. The *Annual Reports* of the IRS are the only regularly published source of such information, and these data are of limited utility because they are so highly aggregated (for example, they do not provide details by filing status or by primary field of activity). The information is organized simply by section of the tax code, and so all public charities are lumped together.[3]

The Business Master File (BMF) is an obvious source of more finely grained data, and the most direct way of proceeding would appear to be to compare successive editions of the BMF. Unfortunately, this approach is impossible because the BMF is constantly updated, and copies of prior versions are not retained. As a result, there is no way to compare cross-sectional slices of the nonprofit universe over time—or, for that matter, to know the size of components of the universe of tax-exempt entities at earlier points in time.[4]

The more complex alternative that we have adopted is to track flows of entrants into the nonprofit universe by analyzing data on the years in which the organizations were granted tax-exempt status ("ruling years"). This mode of analysis has not been used extensively in time-series studies of defined sets of charitable nonprofits, and what follows must be understood as an initial effort to use the BMF data, married to the National Taxonomy of Exempt Entities (NTEE) codes, to examine rates of institutional formation.[5]

The number of new organizations that enter the nonprofit universe each year—the number of annual births, as it were—is clearly a major dimension. While we certainly do not wish to precipitate a debate over "when life begins" in the world of organizations, one has to recognize that it is more difficult to date the birth of an organization than it is to date the birth of a child. Gestation periods are far more varied, the event itself is less distinct, and records are often either missing or inadequate. The best approach, we believe, is to treat the date of recognition of tax-exempt status by the IRS (the ruling year) as a proxy for the time of organizational formation. In a number of cases, ruling year is somewhat later than date of birth, defined in terms of a first meeting of principals, adoption of a formal charter, or incorporation as a legal entity. Ruling year is, however, an accurate measure of formal governmental recognition of tax-exempt status for independent organizations, and it presumably bears a functional relationship to the need of an organization for such recognition. (For further discussion of the ruling-year variable, how it is used here, and some of the attendant complications, see Appendix A.)

Before presenting the results of our analysis, we must alert the reader to two recurring technical issues. First, when counting the number of institutions established in a particular year, one should include those organizations that were born but then subsequently died. If one measures only the number of *surviving* organizations, the true number of institutional births will be undercounted. Moreover, the number of organizations that are missed will be larger for older age cohorts, since they will have had more time to exit the sector.

Our analysis is handicapped in this respect because we have limited information about the number of organizations that ceased operations prior to 1991. We do have partial information, based on the data contained in the inactive portion of the BMF, which we use when possible. However, the inactive file contains only organizations which became inactive since January 1981, which is too short and too recent a period to provide a complete picture. In addition, the organizations in the inactive file have not been systematically coded by field. As a result, when we compare institutional births across fields in the next chapter, we will be able to count only surviving organizations. In the trends described in this chapter, however, we do include data from the inactive file.

What is the actual effect on our analysis of looking only at surviving organizations? The key variable is the magnitude of the exit rates involved. As a way of bounding the range of possible results, we constructed a simulation model that allows us to test the implications of various assumptions about exit rates. Using data from the inactive file, we constructed high and low estimates of exit rates and then compared the number of new entrants under each scenario with the number of surviving entrants alone. The results show that even with a high estimate of exit rates, the observed patterns of change in new entrants are not materially affected. (A complete description of the simulation model is provided in Appendix C.)

Readers should also be aware of a second technical issue: the way we have calculated and construed rates of increase. In describing patterns of institutional formation, we often calculate the average change in entrants from year to year. We consider this rate to be a reflection of the level of activity or interest in a field. It is not, however, an estimate of the growth of the overall size of the field. Even if all entrants were known (not just those that have survived), measuring changes in the number of entrants without taking into account the number of exits would not provide information about the size of the total population. (For example, it is easy to imagine a population with high birth and high death rates, whose size remains relatively constant.) Still, under normal conditions, the number of institutional births should be related to growth in the field. In fact, under the range of assumptions we tested with our simulation model, the average annual increase in entrants proves to be a reasonably good proxy for changes in the overall size of the field.

Grantmaking Foundations

In analyzing trends in the birth of 501(c)(3) organizations, a sharp distinction needs to be drawn between the two basic types of entities identified in Chapter One: grantmaking foundations and public charities. They serve different functions, have been established for different reasons, are treated quite differently under the tax code, and have been affected in dramatically different ways by federal legislation. As a consequence, it is hardly surprising that both the magnitude and the timing of flows of entrants have been very different in these two distinct parts of the 501(c)(3) universe.

Trends in Entrants, Based on BMF Data

The number of grantmaking foundations still in existence in 1991 that received tax-exempt rulings in each year from 1965 through 1990 is shown in Figure 3.1. (As explained in Appendix A, lack of data precludes analysis of trends prior to 1965.) Ignoring for the moment the pronounced ups and

Figure 3.1. Trends in Entrants by Ruling Year, Grantmaking Foundations, 1965–1990.

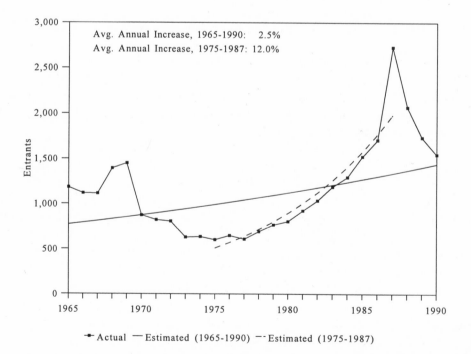

Source: Business Master File, October 1991, active and inactive, independent only. See Appendix G, Table G.3-1.

downs, the average annual growth rate in the number of new foundations established over this quarter century has been 2.5 percent per year.* This overall rate of increase in births of grantmaking foundations is substantially lower than the corresponding rates of increase in entrants for all public charities (6.5 percent per year) and for new business incorporations (approximately 5.0 percent per year).[6]

The overall rate of increase has been far from steady, however, and the most interesting aspect of Figure 3.1 is the sharp fluctuations in numbers of entrants which it reveals. Three main subperiods can be distinguished.

First, there is the evident drop in entrants following the Tax Reform Act of 1969, widely (and, we think, rightly) described as "the watershed legislation regulating private foundations and their activities."[7] Lengthy investigations by Congressman Patman in the 1960s and other revelations combined to create an atmosphere described as "at best skeptical and at worst hostile." In the 1969 act, Congress did the following things:

- Altered provisions concerning the deductibility of gifts by living donors, to provide greater encouragement for donations to public charities than to grantmaking foundations
- Created a series of excise taxes on private foundations, including a 4 percent tax on net investment income
- Imposed a minimum payout requirement to prevent "unreasonable accumulations"
- Sought to limit "excess business holdings," so that foundations could no longer control individual business enterprises
- Restricted lobbying and other activities.

In addition, Congress required much more extensive public disclosure of private foundations' activities. The number of new foundations created each year decreased, from about 1,400 in 1969 (already a depressed rate of new births, as compared with the 1940s and the 1950s) to fewer than 900 in 1970 to a low of around 600 in the early to middle 1970s.

In the second period, beginning about 1975 and lasting until 1987, there was a rebound in entrants (although the previous level was not regained until about 1985). The report of the Filer Commission in 1975, and the positive reaction to it improved the general standing of foundations, and a modest recovery in entrants ensued. There were also adjustments in specific provisions of the 1969 act, including a reduction in the excise tax on net

---

* To obtain the average annual rate of increase, we fitted a least-squares regression line to the natural log of the number of new entrants in each year. (The actual and estimated values for each year are shown in Figure 3.1.) In the subsequent analysis, this methodology is used regularly to derive estimates of average annual rates of change. It avoids the worst problems of arbitrariness and overemphasis on end points implicit in the calculation of simple percentage changes between (for example) the first and last years for which data are available.

investment income from 4 percent to 2 percent. More dramatic growth in the annual number of entrants began in 1980 and continued through 1987, with a huge spurt between 1986 and 1987. Further legislative actions were also helpful. In 1981, a flat 5 percent payout requirement was adopted, and in 1984 the rules governing charitable deductions on gifts to foundations were liberalized. We suspect, however, that improved economic conditions were even more significant. Double-digit inflation ended, and—of great significance for many potential donors to foundations—the stock market enjoyed an unprecedented boom. Over the course of this extended recovery period (1975–1987), foundation entrants increased at an average rate of 12.0 percent per year (see Figure 3.1).

The third and last period shows an abrupt reversal of this trend. There was an exceedingly sharp drop-off in entrants in 1988, with further falls in 1989 and 1990, which together take us almost all the way back to the level of entrants characteristic of the late 1960s. Again, economic developments offer plausible explanations. The stock market crashed in 1987, and even though it recovered nicely thereafter, there were almost surely some effects on the inclination (and ability) of individuals to create new foundations. At the minimum, euphoria about the future of financial markets was dampened. Moreover, the Tax Reform Act of 1986 lowered the highest marginal tax rate from 50 percent to 28 percent, nearly doubling the "price of giving."

A Longer Historical Perspective

These fluctuations and recent trends take on a slightly different coloration when viewed within a longer historical perspective. Thanks mainly to the continuing efforts of the Foundation Center and the Council on Foundations, considerable progress has been made in charting the evolution of at least parts of the universe of private foundations, going back to the early decades of the twentieth century.[8]

Some of the very large private foundations (Carnegie and Rockefeller, for example) were established early in the century, but it was not until World War II and its aftermath that large numbers of private foundations of substantial size were established. Figure 3.2 shows the decade of establishment for foundations with assets of at least $1 million or the capacity to make grants of $100,000 or more in 1990. (This subset represents approximately 30 percent of the foundation universe.[9]) The late 1940s and early 1950s were boom years, and the combination of substantial growth in real income and high levels of taxation were primarily responsible for the unprecedented number of new foundations established then. In the words of Elizabeth Boris, a careful student of this history,

> the high income tax rates that originated during World War II persisted until the Revenue Act of 1963, creating new incentives

**Figure 3.2. Trends in Entrants by Decade of Establishment,
Large Grantmaking Foundations.**

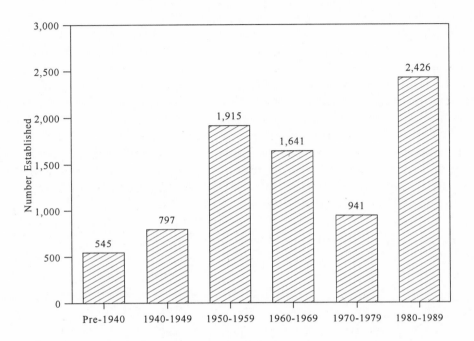

Source: The Foundation Center (1992).
Note: Each bar indicates the number of foundations formed in the period that were still active in 1990. Dates of establishment were not available for 456 foundations. "Large grantmaking foundations" have assets of at least $1 million or make annual appropriations of at least $100,000.

for foundation establishment . . . . Moreover, wealth transfers to family were subject to heavy estate taxes, but charitable transfers to foundations were not . . . . The top income rates were almost confiscatory (above 90 percent), while the top federal estate tax was 77 percent on amounts above $10 million from 1941 to 1971. . . . As historian Robert Bremner observed, "For wealthy people, . . . charity was a bargain because what was given was mainly forgiven taxes. In the upper income brackets the question became not whether one could afford to give, but whether one could afford not to give."[10]

There were also no prohibitions at that time against transferring one's interests in a business to a foundation and thereby maintaining control. An important purpose of the Tax Reform Act of 1969 was to end this practice, and it is significant that "eighty-one percent of foundations created with controlling-interest stock were formed before 1970."[11] An abundant literature grew up on mechanisms for taking advantage of the opportunities offered by the foundation model, and setting up family foundations became the thing to do. Not surprisingly, abuses followed. These led eventually to the Patman hearings, the Tax Reform Act of 1969, and, it appears, the subsequent decline in the rate of formation of foundations.[12]

The volume *America's Wealthy and the Future of Foundations*, published in 1987 and based on data through 1983, represents the most comprehensive effort to date to examine the dynamics of the universe of private foundations. There is, however, a tendency (entirely understandable) to adopt a tone which may have been too pessimistic about the future development of foundations. For example, the authors refer to "the decline in foundation formation over the past three decades" and the need "to understand why there was a declining birthrate for foundations."[13]

With the aid of hindsight, we can now see that the postwar period of rapid growth in the number of large foundations was a phenomenon all its own, not to be taken as a reference point for assessing future developments. One is reminded of the extraordinary expansion in higher education in the 1960s (the "golden years"), which people were also tempted to treat as normal, rather than as highly atypical, in evaluating later developments. If the 1960s are taken as an appropriate reference point for higher education, then it is unlikely that we will ever again regard it as a healthy sector, no matter what happens.

The apparent decline in foundation births is partly due to the methodology underlying presentations such as the one in Figure 3.2, which is misleading in two respects. On the one hand, because it considers only surviving organizations, the presentation underestimates the growth of foundations in earlier years. Although many foundations are established in perpetuity, some have sunset provisions which require them to pay out their principals by a certain date. On the other hand, the methodology used for Figure 3.2 obscures upward trends. The basic problem is that any analysis of "birthdates" for an institutional population defined by a certain size threshold (in this case, assets of at least $1 million in 1990, or grants of $100,000 or more) will fail to allow adequately for the emergence of small foundations, which in turn may become large foundations. Foundations grow over time, as a result both of additional gifts and of the reinvestment of some part of the total return earned on endowment. Hence it is almost inevitable that the large foundations in existence in a particular year will have been formed several decades earlier.[14] A population of foundations with assets of at least $1 million will generally appear older, with fewer recent entrants, than a population of foundations with no cutoff on asset size.

It may also be the case (it almost surely is) that in recent years another kind of shift has been superimposed on this age-maturation effect. All the available evidence suggests that formation of small foundations has increased markedly, relative to formation of large foundations.[15] This development has major consequences for patterns of grantmaking, and for the future of various types of public charities dependent (in differing degrees) on the largesse of large versus small foundations.

Biases exist in both directions, but we believe that the net effect of the methodology used for Figure 3.2 is to minimize births in more recent years. Thus we suspect that the bar for the 1980s, impressive though its height is, underestimates (when seen in relation to bars for earlier decades) the true rate of growth in foundation births in the mid-1980s. We believe that when more time has passed, and when more of the younger foundations formed in the 1980s have grown up, the early and middle parts of this decade will be seen to have been years of exceptional growth for grantmaking foundations.

Public Charities

The category of public charities contains a far more diverse set of organizations than does the category of grantmaking foundations. For that reason, among others, it would serve no purpose to attempt to analyze in detail the overall trend in entrants. As we show in the next chapter, trends among primary fields vary considerably, and it makes more sense to examine them individually. There are several general comments to be made, however, the first of which serves to highlight, as others have done, the dramatic growth in the number of public charities that has taken place in recent decades. When we discuss the overall growth rate for the sector, we are able to speak with certainty only of the period since 1981 because data on exits from the inactive file allow us to estimate the true size of the institutional population. During this period, the universe of public charities grew at an average annual rate of 4.9 percent.

Using the simulation model we have described, we can also estimate growth rates for earlier periods (see Appendix C, especially Figure C.2). These simulations suggest that the number of public charities increased by about 6.9 percent per year between 1965 and 1991. Growth was considerably faster during the first part of this period: estimated annual growth rates between 1965 and 1975 were 8.7 percent, compared to 5.4 percent from 1975 to 1991. During the early period, the population doubled in size in just eight years. By 1991 it had nearly tripled again in size. Even at the reduced growth rate of the 1980s, the total population of public charities can be expected to double again by the year 2005.

The significant growth of public charities is confirmed by an examination of year-to-year increases in the number of entrants (Figure 3.3). The 6.5 percent average annual entry rate for public charities is almost twice the corresponding rate of increase for private foundations and is significantly

Figure 3.3.   Trends in Entrants by Ruling Year, Public Charities, 1965–1990.

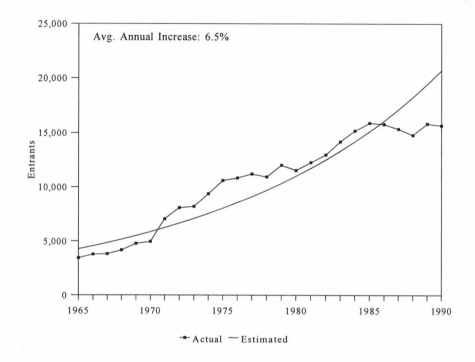

Source: Business Master File, October 1991, active and inactive, independent only. See Appendix G, Table G.3-1.

higher than the rate for business incorporations (which, as already noted, was about 5 percent per year). Judged by any standard, this is a remarkable record of growth, and its extended duration is noteworthy.

It is also interesting to look at the number of entrants in various periods. The period between 1965 and 1975 was one of decidedly above-average formation of institutions: entrants increased at an average annual rate of nearly 13 percent. The 1969 Tax Reform Act, which had such a deleterious effect on the establishment of new grantmaking foundations, had a strongly positive effect on applications for tax-exempt status by public charities. Two specific provisions deserve emphasis.

First, the "15-month rule" of Section 508(a) of the 1969 Tax Reform Act had an immediate impact on rulings issued in 1971 and 1972. With certain exceptions (churches and small public charities), an organization formed after October 9, 1969, was required to file an official application in order to qualify for exemption; otherwise, it would not be eligible to receive tax-deductible contributions. Numerous organizations that had been formed earlier also applied, even though they were not required to do so, because they needed to obtain a *public charity* ruling, not just a 501(c)(3) ruling, in order to attract contributions from individuals, the public sector, and private foundations. We are told, for example, that foundations were generally very cautious in the early 1970s and were reluctant to make grants to organizations that did not have the public charity ruling in hand.[16]

Second, as already noted, the 1969 act tilted gift-giving incentives in the direction of charitable entities that were actively involved in providing services, as contrasted with grantmaking foundations. Potential organizers of new public charities must have taken heart from this change in the law as they estimated the flow of contributions which they might expect to obtain from the general public. (We do not mean to suggest, however, that the tax code was the primary force stimulating the establishment of new public charities; in the next chapter, we discuss the effects of Great Society programs and other factors relevant to specific fields.)

In the years between 1975 and 1985, the average rate of increase in the number of entrants remained positive but was much lower (just over 4 percent per year). Then, in 1985, the year-to-year growth in the number of new public charities came to an end. Indeed, between 1985 and 1988 the number of public charities added to the universe declined each year, before recovering in 1989 and 1990 to the 1985 level of approximately 16,000 per year (see Figure 3.3).

In some respects, the slowdown in the rate of establishment of new public charities in the middle to late 1980s must have commenced earlier in the 1980s, given the lag between establishing an entity and actually obtaining a ruling. Are there global explanations? The political and public policy directions associated with the Reagan years surely played a role, but their effects were more complex than people sometimes assume. Research carried out at the Urban Institute, for example, has corrected the common assumption that more activity by private agencies in the field of social welfare can be expected to compensate more or less automatically for federal cutbacks.[17] Rather, as Lester Salamon has emphasized, this country has seen the development of an extensive public-private partnership in such fields as social welfare, with private entities heavily dependent on governmental funding often developing at precisely the times of greatest governmental activity.[18] Thus, paradoxical as it may seem to some, it is likely that part of the reduction in the rate at which private nonprofits were formed in the 1980s was due to efforts in Washington to reduce the federal role in funding social services.

Another question is whether the exceedingly rapid growth in the overall number of new public charities in the late 1960s and early 1970s, and then the recent deceleration in the growth rate, affected all the major fields of activity in much the same way, or whether there have been significant differences in patterns. It would hardly be surprising if patterns of institutional formation varied considerably between fields as diverse as recreation/leisure and science/technology. The more disaggregated data examined in the next chapter confirm that institutions in the various primary fields have indeed been formed at different rates in different periods, with fields that represent what we call "old enthusiasms" exhibiting behavior quite different from the behavior characteristic of other fields, which represent "new enthusiasms."

Notes

1. For an excellent historical overview of the nonprofit sector, see Hall (1987), which contains an extensive list of references to other historical studies. O'Neill (1989) has also written a broad overview of the sector, and Rudney (1987b) and Weisbrod (1988) have done pioneering quantitative studies.

2. Much more work has been done on the evolution of for-profit industries. See, for example, the careful survey of the literature done by Carroll (1984). The more recent work by Hannan and Carroll (1992) includes only one nonprofit field (labor unions) and no charitable nonprofits among the industries studied.

3. See Table 25 in Internal Revenue Service (1991, p. 35) for an example of how aggregated the IRS data are.

4. An attempt was made by the National Center for Charitable Statistics to determine the number of openings and closings between 1987 and 1989, by comparing the respective BMFs in these two years, but the findings are not plausible because of problems with the coding scheme and the failure to distinguish subordinate organizations from independent entities. (Hodgkinson, Weitzman, Toppe, and Noga, 1992, pp. 186–187 and Table 5.3 on p. 196). We return to the general subject of exits in Chapter Six.

5. There is an earlier study of the evolution of foundations which used "births by year" and which we discuss later in this chapter (Odendahl, 1987b). Also, Weisbrod used the "ruling year" variable in his analysis of the founding of public charities. Since the NTEE system did not exist when Weisbrod was doing his work, however, he had no choice but to use the activity codes on the IRS 990 forms to classify organizations by field (Weisbrod, 1988, pp. 80–84). The use of activity codes is problematic because activity codes are self-reported, and not all organizations classify themselves.

6. The average annual rate of increase for public charities is shown in Figure 3.3. The figure for new business incorporations is based on data from Table 845 in U.S. Bureau of the Census (1992, p. 530).

7. Edie (1987, p. 43). Our discussion of the history of foundations in the United States is based heavily on this reference, and the reader with a broader interest in the effects on foundations of other hearings and other pieces of legislation should consult this excellent survey article.

See also Simon (1987) for an even more comprehensive and finely grained account of the tax treatment of nonprofits.

8. See Odendahl (1987a) and the annual yearbook of the Foundation Center (Renz and Lawrence, 1992).

9. Renz and Lawrence (1992, p. 20, Figure 10).

10. Rudney (1987a, p. 190).

11. Boris (1987, p. 70).

12. Rudney (1987a, pp. 189–196).

13. Boris (1987, pp. 4, 15).

14. Boris (1987). For another study of turnover in the foundation world and a discussion of the importance of the growth phenomenon, see Nelson (1987, especially pp. 133–141).

15. See various Foundation Center publications, especially the annual yearbook, *Foundation Giving* (Renz and Lawrence, 1992), for evidence of a decline in the share of total foundation assets represented by the largest foundations.

16. Personal communication with Robert Gardiner of the Internal Revenue Service.

17. Salamon and Abramson (1982). See also Galaskiewicz (1987) and Liebschutz (1992) for empirical evidence on the impact of federal funding cuts on nonprofit activity.

18. Salamon (1987).

FOUR

Trends in
Twelve Primary Fields:
Old and New Enthusiasms

B y comparing year-to-year variations in entrants between public charities and grantmaking foundations in the last chapter, we were able to
show the powerful differentiated effects of changes in the tax code on
patterns of institutional formation. The overall number of new public charities has grown much more rapidly over the last quarter of a century than the
number of new grantmaking foundations. We now propose, in this chapter,
to look inside the large "black box" of public charities in order to examine
variations in patterns of institutional formation within it.

Our objective is to see what more can be learned by comparing trends
in the number of entrants across twelve primary fields of activity. We examine the same twelve fields discussed in the latter part of Chapter Two (National Taxonomy of Exempt Entities [NTEE] primary codes in parentheses):
arts/culture (A), education (B), conservation/environment (C), animal services (D), health (E,F,G,H), employment (J), recreation/leisure (N), youth
development (O), human services (P), international affairs (Q), community
improvement (S), and science/technology (U). We have chosen these fields
for the reasons given earlier, and because many of the fields we have excluded started from such exceedingly low base values in 1965 (that is, they
had so few known entrants in 1965) that it is difficult to interpret percentage
increases.

In studying rates of institutional formation within these twelve fields, we
are especially interested in knowing the answers to the following questions:

- Which fields have had the fastest rates of increase?
- Have the fields experienced different patterns of institutional formation,

with more entrants recorded in earlier years in some fields and more in later years in others?
- Are there broadly defined forces which appear to have been responsible for the observed trends?

Calculation of annual average rates of increase in entrants for each of our twelve primary fields reveals a considerable range, extending all the way from a low of 0.6 percent per year for youth development to a high of 12.4 percent per year for entities in international affairs. Some other primary fields, which we excluded because they had so few known entrants in 1965, have had even higher growth rates (for example, 14.3 percent per year for food/agriculture, and 15.2 percent per year for disaster relief).

Comparison of trends in the rate of formation of new public charities across fields is intriguing because variations in patterns, both in the rate of growth in entrants and in the timing of spurts in institutional formation, can be related to the major social, economic, and political transformations of the last twenty-five years. There are, of course, time paths and rhythms peculiar to specific fields, but an examination of patterns in all twelve fields suggests that many of the fields experienced a notable transition in the mid-1970s. Therefore, we divided the entire 1965-to-1988 period into two subperiods: the years from 1965 to 1975, and the years from 1975 through 1988. When we calculated average annual rates of increase in entrants for each subperiod for each field, three recognizable groupings of fields emerged, which we labeled *old enthusiasms, new enthusiasms,* and *continuing enthusiasms.* One field, youth development, falls into a category all its own, which we call simply *other,* but which an uncharitable soul might call *no enthusiasm.*

Before discussing each of these groupings, we need to sound two alerts about the data underlying the analysis. The findings reported here must be interpreted with care.

First, there are problems associated with the coding process used to classify organizations into specific NTEE fields (recall the discussion in Chapter Two). We have no reason to believe that the general patterns described below would be invalidated by the substitution of more accurately coded data, but the coding problem is serious enough to justify the raising of a large warning flag. When the recoding process now under way at the National Center for Charitable Statistics has been completed, this analysis should be redone. In time, it will also be possible to extend the analysis beyond 1988, a cutoff imposed on us by the current lack of NTEE codes for many organizations established in more recent years.

The second problem stems from the lack of information about entities that were formed during this period but then died. Because we are able to examine only the ruling years of surviving organizations, we are undercounting the true number of entities established in earlier years. From a theoretical perspective, fields with high exit rates may appear to be young and rapidly growing simply because most of their older organizations have died

and are therefore not included in counts of institutional births. For this reason, it was important to assess how our results might be affected if institutional exits were estimated. To that end, we constructed high and low
estimates of exit rates, using the simulation model referred to in Chapter
Three and described in detail in Appendix C.

To simplify the exposition, we present in the body of this chapter only
the rates of increase for surviving entrants. At the same time, it is reassuring
to report that the general patterns remain unchanged, even with high estimates of exit rates. Specifically, the broad differences in rates of increase between the early and late subperiods are not affected by changing
assumptions about exit rates. In general, higher exit rates accentuate the
contrast between periods for the fields we have labeled *old enthusiasms* and
dampen it somewhat for the fields we have labeled *new enthusiasms*. (Appendix C, Table C.1, contains a full set of alternative estimates of rates of increase, which can be compared with the rates of increase presented below.)

Old Enthusiasms

We labeled six fields sharing certain characteristics *old enthusiasms*: arts/cul-
ture, education, health, employment, human services, and animal services.
Four of these fields (education, health, employment, and human services)
can be identified rather directly with Great Society initiatives, which date
from President Johnson's announcement of this program in May 1964. The
expansion of the field of arts/culture was also very much a product of the
late 1960s and early 1970s, as was animal services (which contains large numbers of humane societies).

Average annual rates of increase in entrants within each of these fields,
shown separately for the two subperiods, are presented in Table 4.1. There
are field-specific differences in rates of increase, of course, some of them
noteworthy, but the similarities are equally striking, especially when we contrast the two subperiods. In general, the old enthusiasms experienced rather
rapid entry rates during the first of our subperiods (1965–1975); then, in the
second subperiod (1975–1988), as Great Society initiatives waned, the rate
at which entities were established in these fields declined dramatically, both
in relation to their own previous rates of growth and in relation to the overall rate for all public charities. Hence the shorthand title *old enthusiasms*
seems appropriate.

More specifically, in the six fields within this first set:

- The average annual rate of increase in entrants for the 1965–1975 subperiod was at least 9.3 percent per year in each field, and the average rate
  of increase for all six fields was 11.6 percent per year.
- The rate of increase for the 1975–1988 subperiod was no more than 5.9

Table 4.1. Average Annual Rate of Increase in Entrants by
Primary Field and Subperiod, 1965–1988.

Primary Field	Average Annual Rate of Increase in Entrants (%)		Difference Between Periods I & II
	Period I: 1965–1975	Period II: 1975–1988	
Old Enthusiasms			
Arts/culture (A)[a]	11.2	4.1	−7.1
Education (B)	9.5	4.7	−4.8
Health (E,F,G,H)	11.9	4.0	−7.9
Employment (J)	9.3	0.3	−9.0
Human services (P)	14.3	3.8	−10.5
Animal services (D)	13.5	5.9	−7.6
New Enthusiasms			
Science/technology (U)	2.1	7.6	5.5
Community improvement (S)	3.2	7.3	4.1
Continuing Enthusiasms			
Conservation/environment (C)	10.1	7.4	−2.7
International affairs (Q)	9.7	14.5	4.8
Recreation/leisure (N)	14.2	7.7	−6.5
Other			
Youth development (O)	2.4	0.7	−1.7
All public charities	11.6	5.9	−5.7

Source: Business Master File, October 1991, active, independent only.
[a] Letters following each field refer to NTEE primary codes.

percent per year in any field, and for all six the average was just 3.8 percent per year.

- As a consequence, differences in rates of increase in entrants between the subperiods (the rate in the second subperiod subtracted from the rate in the first subperiod) were strongly negative and ranged from −10.5 points, in human services, to −4.8 points, in education (see the last column of Table 4.1). For all six fields, rates of institutional formation in the second subperiod averaged almost eight percentage points below the corresponding rates for the first subperiod (−7.8 points, to be exact).

We now look at the annual changes in entrants within these six fields, considered individually. Our purpose is only to suggest some of the major forces at work, not to provide anything approaching a systematic commentary, a task well beyond our capacities and not possible given the limitations of the data. Our emphasis is on the broad patterns that can be discerned. Since we are strangers to many of these fields, we hope that others who are more knowledgeable about them will want to pursue some of the questions we have raised (but surely not answered) with these data and this general discussion.

Arts/Culture

The first of the six old enthusiasms, arts/culture, contains two large subsets of institutions, which together comprise over 60 percent of the field: historical organizations and performing arts organizations. The performing arts include many very small performing arts groups, as well as the larger and better-known professional companies. In addition to these two large groupings, arts/culture also includes museums, cultural centers, organizations active in the visual arts, service organizations, and entities active in the humanities.[1]

To illustrate the pattern generally characteristic of the old enthusiasms, we have prepared a graph which depicts the year-to-year changes in the number of entrants to the arts/culture field between 1956 and 1988 (Figure 4.1).[2] The graph is divided by a dotted line into two parts, to illus-

Figure 4.1. Trends in Entrants by Ruling Year, Arts/Culture, 1965–1988.

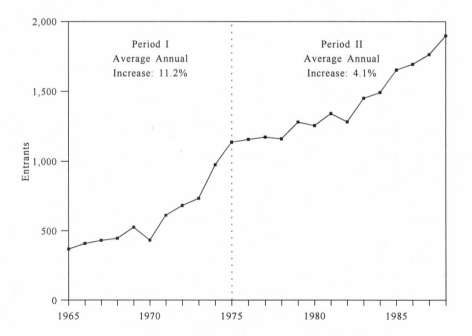

Source: Business Master File, October 1991, active, independent only. See Appendix G, Table G.4-1.

trate the contrast between the two subperiods, with the average annual increase in entrants indicated in each part. A similar graph has been prepared for a typical field in each of the other groups of fields. In addition, Appendix G, Table G.4-1, shows the number of entrants in each year for all twelve primary fields.

The years of rapid growth in arts/culture entities may be related to the Ford Foundation's major performing arts initiatives in the early 1960s and to the establishment of the National Endowments for the Arts and Humanities in 1965. More generally, the heightened interest in the arts stimulated originally by the Kennedy presidency (the "Camelot years") encouraged the formation of new arts organizations. Spending on the arts then received a big boost in the Johnson presidency.[3]

Given the inevitable time lag between the making of initial plans for a new organization, the building of a modicum of institutional support, and the seeking (and obtaining) of a tax-exempt ruling, it is not surprising that the largest spurt in entrants, dated by ruling years, occurred slightly later, during the first half of the 1970s. Moreover, key provisions of the Tax Reform Act of 1969—especially the "15-month rule" (which, as explained in Chapter Three, increased the incentive for organizations to obtain rulings)—led to spurts in the formation of new charitable entities in many fields in 1971 and 1972.

The 1970s were boom years for the establishment of historical organizations, with a peak near 1975. Many of these organizations were local historical societies, reflecting, it seems, a renewed enthusiasm for local history, an interest spawned by planning for the American bicentennial. Furthermore, in 1976 Congress mandated that the state humanities councils established by the National Endowment for the Humanities act as "mini-NEHs," thereby providing a large boost to local-history projects.[4] Another earlier event that affected historical organizations was the passage of the National Historic Preservation Act of 1966, which resulted in the creation of many state-level historical preservation programs.

Education

The flow of entrants into the field of education has been somewhat more erratic. Printouts of the individual organizations included within the education category reveal that the majority of entrants were entities with supporting, advisory, or other ancillary functions; only a minority were new institutions engaged directly in teaching or research. It is also important to remember that the number of nonprofit entities classified as precollegiate is two to three times greater than the number active in higher education—and that, in addition, there are large numbers of libraries and student and educational service organizations.

Between 1965 and 1975, the average annual institutional birth rate was just under 10 percent, and the most rapid growth occurred from about 1967

to 1972. These were years in which there was considerable flight from public elementary and (especially) secondary education, toward new academies
and other independent precollegiate institutions formed in the wake of the
civil rights movement and the integration of public school systems. The unprecedented expansion in higher education during the "golden years" of the
1960s, which was fueled by the demographic consequences of the baby
boom, also led to increased organizational activity, including the establishment of more alumni groups, more honorary and social societies, and more
fundraising entities.

From about 1973 on, the number of entrants into education began to
wane, a trend which continued throughout the 1970s and the early 1980s.
The 1970s were years of retrenchment for many nonprofit institutions operating at all levels of education, and by the end of the 1970s, the year-to-year
increase in the number of entrants had stopped altogether. For the whole of
the period from 1975 to 1988, new entrants increased at an average annual
rate of less than 5 percent—about half the rate characteristic of the first period (see Table 4.1).

In the early 1980s, however, there was a modest spurt in education entrants. At the precollegiate level, there was renewed interest in the formation
of independent schools in the inner cities, at least partly in response to
parental concern about crime and other problems often associated with the
public schools. The Reagan years provided a philosophical underpinning for
privatization. The early 1980s were also marked by improved economic conditions, following the end of double-digit inflation and the arrival of more
favorable financial markets. Many individuals were in a better position to
make contributions to private educational institutions, including libraries
and other ancillary organizations, and endowments increased in real value.

Health

In the large field of health, with 329 entrants in the base year of 1965, the
overall pattern of institutional formation has been generally congruent with
the overall pattern for all public charities. Between 1965 and 1975, in particular, the average annual rates of increase for health and for all public charities were essentially indistinguishable (11.9 percent and 11.6 percent,
respectively). We first thought that the extraordinary congruence between
the health sector and all public charities might reflect a weighting phenomenon, since health is such a large field. In fact, however, the health organizations in our universe made up just 12 percent of total entrants in 1965.
Arts/culture and education both contained more entities than health did,
and the patterns they exhibit do not parallel the figures for all public charities as closely as do the figures for health.

From 1975 on, the growth in new entrants slowed considerably, dropping from almost 12 percent per year to only 4 percent in the more recent
subperiod. As a result, the rate for the two subperiods combined is below the

overall rate for entrants to all public charities. (This may be the only known instance in which a statistic pertaining to the field of health went up at a below-average rate!)

The vast majority of health organizations included in the IRS's Business Master File (BMF) are not hospitals. Recall that the health category is made up of four NTEE primary fields, including organizations having to do with mental health, public health, crisis intervention, elderly care, substance abuse, and medical research, not to mention support services, health associations, and patient-support groups. According to the American Hospital Association, the total number of nonprofit hospitals in 1990 was 3,191, which is fewer than 20 percent of the total number of independent, positive-filer health organizations. Moreover, during the last two decades the number of nonprofit hospitals has actually declined slightly.

At first we thought that the reduction in the number of nonprofit hospitals might be due to rapid institutional growth of for-profit hospitals, or to increases in the capacity of existing institutions. In fact, however, neither of these hypotheses is correct. Since 1972, the number of for-profit hospitals increased only from 738 to 749 institutions. In addition, the total number of hospital beds has declined by over 20 percent since 1972, at the same time that occupancy rates have decreased.[5]

In population-ecology terms, a more probable explanation is that the hospital niche of the health sector has largely been filled. The new institutional formation that is taking place in the health sector (still over 1,000 organizations per year in recent years) presumably reflects the movement toward alternative forms of delivery of health care outside the hospital environment, the greater health needs of an aging population, and the vastly increased attention devoted to such specific health problems as AIDS.

Employment

Of the six fields grouped together under the label *old enthusiasms*, employment experienced by far the slowest overall growth in entrants between 1965 and 1988. Indeed, its overall entry rate of 2.6 percent is second lowest among all twelve of our primary fields. Nevertheless, during the first of our subperiods, and especially during the 1960s, entrants into employment increased more rapidly than entrants into many other fields; it was an "enthusiasm" at that time. The average annual rate of increase in entrants was over 9 percent during the first subperiod. Between 1965 and 1972, there was a significant upsurge in the number of entities involved in job training and in other efforts to improve employment opportunities. The availability of governmental support was no doubt a principal factor behind this growth.

For the last sixteen years, however, the annual number of entrants has fluctuated around a more or less constant level (in the low 100s). The annual number of entrants increased in the first half of the 1980s and then decreased again after 1985. It is possible that for-profit enterprises have taken over some of the functions previously served by nonprofit entities in the employment field. It is also possible that, as in the case of hospitals, the existing entities by now largely saturate the field.

Human Services

The field of human services includes settlement houses, children's and youth services, and family services. Here, we observe an especially large increase in the number of entrants between 1969 and 1974, a plateau between 1974 and 1982, and then above-average increases between 1986 and 1988 (see Appendix G, Table G.4-1). It is entirely appropriate to put this field with the old enthusiasms on the basis of its rapid growth in the late 1960s and the early 1970s, following the Great Society initiatives. Entrants increased at a faster rate in human services (at an average annual rate of 14.3 percent) than in any of our other fields between 1965 and 1975. Its overall rate of institution formation was far lower between 1975 and 1988 (3.8 percent per year), but it has had much more of a resurgence in recent years than many of the other old enthusiasms. This recent increase in entrants may reflect greater awareness of a wide array of social ills.

Animal Services

The last of our six old enthusiasms, the field of animal services, is a cousin to human services, at least in certain respects. Its pattern of institution formation during the late 1960s and the early 1970s can be seen to have followed almost precisely the pattern in human services (see Appendix G, Table G.4-1). Moreover, the rise in interest in the work of humane societies, and in other organizations devoted to the care, protection, and understanding of wildlife during those years, can be thought of as reflecting some of the same broad kinds of social concern that were reflected in the formation of entities intended to provide better human services. For reasons unknown to us, the number of entrants into this field fell precipitously between 1975 and the early 1980s, before enjoying (with human services) something of a renaissance in the 1980s.

New Enthusiasms

The unifying characteristic of the six fields just discussed is that they had much faster rates of institutional formation between 1965 and 1975 than they did between 1975 and 1988. The two fields we now consider—science/technology and community improvement—have precisely the opposite pattern:

- The number of entrants into these fields grew much more rapidly in the second subperiod than in the first one (see Table 4.1).

- Entrants into both fields increased less rapidly during the first subperiod (with average annual rates of increase of just 2.1 and 3.2 percent, respectively) than did entrants into almost all other fields.
- The rate of increase in the 1975–1988 subperiod was over 7 percent per year in both fields (7.6 and 7.3 percent).

Judged by these characteristics, these two fields represent new enthusiasms.

Science/Technology

The pattern of entrants into the field of science/technology, shown in Figure 4.2, is characteristic of new enthusiasms. Overall, new research and service entities in science/technology were established at a slower rate than were all public charities, especially during the first subperiod. In the last few

Figure 4.2.   Trends in Entrants by Ruling Year, Science/Technology, 1965–1988.

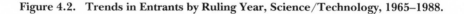

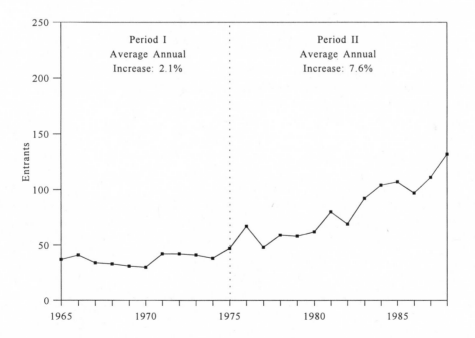

Source: Business Master File, October 1991, active, independent only. See Appendix G, Table G.4-1.

years, however, entrants into this field have increased faster than entrants into all public charities.

The relatively rapid recent growth in nonprofit entities concerned with science/technology has been fed by many currents, including the recurring belief that private initiatives in research and the provision of scientific and technological services are needed to complement governmental activity in these areas. William O. Baker, former president of Bell Laboratories and a leader of research in such fields as condensed-matter physics, observes that research results have outpaced the capacity of government to respond to them. It is possible that the backlog of exciting ideas, which was the product of first-rate applied research, led to the creation of nonprofit entities intended to take advantage of this new knowledge.

Community Improvement

The field of community improvement is intriguing. Included in it are a wide range of neighborhood development and improvement associations, federated giving programs, and business services intended to improve or develop commercial enterprises within communities. Over the entire period from 1965 to 1988, the number of entrants into community improvement has apparently increased much less rapidly than entrants into all public charities. (We say "apparently" to acknowledge again our inability to include organizations which were formed during these years but failed to survive. It is possible that exit rates were especially high in this field because entities in community improvement tend to be small, but there is no way to test this hypothesis.) It is clear, however, that in recent years there has been a pronounced increase in the rate of institutional formation in this field.

We suspect that the sharp contrast between the two subperiods reflects, at least in part, a change in philosophy as to how society should address some of its endemic problems. There has been a pronounced decrease in confidence in the ability of government to address problems of job creation, housing, and so on. Simultaneously, there has been a growing interest in locally based community efforts to help in these areas.[6] In our view, it is not a coincidence that new entities in community improvement were established at relatively modest rates in the earlier subperiod, when new entities in human services and employment were being formed in large numbers, and that these growth patterns were reversed in the more recent subperiod.

In recent years there also appears to have been a decidedly above-average increase in entrants within a related field, which we have not included among our twelve primary fields: philanthropy. We believe that the rapid recent expansion in this field reflects a similar phenomenon—namely, a growing desire to form private-public partnerships (or to encourage purely private efforts) to solve what were once thought to be problems for the state to address.

Continuing Enthusiasms

Three other fields—conservation/environment, international affairs, and recreation/leisure—are distinctive in that the numbers of entrants have increased very steadily throughout both subperiods. They represent *continuing enthusiasms*. These are fields which appeal to a broad spectrum of the population, and their steady growth seems to have been affected relatively little by the forces that drove the creation of entities active in the other fields we have discussed.

Conservation/Environment

As shown in Figure 4.3, entrants into conservation/environment have increased at a remarkably steady rate (with the exception of a small spurt in the early 1970s, when the 15-month rule was enacted). This consistent pattern of growth is typical of the fields we have designated *continuing enthusi-*

Figure 4.3.   Trends in Entrants by Ruling Year, Conservation/Environment, 1965–1988.

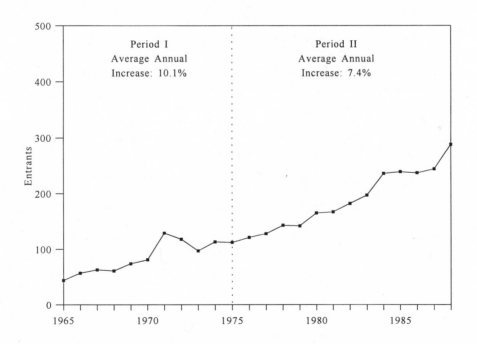

Source: Business Master File, October 1991, active, independent only. See Appendix G, Table G.4-1.

asms. The ever-growing public interest in conservation and ecology is reflected directly in Figure 4.3 and is especially evident in the rapid pace of institutional formation that occurred during the 1980s. One of the major
components of the broad field of conservation/environment is natural resources conservation and protection, and it is this subfield which has been
responsible for most of the entrants in the 1980s.

International Affairs

International affairs includes entities concerned with international cultural
and student exchanges, foreign-policy research and analysis, and human
rights. New entities in this field started from a very low base (we count only
15 entrants in 1965) but then proceeded to increase very rapidly, especially
after 1980. In 1988, there were over 200 entrants.

In the 1960s, there was an explosion of interest in population growth,
economic development, and political modernization. There is such awareness today of the worldwide dimensions of many problems, including disaster relief, population and health issues, and nutrition, that the very term
globalization has become almost a cliché. The exceptionally rapid formation of new entities in the category of international affairs is testimony to
this awareness and to the growing conviction that private nonprofit institutions can make a difference in a world that has been profoundly changed
by new technologies, easy and instant communication, and the end of the
Cold War.

Recreation/Leisure

Recreation/leisure has also been one of the fastest-growing fields during
both subperiods, as evidenced by its average annual rate of increase in entrants (9.5 percent) for the entire period from 1965 through 1988. Physical-
fitness programs, camps and camping programs, and sports-training
activities have all been much in vogue, and the result has been an eightfold
increase in the annual number of entrants over the last twenty-three years.
Noteworthy too is the fact that the rate of increase gives absolutely no indi-
cation of slowing (see the data in Appendix G, Table G.4-1).

Other: Youth Development

It would be difficult to find a field that contrasts more sharply with recre-
ation/leisure than youth development. There has been no sustained growth
in entrants into youth development over the two decades we examined (see
Figure 4.4). The number of surviving entrants has been in the low 100s in
twenty-one of the twenty-four years for which we have data (see Appendix G,
Table G.4-1). Overall, the average annual rate of increase in entrants has

Figure 4.4. Trends in Entrants by Ruling Year, Youth Development, 1965–1988.

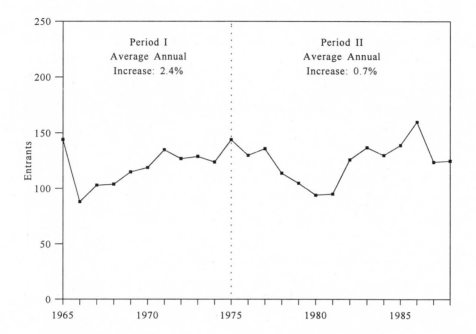

Source: Business Master File, October 1991, active, independent only. See Appendix G, Table G.4-1.

been less than 1 percent. In interpreting this finding, however, it is important to remember that these data are for independent organizations only, and that youth development has an exceptionally high ratio of subordinates to independents (see Table 2.2, Chapter Two). Growth has undoubtedly occurred in the number of subordinate organizations operating under the auspices of such well-established parents as the Boy Scouts of America, the Girl Scouts of America, the Future Farmers of America, the Future Homemakers of America, and so on. But, for reasons explained in our discussion of Ducks Unlimited (see Appendix A), we cannot date the addition of subordinates with any precision. Our main finding is that the omnibus organizations in this field are well established, and there is no evidence of any large wave of new entities.

In concluding this avowedly impressionistic analysis of trends in entrants within selected primary fields, we wish to emphasize the need for much more refined analysis of individual fields and related sets of fields. The twelve primary fields discussed here—and especially the four most populous fields—contain such a wide array of types of organizations that a more disaggregated mode of analysis is called for. In our view, there is much productive research of this kind to be done, especially after the recoding of institutions by field is completed. One challenge is to relate developments specific to the evolution of particular fields to broader currents affecting all public charities (and, for that matter, society at large). We also believe that the concepts of population ecology and organizational ecology have much to contribute to the understanding of phenomena of this kind.

In this chapter, we have been able to do no more than organize the rudimentary data that exist and propose a few explanations for some of the most distinct patterns. In the next chapter, we attempt to take another step by illustrating ways of using a more disaggregated type of analysis within three very different sectors: higher education, civil rights, and the performing arts.

Notes

1. See Appendix B of *Nonprofit Almanac, 1992–93* (Hodgkinson, Weitzman, Toppe, and Noga, 1992, pp. 593–613) for a detailed explanation of the criteria for inclusion in each primary field.
2. Comparable figures using high and low exit-rate assumptions are shown in Appendix C, Figure C.1.
3. See Chapter Five for a fuller discussion of the evolution of the performing arts fields.
4. Phillips and Hogan (1984, pp. 27–28).
5. Table 167 in U.S. Bureau of the Census (1992, p. 112).
6. Steinberg (1987) and Milofsky (1987). Our colleague Joan Gilbert points out that a back-to-the-city movement began in the late 1960s and was subsequently fueled by governmental block-grant programs, which were initiated in 1974.

FIVE

A Closer Look at
Higher Education, Civil Rights,
and Performing Arts

I n the last chapter, we compared trends in the number of entrants across twelve primary fields of activity. In this chapter, we look more intensely at the patterns of institutional formation in three specific sectors: higher education, civil rights, and performing arts. These fields are quite different, in terms of their histories and general characteristics, and thus illustrate the advantages of more disaggregated analysis.

Higher education is interesting because it permits an analysis, over long periods of time, of the establishment of a variety of templates, with different types of institutions established in successive waves. Civil rights is a much younger field, and it allows us to investigate the ways in which increasing specialization has shaped the kinds of new entrants that have predominated in recent years. Performing arts is itself an amalgam of activities, and differences in patterns of institutional formation (between, for example, theater and opera) reflect the preferences of influential funders, the cost structures of the respective fields, and competition for audiences and financial contributions across fields.

Higher Education: Waves of Institutional Formation

Of all the major nonprofit sectors, higher education is, along with religion, the oldest and the most institutionalized. Nearly 60 percent of all existing four-year colleges and universities were established prior to the start of the twentieth century, and many are well over one hundred years old. The longevity of this set of institutions is truly striking. For this reason, higher ed-

ucation is especially amenable to an analysis of the long-term evolution of
the varied subsets of institutions that together comprise what we loosely call
a sector.

Another feature of the higher education sector that makes it particularly productive to study is the existence of directories such as the *Higher Education Directory,* a comprehensive listing of accredited colleges and
universities. As explained more fully in Appendix D, we use the *Directory*
rather than the Business Master File (BMF) for our analysis of the evolution
of higher education, for three reasons. First, we are unable, with the still imperfect National Taxonomy of Exempt Entities (NTEE) codes, to separate
the bona fide colleges and universities in the BMF education field from the
many ancillary organizations and primary and secondary schools. Second,
the *Directory* includes both private and public institutions. In higher education, arguably more than in the other sectors examined here, establishments
of public and private institutions need to be studied together if the development of the overall system is to be understood. Ideally, we would have included public institutions in our studies of other sectors, but we could not
identify all-inclusive sources (such as the *Higher Education Directory*) outside
of education. Third, because the higher education sector is so old, the establishment dates in the *Directory* are much more revealing than the ruling
years in the BMF.

As in earlier chapters, we limit our analysis to organizations that have
survived. In the field of higher education, it is possible to compare data based
on the establishment dates of surviving institutions, with other data showing
the total number of institutions in existence in earlier years, *including those
that subsequently died.*[1] This comparison can be made at ten-year intervals,
from 1869 to 1989. We find that the two series are highly consistent: both
decade-to-decade changes and the absolute levels are very similar. For example, the count of all institutions in existence in 1869 was 563, whereas our universe of surviving institutions (that had been established by 1869) was 514—a
believable difference in the right direction. In 1939, the corresponding numbers were 1,708 and 1,714; in 1979, 3,152 and 3,111. This comparison is most
reassuring. Our inability to consider the birthdates of individual colleges and
universities that failed to survive until the present day does not appear to have
had any major distorting effect.

Our purpose in this chapter is not to present anything approaching a
comprehensive analysis of the higher education sector. Rather, we wish to
illustrate a basic characteristic of institutional development: the tendency
for subsets of institutions within the sector to be created in spurts or waves,
each responding to new needs and opportunities. In order to keep this discussion within proper bounds, we concentrate on the three most readily
identifiable waves of institutional foundings: Liberal Arts I colleges, Re-
search/Doctorate universities and Two-Year colleges.[2] (See Appendix D for
definitions of these types of institutions, which are based on the Carnegie
Classification system.)

General Concepts

The wave phenomenon at work here is by no means peculiar to higher education and is well understood by scholars who have studied organizational life cycles. As Arthur Stinchcombe explained in a classic article written almost thirty years ago,

> the organizational inventions that can be made at a particular time in history depend on the social technology available at that time. . . . Then, both because they can function effectively with those organizational forms, and because the forms tend to become institutionalized, the basic structure of the organization tends to remain relatively stable. . . . An examination of the history of almost any type of organization shows that there are great spurts of foundation of organizations of the type, followed by periods of relatively slower growth, perhaps to be followed by new spurts, generally of a fundamentally different kind of organization in the same field.[3]

Thus we would expect the evolution of a sector to proceed in three phases: (1) introduction of an institutional model appropriate to the needs and circumstances of the time; (2) relatively rapid replication of it; and (3) a slowdown in the rate of entry as competition increases and the organizational niche becomes filled. A corollary is that it is generally much easier to replicate an existing organizational form than to develop a new type of entity—it is easier to copy than to create a new template. After some point, however, when the need for the initial type of organization has been largely satisfied, the resumption of rapid institutional growth depends on the introduction of a new template.

Liberal Arts I Colleges

These ideas have direct applicability to the founding of distinct types of institutions of higher education in this country. For instance, the selective Liberal Arts I colleges of today were established largely in the nineteenth century and comprise the oldest field within American higher education (Figure 5.1). Well-known examples include Amherst, Dickinson, Oberlin, Reed, and Smith Colleges. These institutions often evolved from small "literary colleges," and they served a wide variety of religious, political, and economic purposes in eighteenth- and nineteenth-century America. Their small scale was appropriate to the times, as were the kind of education they offered and their commitment to serve what were primarily local and regional needs.[4]

These colleges are of continuing importance, as exemplars of high-quality education for students with broad interests in the liberal arts and as feeders for doctoral and professional programs of all kinds, but they now en-

Figure 5.1.   Trends in Entrants by Date of Establishment, Liberal Arts I Colleges.

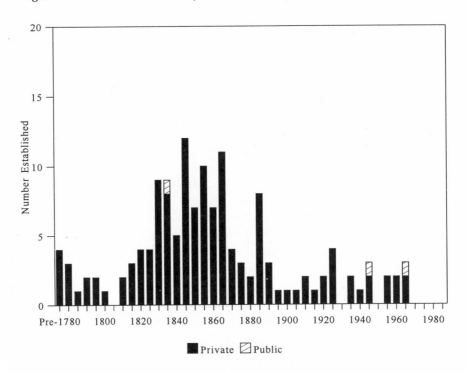

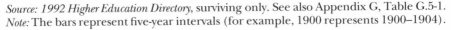

Source: 1992 Higher Education Directory, surviving only. See also Appendix G, Table G.5-1.
Note: The bars represent five-year intervals (for example, 1900 represents 1900–1904).

roll less than 2 percent of all college students (and less than 3 percent of all
students attending four-year institutions). It is surely significant that of the
142 Liberal Arts I colleges listed in the *1992 Higher Education Directory,* only
25 were founded in this century. The institutional niche which they occupy
appears to have been largely filled by the late 1800s, when a new and quite
different wave of institutional formation began.

Research/Doctorate Universities

In the second half of the nineteenth century, it became increasingly clear
that the traditional colleges, valuable as they were, could not meet all the
needs of a changing, increasingly complex, industrialized society. The claims
of science, and of applied studies of all kinds, were becoming more insistent,
and the hold of religion on institutions of higher education weakened. In addition, the example of graduate education abroad, especially in Germany,
was widely admired in the United States. These developments had major effects on the evolution of both private and public higher education.

By 1870, the number of new Liberal Arts I colleges being founded had dropped off sharply (see Figure 5.1), and energies shifted to the establishment of other types of institutions. The founding of Johns Hopkins University, in 1876, launched what has been called the "university revolution," and from 1876 to 1895 this revolution was in full swing.[5] Prior to the founding of Johns Hopkins, all attempts to establish universities as we know them today had failed.

Subsequently, new institutions were established (including many new public institutions, as noted below), and many existing private colleges transformed themselves into Research/Doctorate universities by adding graduate and research programs. Such organizational transformations are not uncommon. Fundamental changes (for example, in mission) are unlikely to occur, but less radical adjustments (such as the addition of graduate degrees) are to be expected.

Organizational transformation can significantly complicate an analysis of foundings. For example, most of the private research universities in existence today took on their present-day character in the last third of the nineteenth century. Thus, in one important sense—when defined as Research/Doctorate universities—they are not nearly as old as they appear to be. Harvard, Columbia, the University of Pennsylvania, Princeton, and other private universities that have establishment dates prior to 1870 were originally established as small colleges. Nomenclature sometimes captures the evolution of an institution. The legal name of Harvard University, for example, is still "The President and Fellows of Harvard College."[6] Because many private Research/Doctorate universities were originally liberal arts colleges, the pattern of their founding dates, shown in Figure 5.2, dramatically understates the bunching or replication phenomenon that occurred in the 1870s, 1880s, and 1890s.

The parallel pattern, whereby publicly supported universities (the state universities, as some refer to them) were established, sometimes by modifying the purposes of existing institutions and sometimes by creating entirely new institutions, was stimulated by the passage in 1862 of the Land Grant College Act, known as the Morrill Act. This bill granted each state thirty thousand acres for each senator and representative in Congress, the proceeds of which were to be used to support at least one college. Reflecting the same social and economic forces alluded to above, the primary aim of these new institutions was "to teach such branches of learning as are related to agriculture and the mechanic arts . . . without excluding other scientific and classical studies." Although a number of state universities had been started prior to the act, they had suffered from lack of funds and were still strongly influenced by religious denominations.[7] The profound impact of the Morrill Act can be seen directly in Figure 5.2 (the growth in the number of public universities is shown by the striped bars). Between 1865 and 1895, 54 public Research/Doctorate universities were founded, 40 percent of the total number in existence today.

Figure 5.2.   Trends in Entrants by Date of Establishment,
Research/Doctorate Universities.

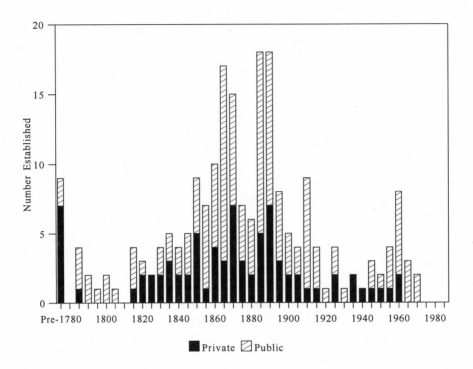

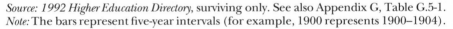

Source: 1992 Higher Education Directory, surviving only. See also Appendix G, Table G.5-1.
Note: The bars represent five-year intervals (for example, 1900 represents 1900–1904).

The Research/Doctorate universities, then, constitute the second wave of institutions formed to meet the needs of society for postsecondary education. While younger than the Liberal Arts I colleges, these universities are also old by the standards of nonprofit entities. Indeed, all but 61 were founded before 1895. After that date, the rate of establishment of new Research/Doctorate universities declined markedly. The modern research university is an interesting example of an institutional type that developed initially within the private, nonprofit sector and then spread to the public sector, once workable models had been established.

Community Colleges

If the establishment of Liberal Arts I colleges dominated the early history of higher education in America, and the founding of Research/Doctorate universities shaped the landscape of higher education in the latter part of the nineteenth century, the development of Two-Year colleges has certainly been the single most dominant feature of the post–World War II period. The overwhelming majority of these institutions are public entities, under the control of a state, a county, or a municipality (see the striped bars in Figure 5.3).

The growth in the Two-Year college field that has taken place, especially during the 1960s, is nothing less than phenomenal. (Note that the scale in Figure 5.3 is twenty times the scale in Figures 5.1 and 5.2.) To be sure, the concept of Two-Year, or junior, colleges as separate institutional entities began to emerge much earlier, really at the end of the nineteenth century, when these were primarily private institutions. The term *junior college* was first used in 1896, and by 1915 the idea had spread so rapidly that references to the "junior college movement" began to appear. In 1920, the U.S. commissioner of education called a national meeting of junior college leaders. The next year, the American Association of Junior Colleges was established. These events are reflected in the jump in entrants during the 1920s.[8]

Figure 5.3.   Trends in Entrants by Date of Establishment, Two-Year Colleges.

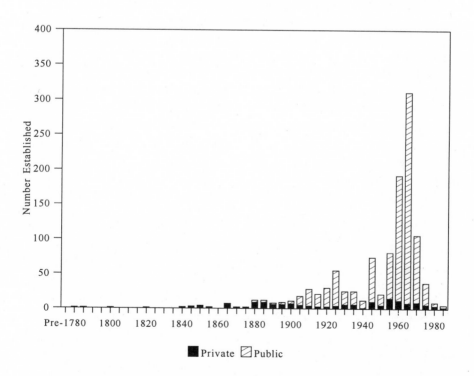

Source: 1992 Higher Education Directory, surviving only. See also Appendix G, Table G.5-1.
Note: The bars represent five-year intervals (for example, 1900 represents 1900–1904).

The second peak in entrants took place after World War II, between 1945 and 1950. This spurt was a direct result of the G.I. Bill and the thousands of returning veterans who sought places in the nation's colleges and universities—places which the combination of private and state institutions then in existence simply could not provide. In 1947, the Truman Commission gave new support and credibility to junior colleges. In addition to proposing a new name—*community colleges*—the commission proposed that every state that had not already done so allow school districts to extend their schools through the fourteenth grade. By 1955, the number of new institutions had begun to grow dramatically, with a third and final peak occurring between 1965 and 1970, when over 300 new institutions were created.

It is difficult to imagine how such an extraordinary spurt in institutional formation could have occurred without substantial governmental funding. In this respect, the establishment of community colleges in the postwar period represents a dynamic different from anything else we have seen. The Two-Year colleges were a direct response to the national need for a rapid expansion in the overall capacity of the system of higher education—for new places that could accommodate many students, including many "nontraditional" students, at a reasonable cost. In effect, a new institutional niche opened up, and the Two-Year colleges filled it.

As was the case with other waves of institutional formation, a rapid deceleration in the growth of Two-Year colleges then ensued. Still, it is important to recognize that over 100 new entities were established as recently as 1970–74. However, relatively few new Two-Year colleges have been founded since 1980, and it would appear that this wave of institutional formation has now crested.

In more recent years, some of the most interesting developments in higher education have concerned the establishment and growth of for-profit institutions providing specialized forms of advanced training. This development deserves much more attention than it has received to date, in part because it illustrates how the nonprofit and for-profit sectors intersect.

We have assembled in Figure 5.4 the founding dates of all the institutions of higher education, regardless of type, which are represented in the *1992 Higher Education Directory*. By superimposing on this figure the median year of establishment for the sets of institutions described in this section, as well other types of schools, we are able to show graphically the successive waves of foundings, which together have shaped this country's system of higher education. The median founding years range from 1856 for Liberal Arts I colleges to 1962 for Two-Year colleges. We are persuaded that this way of thinking about the evolution of the sector provides a much richer understanding of patterns of institutional development than would a more aggregative approach.

Figure 5.4. Trends in Entrants by Date of Establishment,
All Institutions of Higher Education.

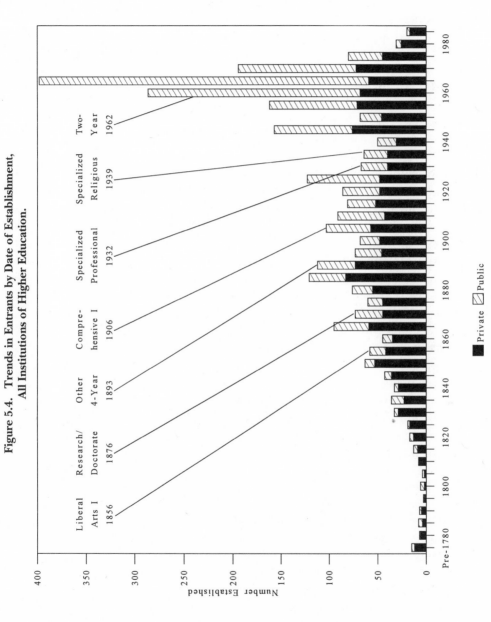

Source: 1992 Higher Education Directory, surviving only. See also Appendix G, Table G.5-1.
Note: The bars represent five-year intervals (for example, 1900 represents 1900–1904).

Civil Rights: Effects of Specialization on Institutional Formation

It would be hard to conceive of a category that differs more from higher education than civil rights does. Whereas higher education is notable for the age of so many of its institutions, civil rights is one of the youngest and (still) most rapidly changing of all the NTEE primary fields. Higher education is heavily institutionalized and contains many large as well as long-established institutions; civil rights is much less formally constituted and contains many small organizations, which are often loosely organized. Higher education is clearly structured, with individual institutions fitting fairly neatly within an understood framework; civil rights, broadly defined, is far more heterogeneous and diverse, both in the population groups and in the missions which it serves.

These extreme differences are one reason why it seems desirable to complement the discussion of higher education by conducting another kind of exploratory probe. Another reason for devoting special attention to civil rights is, of course, the intrinsic importance of the field in our society today. The difficulties in defining the field, enumerating its members, and charting its growth are real, but they should not be excuses for ignoring it.

These difficulties do mean, however, that the caveats associated with any provisional probe of this kind must be underscored. We are not in a position to come to strong conclusions. This analysis is intended primarily to raise questions and stimulate more research by individuals with special knowledge of institutions active in civil rights.

We do have a thesis to propose, however—namely, that the recent pattern of institutional formation within civil rights illustrates and exemplifies a growing social fragmentation within American society. Increasingly, it seems to us, new organizations have been designed to deal with the special needs of rather precisely defined population groups (for example, the problems encountered by immigrants from country X, rather than with the problems of immigrants in general or with the problems of the disenfranchised or disadvantaged defined even more broadly).

Subsectors Within the Civil Rights Field

After much examination of the organizations assigned to various fields and subfields within the NTEE classification system, we identified five subgroups which, taken together, constitute our operative definition of the civil rights field. (See Appendix D for an explanation of how we defined and then divided our civil rights universe.) The first of these subgroups consists of 828 organizations concerned with the provision of *legal services*. This group includes, for example, the Legal Aid Society of Birmingham, Alabama; Ozark Legal Services of Fayetteville, Arkansas; and the Los Angeles Center for Law and Justice. Next comes a slightly larger cluster of 876 entities concerned with *minority/immigrant rights*. (Some finer breakdowns can also be made, as we discuss below.) The third subgroup consists of 575 entities which either are *women's centers* or are concerned with *women's rights*. The fourth subgroup consists of 252 *abortion-related* entities and includes both right-to-life organizations and reproductive rights (or prochoice) groups. The right-to-life organizations predominate in this category, with 230 of the total of 252 organizations, presumably because many of the prochoice groups function under the broader heading of women's rights. Finally, we have the inescapable *other civil rights* category, which consists of 501 entities, two-thirds of which are concerned generally with civil rights and with the advocacy of civil liberties. The remaining one-third is concerned with special interests not represented by one of our main subgroups (such as the rights of people with disabilities, senior citizens, children, and homosexuals).

Trends in Entrants

Of the 3,032 civil rights entities included in this analysis, only 159 have pre-1965 ruling years, and fully four-fifths of these older organizations are in either the legal services or women's centers/rights subgroups. In other words, nearly 95 percent of the surviving institutions coded as falling within the boundaries of the civil rights field, as it is defined here, were granted tax-exempt rulings by the IRS in the last twenty-five years. From this perspective, it is indeed an extremely young field.

The civil rights field also appears to have grown very rapidly. Entrants into the field increased at an average annual rate of 8.9 percent per year between 1965 and 1988. Especially striking is the very large increase in 1987, when the number of entrants jumped to 211 (Figure 5.5). This exceptionally high level of entrants was more than sustained in 1988, and the fragmentary evidence available suggests strongly that it continued into at least 1989 and 1990. More generally, Figure 5.5 shows very rapid rates of increase in entrants in the 1970s (12.2 percent per year, on the average), a distinct slowdown during the first half of the 1980s (an average increase of just 3.7 percent per year), and then the sharp spurt in 1987.

The trends for the subgroups within the civil rights sector are quite different, and legal services differs most dramatically from the others (Figure 5.6). From 1965 to 1970, it had by far the largest absolute number of entrants each year, and entrants into legal services increased steadily during the 1970s (reaching a peak of 47 new organizations in 1979). The large number of new legal services entities that received tax-exempt rulings during this period directly reflects the country's awakened social concern for the importance of protecting the legal rights of disadvantaged groups, especially minorities.

After 1978, however, the number of new legal services entrants—in sharp contrast to the other civil rights subgroups—declined rather steadily. One possible explanation for this drop is that by the late 1970s the legal services niche was largely filled. The interest in forming new legal services entities may have diminished, relative to the interest in forming other kinds of civil rights organizations, because of a perceived need to move beyond

Figure 5.5. Trends in Entrants by Ruling Year, Civil Rights, 1965–1988.

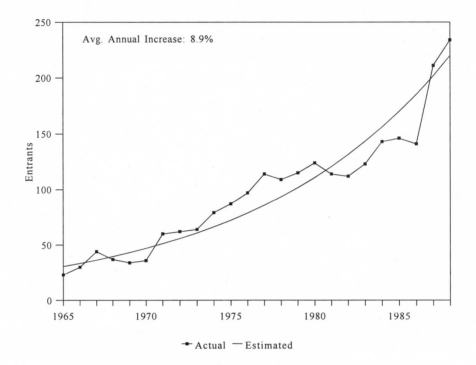

Source: Business Master File, October 1991, active, independent only. See also Appendix G, Table G.5-2.

legal challenges if some of the most pressing problems facing minority groups were to be addressed effectively in such areas as schooling, jobs, housing, health, safety, and family and community life. A related hypothesis is that as more public funding became available for legal services, more organizations survived, thus reducing the need for new organizations. In any case, during the entire period from 1965 through 1988, the number of new entities in legal services increased at an average rate of less than 3 percent per year.

Entrants into all other kinds of civil rights subgroups—which started, to be sure, from much lower bases—grew at average rates of at least 10 percent a year. Women's centers, and organizations concerned with women's rights, for example, grew very rapidly during most of this period (at an average annual rate of 14.1 percent, from 1965 to 1988). The women's movement (and the pro-choice movement) really took hold during these years, and it is not surprising that the formation of nonprofit entities responded accordingly.

Figure 5.6.   Trends in Entrants by Ruling Year, Legal Services,
1965–1988 (Three-Year Moving Averages).

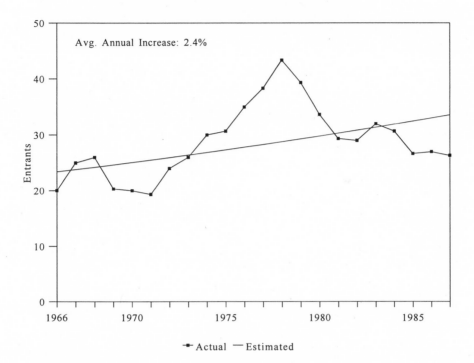

Source: Business Master File, October 1991, active, independent only. See also Appendix G, Table G.5-2.

Abortion-related organizations did not come into being in a significant way until 1971, which was the beginning of a period of fairly rapid growth. An even larger spurt took place in the mid-1980s, but the rate of growth now seems to have leveled off again (Figure 5.7). The early part of this pattern of institutional formation appears to be directly related to the *Roe* v. *Wade* Supreme Court decision. That historic decision was not announced until January 22, 1973, but the Texas law was declared unconstitutional in June of 1970, and the entire sequence of events followed. Hence it is not surprising that the first tax-exempt rulings were granted in 1971. The second surge of new right-to-life entrants, in the mid-1980s, presumably reflects the heightened political interest in the abortion issue during the Reagan presidency.

On the surface, the increases in new entrants into the final two civil rights subgroups—"other civil rights" and minority/immigrant rights—resemble the women's rights and abortion-related fields. Both subgroups grew

Figure 5.7.   Trends in Entrants by Ruling Year, Abortion-Related, 1965–1988 (Three-Year Moving Averages).

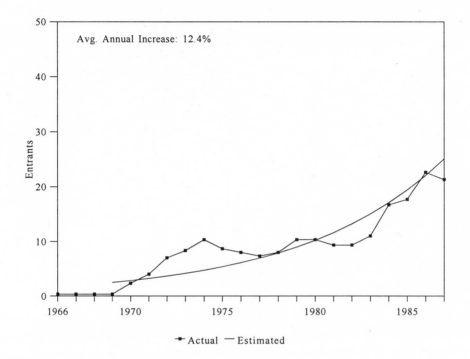

Source: Business Master File, October 1991, active, independent only. See also Appendix G, Table G.5-2.

Note: The "estimated" line begins at 1969 because there were no entrants in earlier years.

steadily and rapidly over the entire 1965–1988 period, in the case of "other civil rights" at an average annual rate of 11.5 percent, and in the case of minority/immigrant rights at a rate of 11.9 percent. It is impossible to understand what has occurred, however, by working with such aggregative data. A closer examination of the components of "other civil rights" and minority/immigrant rights is revealing, and it takes us directly into the last part of this commentary.

Evidence of Increased Specialization

It is instructive to divide the amorphous "other civil rights" subgroup into two parts: the truly general organizations established to address broad-based concerns, and organizations formed to meet highly specific needs. Of the 70 organizations in the "other civil rights" subgroup founded prior to 1975, less than 16 percent fell into the "specific" category. This percentage more than doubled in the 1975–1984 period, rising to 33 percent (66 out of 200). In the most recent four years, 1985 to 1988, fully 42 percent of new organizations fell into the "specific" category (54 out of 129).

This increase in specialization may be due in part to a proposition concerning organizational life spans: in general, broadly defined organizations can be expected to survive longer. Since our data capture only surviving organizations, we would expect to find—and do find—that the majority of older organizations have broad missions.

There has also been, we suspect, an increase in specialization that is independent of this life-span hypothesis. Greater specialization is evident not only in the "other civil rights" field, but also among minority/immigrant rights entities. Between 1980 and 1988, the minority/immigrant rights entrants increased at the dramatic rate of 17.3 percent per year, and most of these new entrants have been formed to meet the needs of specifically defined subsectors of the population. When we divide the organizations within the minority/immigrant rights subgroup according to their target populations, we find that 85 percent of entrants since 1980 were in one of three "specific" fields (*all Asian, all Hispanic,* or *other specific*) while 15 percent were not targeted to a specific group (Appendix G, Table G.5-2).

Additional supporting evidence for our specialization thesis is found when we look inside the "all Asian" category. Again, we find distinct patterns of institutional formation, with Vietnamese organizations, for example, having been formed in relatively large numbers in the early 1980s. Since 1982, however, by far the largest number of entrants have consisted of "other Asian"—organizations representing people from such nations as Laos, Korea, and Cambodia.

The trend toward specialization is present in other fields as well. Thus there is evidence, in recent years, of rapid growth in organizations concerned specifically with particular sexual orientations. For example, the membership of the Lesbian and Gay Coalition in New Jersey, a consortium of nonprofits devoted to lesbian and gay issues, is said to have doubled to 40 members in a single year.[9] In our database, the earliest ruling year for a lesbian/gay organization is 1974.

A very different kind of example, outside the civil rights field, is provided by the recent popularity of the Jewish Museum, in New York. In the 1970s, it was described as "a backwater in the bustling New York art scene; for many in the art world, it virtually ceased to exist. But now, when widening ethnic rifts shape urban politics and multiculturalism dominates intellectual debate, the institution's emphasis on ethnic identity and social history has become downright trendy."[10]

Whether the identifying phrase has to do with country of origin, racial group, sexual orientation, or religious belief, the general pattern seems clear: each group, however defined, has created a specialized tax-exempt organization devoted to its own history and current concerns, to ensure that its interests are addressed. Institutions that represent a broad range of interests appear to be losing some of their constituents to organizations that serve more homogeneous populations. We have seen how this trend has manifested itself within the minority/immigrant rights subgroup, and in the growing number and specialization of what we have called "other civil rights" entities. It is also probably part of the explanation for the decreasing number of entrants into the legal services subgroup. It will be important to observe how these new, more precisely focused organizations, as well as the older, more broadly based groups, fare in the 1990s.

Finally, there is the question of whether the civil rights sector will continue to proliferate or whether some of the subgroups will find that their niches have been filled and that a certain amount of reconsolidation will ensue. It is hard to know whether the newer organizations will remain as targeted as they are at present or will broaden their focus. These issues are linked to still deeper questions concerning the character of American society, especially the degree of integration which is desired.

Performing Arts:
Varieties of Institutional Formation Within a Single Sector

If higher education and civil rights represent two extremes of the nonprofit universe, then performing arts is perhaps a more typical sector, including old and young as well as large and small organizations. Because the performing arts are so varied, an examination of the evolution of five major performing arts fields—theater, dance, ballet, orchestra, and opera—illustrates similarities and differences in rates of institutional formation within a single broad sector. (See Appendix D for an explanation of how we extracted these fields from the BMF.)

In analyzing trends in entrants into the performing arts, we were able to include not only all active entities but also those classified as inactive since 1981. This approach, which we would have preferred to use in other sectors as well because it permits a more inclusive analysis of institutional births, was possible here because of our recoding of a portion of the inactive file (discussed at some length in Chapter Six).

Three themes run through our analysis of the performing arts. First, in examining trends in entrants, we are struck by the critical role played by external funders, particularly the Ford Foundation and the National Endowment for the Arts (NEA) in shaping the development of the sector. Although these two funders never provided more than a small fraction of support to any field, their influence was much greater than the dollar value of their contributions might suggest. They entered many of the fields early and encouraged organizations to leverage their monies; in the cases of dance and ballet, Ford and the NEA actually helped to define the fields.[11]

Second, the economic cost structure of performing arts fields—in particular, the ease (or difficulty) of starting new companies—affects their development. In fields with low start-up costs, such as dance, new organizations tend to be formed; in fields with high start-up costs, such as opera, institutions tend to expand (for example, by staging more productions or extending seasons). Similarly, in such fields as theater that are able either to use amateurs extensively or to rely on other institutions (usually universities) to train performers, the number of new entrants would be expected to increase much more rapidly than in such fields as ballet, which require rigorous professional training.

Finally, competition among performing arts organizations influences the development of fields in significant ways. Anecdotal evidence about this competition abounds. Writing in 1986, Mark Freedman made the following observation:

> It is difficult to overestimate the intensity with which many performing arts organizations view themselves to be in competition with other companies, for audiences and, more fiercely, for contributed income. This competition has a visceral feel to it and can be traced in large measure to survival instincts and the constant, gnawing sense of not having enough money to continue operating in a viable manner. Under these circumstances, most groups perceive a frustrating dynamic in which the gains by one organization in grants or audiences must come at the expense of the others.[12]

Although Freedman acknowledged that the evidence on competition was far from clear, he nevertheless believed that the widespread perception of competition was a major factor preventing performing arts organizations from sharing management services. Such a perception may also help account for slowdowns in entrants into specific performing arts fields.

Sizes and Distinct Histories of the Fields

The sizes of our five performing arts fields differ dramatically. As of October 1991, theater was the largest, with 3,726 organizations. Orchestra was the next largest, with 1,195 organizations, followed closely by dance, with 957 organizations. Ballet and opera were much smaller, with 521 and 418 organizations, respectively. The different sizes of the fields reflect both unique histories and special characteristics.[13]

Theater, by far the largest field, has a well-established tradition in the United States. The first permanent American theater was built in 1716 in Williamsburg. By 1900, "nearly every crossroads town had its own theater."[14] The popularity of theater, however, declined with the coming of the automobile and the motion picture. Many professional actors began to concentrate on film, and so community theater was left to amateurs while Broadway came to dominate professional theater. It was not until after World War II that a resident professional noncommercial theater reemerged, with the establishment of Theater '47, in Dallas; the Alley Theater, in Houston; Arena Stage, in Washington, D.C.; and Actors' Workshop, in San Francisco. With support from the Ford Foundation, these new theaters provided a basis for the resurgence of professional nonprofit theaters in the 1960s.[15]

Orchestra also has a long history in the United States. Many of the major orchestras were established in the 1800s, including the New York Philharmonic, in 1842; the Boston and St. Louis Symphonies, in 1881; the Chicago Symphony, in 1891; and the Cincinnati Symphony, in 1895. Because orchestras historically had been supported by a few wealthy patrons, however, and because they still involve many more performers and therefore have higher operating costs than theater does, there are not nearly as many orchestras as there are theater companies.

Dance is a much younger field than either theater or orchestra. The first modern American dance troupes were established in the 1930s. Although many American dancers gained acclaim overseas, they danced in near obscurity here until the late 1960s. Martha Graham, for example, universally regarded today as one of the premier modern dancers, toured exclusively overseas during the 1950s and the early 1960s. When United States audiences finally embraced modern dance, in the early 1970s, the field grew rapidly because of its relatively low cost and the ease with which troupes could tour.

Ballet also was not firmly established in this country until the 1930s, when the first professional ballet schools and companies were founded. Regional or civic ballet became popular in the 1950s, but it was not until the 1960s, again with support from the Ford Foundation, that a national ballet program was established. Because Ford and subsequent funders wanted to build a strong foundation for ballet in America, and because they appreciated the rigorous training required of top ballet performers, they concentrated their resources on a few national companies with established schools.[16] Thus the number of professional ballet companies remains relatively small.

The opera field also remains small, despite its long history in the United States. The first opera was presented in America in 1735, and *Tammany*, the first American opera, was staged in 1794. Until quite recently, operas relied almost exclusively on wealthy people to fill their seats and their coffers. Supertitles and the televising of operas have made opera more accessible, but its sheer complexity (the combination of singing, orchestral playing, acting, dancing, and extensive set design) has precluded it from expanding more extensively. Opera companies are large and costly to maintain.

The distinct histories and characteristics of the performing arts fields account for their different sizes. These features, among others, also explain the varied development of the fields over the last three decades. It is to these trends that we turn now.

Trends in Entrants: General

Between 1965 and 1988, the number of organizations in all five fields increased. The rates of change and patterns of entrants varied substantially, however. Dance, with a 12.6 percent average annual entry rate between 1965 and 1988, and theater, with an 8.2 percent rate, increased more rapidly than all public charities (which had a rate of 6.5 percent when we included the inactive organizations). Ballet (5.3 percent), orchestra (4.2 percent), and opera (3.3 percent), however, increased at significantly slower rates.

Trends in Entrants: Theater

The evolution of the theater field between 1965 and 1988 can be divided into four distinct periods (Figure 5.8). Between 1965 and 1970, about 50 theater groups were established each year. During this period, the Ford Foundation and the National Endowment for the Arts were the primary national funders of performing arts organizations. Between 1959 and 1968, the Ford Foundation spent more than $10 million to develop resident nonprofit theater as an alternative to Broadway. Beginning in 1966, the NEA also provided funds to strengthen regional theater. Much of the early support provided by both of these funders focused on existing theater companies, enabling them to retain actors and expand their seasons. Therefore, it is understandable that the increased support during this period was not reflected in a rise in theater entrants.

Beginning in 1971, the number of new theater groups did begin to increase, and by 1975 there were 199 entrants. Although some of the increase evident in 1971 and 1972 is undoubtedly due to the change in IRS regulations described in Chapter Three (the "15-month rule"), it is notable that the growth in entrants actually accelerated after 1973. To a large degree, the increase in theater entrants (and, in fact, in most of the performing arts fields) during the early and mid-1970s can be attributed to the greater funding available to performing arts organizations during those years. Between 1970 and 1971 the NEA budget increased from $8.25 million to $15.1 million. This rapid growth continued through the late 1970s, so that by 1979 the NEA had a budget of almost $150 million.[17] State support also grew substantially during the 1970s, from $3 million in 1968 to more than $120 million in 1981.[18]

Resident theater in the early 1970s was in an economic position very different from the one it had been in in 1965 for another reason: in 1967, the Arena Stage's *The Great White Hope* became the first of many plays developed at resident theaters to achieve commercial success, and the possibility of producing a commercial hit, as well as the encouragement of funding sources (particularly the NEA), prompted resident theaters in the early 1970s to break away from the classics and focus on the development of new plays.

The number of theater entrants continued to increase between 1975

Figure 5.8.   Trends in Entrants by Ruling Year, Theater, 1965–1988.

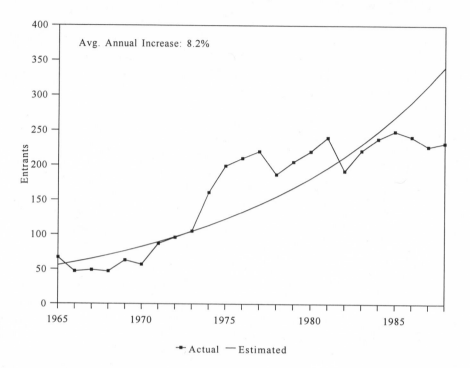

Actual ── Estimated

Source: Business Master File, October 1991, active and inactive, independent only. See also Appendix G, Table G.5-3.

and 1985, but at a slower rate. Again, a change in the funding climate seems to have been responsible. In 1975, Ford was forced to cut back its support of theater as part of an across-the-board reduction in its grantmaking. Shortly thereafter, the NEA budget stabilized at between $145 and $165 million, where it remained through the late 1980s.[19] Corporate and foundation contributions also leveled off in the late 1970s, at $400 million and $300 million, respectively.[20]

The number of theater entrants peaked at 249 in 1985, and then fell gradually over the next three years. This decrease in entrants may be attributed, at least in part, to greater competition. By 1985, third-generation theater companies were competing vigorously with first-generation theater groups for both audiences and funds. Meanwhile, both new-play production and audience interest seemed to have leveled off, prompting the NEA to write in 1990:

It may be likely that major, fundamental change will be required in both the commercial and not-for-profit systems if theater art is to prosper. . . . The accepted model of not-for-profit theater that has been perpetuated since the 1960s may not still be feasible in all cases. We may perhaps need to consider the notion of an alternative *project* investment of limited duration in the not-for-profit sector, as opposed to the continuing emergence of new *institutions* that in all cases must assume permanence.[21]

The NEA's remarks can be restated in terms of Hannan and Freeman's theory of sector evolution, described in the higher education section of this chapter: by the late 1980s, the nonprofit theater niche had become filled; in order for it to grow further, a new template needed to be developed.

Trends in Entrants: Dance

In many ways, the evolution of dance between 1965 and 1988 resembles the evolution of theater. Just as the theater field developed by spawning new theater companies, so too did dance seem to grow more by institutional formation than by institutional expansion. Dance troupes characteristically remained small, since they depended heavily on touring to attract audiences and generate revenues.

The increase in the number of modern dance companies between 1965 and 1988 is remarkable. Dance's average rate of increase in entrants—12.6 percent per year—is almost double the rate for public charities overall. To be sure, this high rate is due in part to the small size of the field in 1965. Only 10 modern dance troupes with known ruling years in our data had received IRS rulings by 1965. Still, even given this small base, the proliferation of dance troupes during this period was unprecedented. What we cannot determine, because we have a record of inactive organizations going back only to 1981, is to what extent the new troupes represented real growth in the field and to what extent they replaced organizations which had died.

As shown in Figure 5.9, between 1965 and 1971 the number of dance entrants increased moderately, from 3 to 12 per year. Initial support from the Ford Foundation and then the NEA enabled established artists to present more performances in the United States and thus to begin to build an audience at home. In 1965, the Rockefeller Panel estimated that the American public for dance did not even approach 1 million.[22]

During the 1970s, the number of entrants grew much more rapidly, from 12 entrants in 1971 to 76 entrants in 1980. Increased funds from corporations, foundations, individuals, and all levels of government certainly contributed to this increase. At least as important, however, may have been the more widespread audience interest in modern dance. Beginning in 1967–68, the NEA sponsored its Dance Touring Program, which exposed communities across America to modern dance (many for the first time). Public television, especially the popular "Dance in America" series, which began

Figure 5.9.   Trends in Entrants by Ruling Year, Dance, 1965–1988.

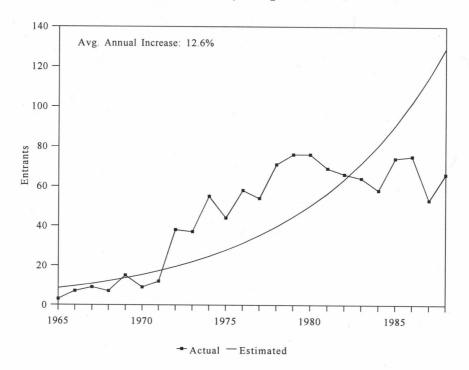

Source: Business Master File, October 1991, active and inactive, independent only. See also Appendix G, Table G.5-3.

in 1976 and continues today, also contributed to the increased visibility of modern dance.

The number of dance entrants slowed markedly in the late 1970s and actually began to decline in 1981. Although the number of entrants surged briefly in 1985 and again in 1988, the field never again reached its 1980 level of 76 entrants. As discussed earlier, funding sources for the performing arts in general stabilized in the late 1970s. At the same time, modern dance was becoming more expensive to produce. In particular, touring fees no longer adequately covered touring expenses. Attendance also dropped off because audiences could now choose from an abundance of dance performances. Competition for audiences, as well as for funding, was much keener.

Trends in Entrants: Ballet

Ballet, between 1965 and 1988, experienced an evolution markedly different from that of the other forms of dance. This difference reflects the priorities of the major funders and the artistic requirements of ballet, particularly the need for advanced classical training. Whereas the number of dance entrants grew at an unparalleled rate between 1965 and 1988, the number of ballet entrants grew at an average annual rate of only 5.3 percent—less than the rates for all public charities and arts/culture. However, this modest overall rate obscures significant growth within individual ballet companies during the same period.

The establishment of a national ballet program was one of Ford's first major funding priorities in the performing arts. Ford's efforts here were in many ways the reverse of its efforts in the theater field. In theater, Ford sought to provide a regional nonprofit alternative to the highly centralized world of Broadway; in ballet, Ford set out to stabilize what was already a decentralized field, with many small community ballets scattered across the country. It sought to achieve this objective by "supporting a series of resident and professional companies and schools throughout the country, ensembles that would transcend the community ballets."[23] Such centralization was necessary, given the importance of high-quality classical training for aspiring professionals and the scarcity of master teachers from Russia.

In 1963, Ford appropriated $8 million to begin its ballet initiative—which, as W. McNeil Lowry noted, "at that point represented the largest sum ever allotted by a foundation to a single art form."[24] The New York City Ballet and The School of American Ballet received $4.4 million. Another $1.5 million was set aside to provide regional and local scholarships for promising young dancers. The balance went to seven large regional ballets.

From 1965 to 1972, the number of ballet entrants doubled, from 9 to 18 (Figure 5.10). Was this increase the result of the indirect support to civic ballets provided by the local scholarship program? The graduation of a new wave of highly trained students able to perform and to teach? A heightened general interest in ballet? The answers cannot be determined from our data, but all three explanations are plausible. The NEA probably also contributed to the increase in ballet entrants by supporting the efforts of such organizations as the National Association for Regional Ballet and subsidizing tours by the Joffrey Ballet and other large companies.

The number of new organizations that were granted tax-exempt rulings doubled again between 1972 and 1973, most likely because of the change in the tax law. The number of entrants then hovered in the low 30s before dropping to 25, in 1977. It is curious that while the number of entrants into all the other performing arts fields grew in the 1970s, the number of entrants into ballet did not. Rather, the number of ballet entrants showed moderate growth between 1977 and 1980 before falling off, in the 1980s. Rising costs and increased competition for audiences and funds—in this case, not only with other ballet companies but also with the many new modern dance ensembles—were probably responsible for this slowdown.

Figure 5.10. Trends in Entrants by Ruling Year, Ballet, 1965–1988.

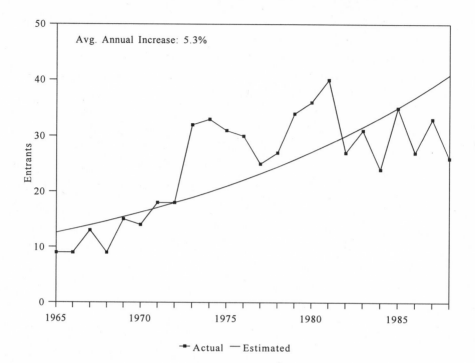

Source: Business Master File, October 1991, active and inactive, independent only. See also Appendix G, Table G.5-3.

Trends in Entrants: Orchestra

Between 1965 and 1988, the number of orchestra entrants grew by an average annual rate of only 4.3 percent, less than all public charities. As in the case of ballet, however, this low rate of institutional formation obscures the substantial growth of existing orchestras during the period. Moreover, this low rate may also fail to reflect growth of another kind—namely, the formation of orchestras affiliated with other nonprofits. Many orchestras, particularly youth, chamber, and student orchestras, do not have independent tax-exempt status, because they are affiliated with universities, colleges, or larger orchestras.

At the beginning of the 1960s, orchestra was by far the best-established performing arts field. Indeed, a 1965 Rockefeller Panel report on the future of theater, dance, and music in America stated, "Of all existing professional organized activity in the performing arts, the longest established, most widely dispersed and most stable is the symphony orchestra."[25] Recognizing this situation, the Ford Foundation initially focused its funds on stimulating the development of a repertory of contemporary music and on improving the situation of conductors, rather than on institutional development. When the foundation realized larger-than-expected capital gains in the mid-1960s, however, the board of trustees authorized a ten-year, $80 million series of grants for endowment and operating support to sixty-one major and metropolitan symphony orchestras.[26]

This considerable influx of monies is not reflected in any apparent surge in entrants (Figure 5.11). In fact, between 1965 and 1972 (with the exception of 1971), the number of orchestra entrants remained fairly steady, at between 20 and 30 per year. What the figure does not show, however, is the substantial growth within existing orchestras. During the late 1960s, existing orchestras grew in two related ways—by lengthening their seasons, and by expanding their budgets. In 1965, even the major symphonies did not have year-round seasons. Most major orchestras performed for twenty-two to forty

Figure 5.11. Trends in Entrants by Ruling Year, Orchestra, 1965–1988.

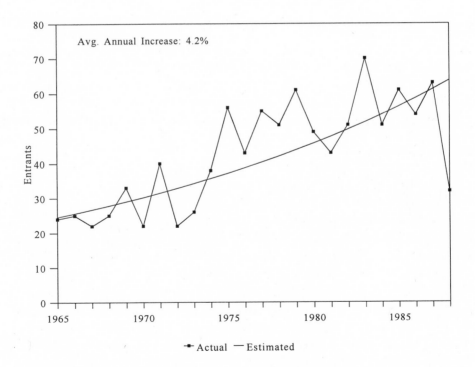

Source: Business Master File, October 1991, active and inactive, independent only. See also Appendix G, Table G.5-3.

weeks, and the metropolitan orchestras had seasons only sixteen to thirty-three weeks long.[27] When the orchestras expanded their seasons, their budgets grew substantially. As Lowry notes, "In 1957 the average annual budget even of a 'major' orchestra was around $600,000. By 1971, it had moved, in constant dollars, to $2.8 million."[28]

In the early 1970s, the number of orchestra entrants did begin to rise, so that there were fifty-six entrants by 1975. This increase was due mostly to the establishment of semiprofessional orchestras in small cities, such as Albuquerque, New Mexico; Lawrence, Kansas; and Rochester, Minnesota. The influx of these smaller orchestras led the American Symphony Orchestra League to add "regional orchestra" to its budget categories in 1976.

The rise in orchestra entrants leveled off during the late 1970s and 1980s as both funding and audience interest plateaued. One interesting development during this period was the increased popularity of chamber orchestras, in response to the growing costs of maintaining a full-scale symphony and the advent of compact discs. Only 15 percent of the 120 chamber orchestras in the BMF have ruling dates before 1975, and over 60 percent of them have ruling dates in the 1980s—a significant difference, even though before 1981 we have data on only surviving organizations.

Trends in Entrants: Opera

The final performing arts field that we examine is opera. The number of entrants into this field increased the least between 1965 and 1988. As in the cases of ballet and orchestra, however, the data for entrants tell only part of the story.

As shown in Figure 5.12, the pattern of opera entrants was sporadic between 1965 and 1971. The overall downward trend in entrants during this period is not readily explainable, although the new attention being paid to the other fields—by audiences, funders, and even aspiring performers—may have contributed to opera's decline.

The number of opera entrants rose from 5 in 1971 to 31 in 1978. Public and cable television began to broadcast opera during the 1970s, and these broadcasts were extremely popular. As in all the other performing arts fields, the number of entrants into opera declined in the 1980s (but, in the case of opera, not consistently). According to the NEA's 1982 and 1985 surveys of public participation, the percentage of adults who had seen opera live within the last year declined, from 4 percent to 3 percent, between 1982 and 1985. Of particular concern to opera administrators was the relatively advanced age of opera audiences. More encouraging, however, was the fact that, in 1985, 12 percent of adults saw opera on TV, 7 percent heard opera on the radio, and 7 percent purchased operatic recordings. Nevertheless, the availability of opera through these mediums made it difficult for opera administrators to raise ticket prices, even though their own costs were increasing rapidly.

Figure 5.12.   Trends in Entrants by Ruling Year, Opera, 1965–1988.

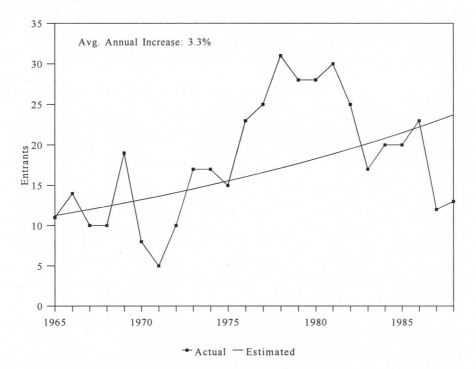

Source: Business Master File, October 1991, active and inactive, independent only. See also Appendix G, Table G.5-3.

This chapter concludes our discussion of entrants into various nonprofit fields. The evolution of any sector depends, of course, on exits as well as on entrants, and so we turn in Chapter Six, to the subject of institutional demise.

Notes

1. The source of these data is Table 224 in U.S. Department of Education (1991, p. 230).
2. We skip over entirely other waves of institutional foundings, including the establishment of Comprehensive institutions (which are larger than liberal arts colleges, and which offer graduate education through the master's degree), Specialized institutions (religious and other), historically black colleges and universities, and women's colleges. We are at work on a companion study of the evolution of American institutions of higher education, and the discussion presented here is drawn from that much more comprehensive analysis.

3. Stinchcombe (1965, pp. 153–154). See also Aldrich (1979), Carroll (1983, 1984), Hannan and Carroll (1992), Hannan and Freeman (1977), and McPherson (1983). Hannan and Freeman applied concepts of population ecology to the study of the formation of labor unions between 1836 and 1885. They predict (and confirm) that "the founding rate rises initially and then falls with increasing density." This phenomenon is explained in part as a result of the training of new founders: "Knowledge about organizational strategies and structures is often available only to insiders (those already participating in such organizations). . . . Existing organizations are the training grounds for organization builders. . . . [Also,] legitimation of a form increases its founding rate." However, once a certain number of organizations of a given type has come into existence, competition within the population causes the founding rate to decline (Hannan and Freeman, 1987, p. 918).

4. Rudolph (1990) is the best-known one-volume history of higher education, which devotes a great deal of attention to the literary colleges. See also Burke (1982) for a critique of some of the ideas advanced by Rudolph. Burke is particularly persuasive in stressing the capacity of literary colleges to adapt to local needs at a time when transportation was limited and many families could not afford to send children to more distant—and more expensive—institutions.

5. Berelson (1960, p. 9). For general discussions of the founding of research universities, see also Rudolph (1990) and Veysey (1965).

6. The phenomenon of institutional adaptation is fascinating, and highly important in its own right. In the larger study of higher education in which we are involved, we make a major effort to track the historical record of institutional adaptation.

7. See Cowley and Williams (1991, pp. 120–123) for a summary of the Morrill Act.

8. For a discussion of the beginnings of the junior college movement, see Cowley and Williams (1991, pp. 151–156, 169–170, 177–178, 189–190).

9. Soderlind (1992, p. 1).

10. Kimmelman (1993a, p. 1).

11. One of the major goals of Ford's arts program was to "pull into the arts on a more systematic basis available non–Ford Foundation funds from private and corporate sources throughout the country" (Ford Foundation, 1986, p. 14). Similarly, the 1965 legislation that created the NEA encouraged nonfederal contributions by mandating that the endowment support not more than 50 percent of a project's cost and by establishing a treasury fund, outside the NEA's budget, for which applicants could qualify with a private match (Lowry, 1978, p. 19).

12. Freedman (1986, p. 207).

13. The historical information in the performing arts section of this chap-

ter is drawn from many sources, including Lowry (1978), National Endowment for the Arts (1988, pp. 31–122), Rockefeller Panel Report (1965, pp. 20–24, 27–48), Baumol and Bowen (1966, pp. 15–32), and Heilbrun and Gray (1993, pp. 23–31). In addition, we relied on a number of Ford Foundation reports on specific fields. These reports are cited in the appropriate places throughout the text.

14. Ford Foundation (1977, p. 2).
15. For a more detailed description of the history of theater in the United States, see Ford Foundation (1977).
16. See Kendell (1983) for an extensive history of American ballet (pp. 7–18) and an overview of Ford's ballet initiatives (pp. 19–38).
17. National Endowment for the Arts (1992, pp. 361–363).
18. Ford Foundation (1986, p. 9).
19. National Endowment for the Arts (1992, pp. 361–363).
20. Ford Foundation (1986, pp. 8, 11).
21. National Endowment for the Arts (1988, p. 116).
22. Rockefeller Panel Report (1965, p. 44).
23. Lowry (1978, p. 61).
24. Lowry (1978, p. 61).
25. Rockefeller Panel Report (1965, pp. 20–21).
26. The American Symphony Orchestra League (ASOL) used to classify orchestras according to the sizes of their budgets and professional staffs. In 1965, ASOL recognized 1,401 symphony orchestras: 25 major, 29 metropolitan, 1,059 community, and 288 college and university (Rockefeller Panel, 1965, p. 21).
27. Rockefeller Panel Report (1965, p. 22).
28. Lowry (1978, p. 14), citing Ford Foundation (1974).

SIX

Closings of
Nonprofit Institutions

A balanced picture of the evolution of the nonprofit sector must include organizational deaths as well as entrants. However, while considerable energy has been devoted to tracking the rate of failure among for-profit corporate entities, discussion of rates of closings among nonprofits has been sparse.[1] This lack of attention is a serious void: for policy purposes, as well as for our understanding of the population dynamics of fields, it is important to know the frequency of exits, the reasons for closures, and the consequences.

Obvious questions include the following:

- How should exits be defined? Are there differences in relevant definitions between the for-profit and nonprofit sectors?
- Are there reasons to expect exit rates in the nonprofit sector to be higher or lower than exit rates in the for-profit sector?
- What does the evidence show? How do overall exit rates compare in the two sectors?
- Are nonprofits that are operating in certain fields more likely to close than those operating in other fields? If so, why?
- Are nonprofit institutions more fragile—more likely to die—at particular stages in their development than at others? Is there a "liability of newness"?
- Are there reasons to believe that nonprofit institutions sometimes live too long? Are the incentives to keep going too strong? In determining length of life in the nonprofit world, what roles are played by legal strictures and economic incentives?

In this chapter, we address some of these questions more fully than others. Our objectives are, first, to set forth a framework for analysis, focusing on comparisons with the for-profit sector; and, second, in the last section of the chapter, to provide new empirical evidence on exit rates in the nonprofit sector.

Concepts

We define *exits* as the number of organizations that cease independent existence over some specified period of time. Viewed in this broad way, exits take many forms: liquidation of assets, takeover by another entity, voluntary closings, and bankruptcy. *Failure* and *closing* are not synonymous terms. In general usage, *failure* implies a loss to creditors, while *closing* is a more general term, which also includes voluntary exit without loss to creditors.

Normative Questions

We understand, at least conceptually, the conditions that precipitate failure in the for-profit world,[2] but the situation is far more complex in the nonprofit world, where it is often impossible to quantify outputs, much less make a determination as to whether they are produced in the "right" quantities by the "right" number of firms. In the nonprofit sector, technologies rarely become obsolete, and it is nearly impossible to determine excess supply, so long as there is still a constituency which values the activities of the entity. Consider several hypothetical cases:

- A historical society is open on a regular schedule, but the number of people who visit the collections is quite small and highly specialized (mostly scholars). The visiting scholars, although they do not pay directly for the privilege, place a high value on the services they receive, which are very costly to provide. Is the mode of delivering this service efficient?

- A cancer research institute discovers the ultimate cure for the disease. Such a discovery is hardly a failure, but the institution's stated mission is now obsolete. This scenario is perhaps the clearest example of obsolescence in the nonprofit world. Are we to conclude that the institution should cease functioning? Or should it redeploy its resources and allow its infrastructure to serve another cause? One example of this type of transformation is the March of Dimes. Founded in 1938 by Franklin D. Roosevelt, with the aim of finding a cure for polio, the March of Dimes in more recent years has sought to prevent birth defects.

- A dance troupe presenting alternative work does poorly at the box office. Is this a sign that there is an oversupply of opportunities to see dance? That this troupe is of poor quality? Or that it has artistic merit, is simply ahead of its time, and should continue to function as a provider of a public good?

These hypothetical cases illustrate how difficult it is to answer the question of when a nonprofit firm should cease its activities. John C. Whitehead, now chairman of AEA Investors and former Deputy Secretary of State and comanaging partner of Goldman Sachs, has summarized succinctly an essential difference between the obligations of directors or trustees in the two sectors: "A for-profit board has an obligation to *get out* of a bad business while a nonprofit board may have an obligation to *stay in*, if it is to be true to its mission."[3]

We do not pursue this normative question any farther here, but we are left with the basic empirical fact that organizations do in fact die, in the nonprofit and for-profit sectors alike. To understand the data that are reported, it is necessary to consider types of closures and the mechanisms leading to closures, which differ between the two sectors.

Types of Exits and Legal Mechanisms

Broadly speaking, it is useful to distinguish between closures that result from the inability of an entity to satisfy its creditors (and which often involve bankruptcy proceedings) and closures that reflect the decision either to merge with another entity or simply to liquidate (voluntarily) the assets of the entity in the absence of pressure from creditors. In the most general sense, bankruptcy occurs when the assets of the firm are insufficient to meet the fixed obligations of the debtholders. In the for-profit world, firms may seek court supervision for reorganization under Chapter 11 of the federal statutes and eventually may emerge from bankruptcy without ever having closed. Bankruptcy may be terminal, however, when there is a permanent loss of economic viability and assets are sold under Chapter 7 of the law.

In the nonprofit world, the condition of "assets less than obligations" loses much of its clarity. Consider, for example, the case of a museum whose assets consist of cash and other liquid assets, a building, and a large collection of valuable paintings and other art objects. If such an institution cannot meet its operating expenses—cannot "make payroll"—it is most surely in poor financial health, but it cannot be judged bankrupt by the standards that apply to for-profits. Recognizing this reality, the operative parallel for nonprofits is "equity insolvency," defined as the "inability to pay bills in the regular and ordinary course of business."[4]

Whereas for-profits can be forced into bankruptcy by creditors, involuntary bankruptcy does not apply to nonprofits under federal law. Instead, creditors must follow proceedings mandated by state law pertaining to insolvent nonprofit organizations, and the Model Non-Profit Corporation Act contains provisions for involuntary dissolution.[5] In the case of voluntary bankruptcy, the nonprofit must file a written petition, asking to be adjudicated bankrupt. In such circumstances, bankruptcy statutes and federal district courts may be used. Involuntary closure of a nonprofit may also be precipitated by state authorities (usually the attorney general's office) when there is evidence of fraud or abuse of authority.

In general, bankruptcy and losses to creditors are much more common in the for-profit world than among nonprofits. We make this assertion with confidence, but we must also acknowledge that it *is* an assertion, since we know of no data that permit us to test this proposition for nonprofit entities.

Voluntary liquidations and mergers constitute the second main type of closure. Here, too, circumstances differ between the nonprofit and for-profit sectors. Liquidation of a for-profit firm occurs when the firm's principals—generally, the members of the board of directors—decide that the value of the firm's assets, sold piecemeal, exceeds the value of the stream of returns offered by the firm as a going concern. In this sense, liquidation may be a recognition that the firm is "worth more dead than alive."[6] In such cases, the liquidation process is relatively straightforward, at least in principle: assets are sold to the highest bidder, creditors are paid, and excess proceeds are distributed to the equity holders.

Variants on liquidation include such additional forms of corporate restructuring as mergers, acquisitions, and takeovers, all of which are mechanisms for transforming two independent entities into one. In the for-profit sector, these mechanisms are used when investors believe that there are opportunities for synergy between two firms, or when the principals of one entity believe another is undervalued. Such actions may be either friendly or hostile: two firms may agree that there is an opportunity to increase value, or one may use the proxy mechanism (or the threat of it) to gain control in a more predatory fashion.

In the case of a nonprofit, liquidation is less likely to be straightforward. First, the charter of a charitable organization usually requires that the assets be held in trust to serve the charitable purpose; thus it may not be possible to use the market mechanism—sale to the highest bidder—to reposition assets. Second, there are no equity holders in a nonprofit, and thus there is no unambiguous answer to the question of who should receive the proceeds obtained by liquidation of assets.[7]

For nonprofits, the path to liquidation is murky indeed, and the required steps depend on state-specific legislation. The benefits of tax exemption and tax-deductibility of contributions imply a public interest in the dissolution of a nonprofit and the distribution of its assets, and this public interest is generally exercised through the courts and appropriate state officers (usually the attorney general). As some dramatic experiences attest, seeking to merge with another enterprise, to take in a new partner, or to dissolve can be highly contentious acts.[8]

While the basic mechanisms of merger and acquisition can be utilized in the nonprofit sector, such actions must also be consensual; there is no provision for hostile action. Moreover, the absence of stockholders and takeover specialists reduces the incentive to merge.[9] For example, no other nonprofit institution (such as the New York Public Library or New York University) could launch a takeover bid for the library of the New-York Historical Society, even though the future of this great library is known to be in jeopardy. The boards of the respective institutions, as well as the state attorney general, would need to agree to any reorganization.

In general, then, mergers in the nonprofit sector are less common than in the for-profit sector. When they do occur, they frequently are "last-resort efforts to survive . . . rather than well-planned and well-executed growth strategies."[10]

Expected Differences in Exit Rates

Given these types of closures and legal mechanisms, we can now ask what *a priori* propositions might help us predict differences in rates of exit between the two broad sectors and among particular fields within the universe of charitable nonprofits. Two considerations are relevant: adaptability, and incentives for continuing, combined with costs of exiting.

Economic failure is often thought to be inversely related to the ability of firms to adapt to new technologies and changing circumstances. A failed firm is the dinosaur that becomes extinct. In the business world, competitive markets are thought to stimulate adaptation and thus to reduce the likelihood that enterprises will remain dormant so long that they eventually die. Many nonprofits operate far from the competitive model, and it has been argued that the lack of competition may slow adaptation.[11] This line of argument would lead us to expect, other things being equal, that exit rates would be higher among nonprofits than among for-profit firms.

A second set of considerations, having to do with the incentives to carry on and the costs of exiting, leads to precisely the opposite expectation about the relative frequency of exits in the two sectors. Because nonprofits have both greater incentives to persist and higher costs of exiting, we would expect them to be much more likely to resist closure. This second set of considerations is far more significant, we believe, than the adaptability effect.

Exiting is far from a cost-free process in any sector or any field. Lawyers must be hired, papers filed, and effort expended on the distribution of assets. Still, in relative terms, expected costs are far higher in nonprofit settings than in for-profit settings. The incentive simply to carry on is also stronger in nonprofit settings. Nonprofit managers and directors cannot profit from opportunities to liquidate or merge, as can managers and boards in the for-profit sector. In addition, many leaders of nonprofits understandably wish to retain their jobs and avoid the occurrence of a closure on their watch.

The mechanisms available for achieving closure are much more difficult and cumbersome in the nonprofit sector than in the for-profit sector, and this difference alone would lead one to predict lower exit rates among nonprofits. For-profits have the great advantage of access to markets. Assets can be sold, and relatively simply; so long as a reasonable price is obtained for them, no one will question their sale. For-profit entities are spared any obligation to justify departing from a stated mission when it seems impractical to serve it effectively any longer.

Nonprofits, by contrast, face the prospect of lawsuits if they seek to declare that they have served their purposes and that their remaining assets should be put to other (better) uses. Similarly, proposed mergers are subject to all kinds of attacks. At Wilson College, for example, the trustees voted overwhelmingly to close the college and use the remaining endowment to provide scholarships for women students, rather than "fritter [the remaining assets] away on a nearly hopeless effort to keep the college going in any form."[12] A group of alumnae objected and sued the trustees. On April 25, 1979, the judge at the Franklin County Orphans Court released a *decree nisi* against the trustees, enjoining the closing of the college on any date without prior court approval, removing the president and another member of the board, and ordering the trustees to pay the costs of the court proceedings. Similarly, the trustees of the University of Bridgeport are still ensnared in lawsuits growing out of their (reluctant) decision to accept support from the Reverend Sun Myung Moon.[13] Is it any wonder that trustees will do almost anything to keep their organizations in existence?

For a nonprofit, generally speaking, the worst consequence of remaining alive (from the perspective of the CEO and the board) is that the entity will survive for another ten years as it finances annual deficits by spending down all monetary assets which are unrestricted. The sad corollary is that the tendency of nonprofit boards to resist closure rarely produces the best result for society at large, since so many valuable assets may in effect be wasted, at the same time that opportunities to achieve more lasting solutions are missed. As the economic condition of a nonprofit continues to deteriorate, it becomes harder and harder to find good ways to rescue it or dispose of its assets in a socially productive way. In our view, the tendency of some nonprofits to live too long is a major public policy problem which by no means has been solved.

The problem of proper disposition of assets may be nearly overwhelming for a nonprofit contemplating closure. It follows that the cost of closure may be especially high for large, capital-intensive, nonprofit institutions. In such cases, managers and boards will have an exceptionally strong incentive to stave off closure, hoping for better times, rather than to expend significant time and resources in the process—an often embarrassing process—of determining what they believe should be done with paintings, buildings, endowments, and so on.

We conclude by advancing two hypotheses: First, nonprofits are more likely to resist closure and simply hold on in the face of economic setbacks than are for-profits, which may see economic benefit in combinations or even liquidations. Second, nonprofits with substantial assets are less likely to close than are other nonprofits.

Empirical Findings

Overall Comparisons with the For-profit Sector

Sadly, the elementary statistics needed to confirm or reject the first of our two hypotheses in any definitive way do not exist. The primary source of data on exits in the for-profit sector is Dun's *Census of American Business.* These widely published data report trends in new incorporations, failures, the number of active entities, and mergers. The data suffer from severe limitations, however. For example, "failures" consist only of situations in which there was a "loss to creditors." Closures which resulted only in the loss of equity to owners, or which involved no loss to anyone, are not counted. Dun's estimate of failures is therefore only the tip of the proverbial iceberg. Defined in this limited way, the annual failure rate of for-profits was about 1.2 percent of all business establishments between 1984 and 1987 and 0.8 percent between 1989 and 1990.[14] We have no figure for nonprofits comparable to the failure rate of for-profits, but if we had such a number, we are confident that it would be much smaller.

The main published source of information on exits in the nonprofit sector is annual counts of the number of entities moved from the active to the inactive part of the Business Master File (BMF). These counts are subject to limitations of many kinds, especially as measures of annual changes in the number of exits. A 501(c)(3) may cease functioning, in practical terms, without surrendering its tax-exempt status. Thus organizations may reside in the active file in a comatose condition for a considerable period, and it is impossible to distinguish such functionally deceased organizations from entities which operate by design on a scale below that of the filing requirement.[15] Given all these qualifications, the overall exit rate for all 501(c)(3)s over the last nine years has been quite steady and has averaged 2.3 percent per year (see Table 6.1).

The fact that this rate is two to three times higher than the failure rate among for-profit enterprises proves nothing, however, because the "exit" category for nonprofits is so much more inclusive. As noted above, the for-profit figure does not include any estimate of the incidence of liquidation without loss to creditors. Available evidence does suggest that voluntary liquidations are infrequent among large corporations,[16] but it is reasonable to suppose that the liquidation rate among smaller firms is far higher.

Another complication is that mergers appear to be far more common among for-profits than among nonprofits, although here again data limitations preclude any precise statistical comparisons. In the nonprofit sector, mergers were about 2.0 per 10,000 in 1990 and about 2.6 per 10,000 in 1991. (These calculations are based on detailed tabulations provided by the IRS). In the for-profit sector, merger rates have been more than twice as high throughout the decade, and the for-profit measure is itself a considerable underestimate, since it excludes those transactions valued at less than $1 million.[17]

Table 6.1. Annual Exit Rate for All 501(c)(3)s, 1984–1992.

Year (ended September 30)	Number of Active Entities at Start of Year	Number of Exits During Year	Exit Rate (%)
1984	312,416	9,459	3.0
1985	330,625	8,775	2.7
1986	342,696	4,448	1.3
1987	369,147	7,611	2.1
1988	395,936	9,266	2.3
1989	418,163	9,295	2.2
1990	432,698	9,966	2.3
1991	455,907	9,847	2.2
1992	481,241	11,470	2.4

Source: Based on tabulations supplied by the IRS.

Note: "Exits" include all organizations, including subordinates, assigned to inactive codes 20, 21, 22, 23, 24, 25, 26, 28, and 29 during the year (see Appendix A).

In the face of these grossly inadequate data, we are thrown back on *a priori* considerations and anecdotal evidence, which we trust more than the limited and noncomparable information currently available. We continue to believe that overall exit rates among nonprofits are appreciably lower than exit rates among for-profits of comparable scale. A real test of this hypothesis would be most welcome but would require data not now available.

Field-Specific Exits Among Nonprofits

Fortunately, it is possible to speak with more confidence about differences in exit rates among certain fields within the universe of charitable nonprofits. We are particularly interested in three questions: Does the probability of exit differ by field? If so, do measures of capitalization (differences in fixed assets) explain these differences? Does institutional age affect exit probabilities?

In order to answer these questions, we first had to code part of the inactive portion of the BMF. We identified organizations in the inactive file that belonged to eight fields—dance, theater, opera, ballet, higher education, job training, museums, and historical societies—and then replicated the methodology of the National Taxonomy of Exempt Entities (NTEE) coding process for these fields and checked the resulting lists for consistency.*

Analysis of these new data provides a unique opportunity to assess the characteristics of a subset of nonprofits that have ceased operation. Specifically, we are able to look inside the aggregate figures presented in Table 6.1

---

*The data presented in this section are limited to exits among independent and parent organizations. Subordinates are not tracked, because such changes often reflect broad changes in corporate organization, rather than actual closures. Exits appearing in this file are also limited to organizations assigned status codes 20 and 21 (notification of closure, and failure to respond; see Appendix A).

and compare particular fields. We know the ruling year for each organization included in the analysis, whether it exited in the 1980s, and other descriptive characteristics, such as location and assets (if the organization filed a return with positive financial data). While we are also given year of exit, this information is highly subjective, representing administrative cycles in enforcement. For this reason, we group all entities that exited at any time during the 1980s.

There are considerable differences in the incidence of exits among fields (Table 6.2). The highest overall rate of exit over the decade occurs among job training institutions in the primary field of employment (26.5 percent), and the lowest exit rate is found among historical societies (6.9 percent). These figures translate into annual exit rates of about 3.2 percent per year among job training organizations, between 2.4 percent and 3.0 percent per year among the performing arts organizations, and about 1 percent per year for museums and historical societies (see the right-hand column of Table 6.2).

This pattern of results is roughly consistent with what one would expect, given differences in capitalization. Job training entities and performing arts organizations of all types tend to be much less capital-intensive than either museums or historical societies, which usually have fixed assets of considerable value. Disposing of the collections of a museum is a much more daunting task than dissolving a dance troupe, and on that ground alone one would expect exit rates to be lower among museums, as is the case.

Exit rates also vary with the relative importance of earned income as a source of revenue. This finding is also consistent with expectations, since organizations such as theaters, which must depend heavily on their continuing appeal at the box office, are more vulnerable to sudden shifts in taste than are organizations which depend more heavily on endowments or regular contributions from a known base of donors. Similarly, the substantial dependence of job training organizations on specific governmental programs may have made their survival hostage to political vicissitudes.

Within the performing arts, theater and dance belong to a regime in which relatively large numbers of exits are offset by relatively high rates of entry, leading to net increases in the number of new organizations in these fields of 4.3 percent and 4.8 percent, respectively (see Table 6.2). For opera and ballet, lower rates of institutional formation imply that the total institutional populations in these fields are growing more slowly—about 1.8 percent per year in opera and 2.5 percent per year in ballet.

The one apparent anomaly in the ranking of types of nonprofits by exit rate is the field of higher education. This field appears to have a relatively high exit rate (20.2 percent over the decade, or an implied annual exit rate of 2.3 percent), even though one generally thinks of the population of private colleges and universities as both capital-intensive and quite stable over the last two decades. Looking at National Institute of Independent Col-

Table 6.2. Exit Rate by Field, 1981–1991.

Field	Number of Institutions					Total Exit Rate (%)[a] 1981–1991	Implied Annual Rate (%)				
	Exited 1981–1991	+	Active in 1991	=	Base Population		Gross Entrants	–	Surviving Entrants	=	Exits[b]
Job training	686		1,901		2,587	26.5	4.4		1.3		3.2
Ballet	175		521		696	25.1	5.5		2.5		3.0
Opera	123		418		541	22.7	4.5		1.8		2.7
Dance	274		957		1,231	22.3	7.4		4.8		2.7
Theater	951		3,726		4,677	20.3	6.7		4.3		2.4
Higher education	408		1,616		2,024	20.2	1.4		–0.9		2.3
Museums	271		2,484		2,755	9.8	6.1		5.0		1.1
Historical societies	522		6,998		7,520	6.9	5.7		4.9		0.8

Source: Business Master File, October 1991, active and inactive, independent only.

Note: Organizations with foundation codes 4 and 17 are excluded.

[a] "Total exit rate" is the number exited between 1981 and 1991 divided by the base population.

[b] Annual exit rates are computed by first calculating the average annual rate of increase in the total number of new entrants (gross entrants) between 1981 and 1991. We then calculate the average annual rate of increase in the number of still active organizations (surviving entrants). The average annual exit rate is the difference between these measures.

leges and Universities (NIICU) data on closings of colleges and universities in the 1980s for external verification of this high exit rate, we find that the NIICU universe, which includes only accredited institutions, is characterized by a much lower incidence of closing.[18] Of the 408 institutions in the field of higher education that are in the BMF inactive file, only about 10 percent are also recognized by the NIICU as having closed.

The implication is that a large number of exits in the inactive portion of the BMF are those of nonaccredited institutions. Examples include the North American College of Natural Health Sciences, the Florida School of Professional Psychology, the Interstate College of Personology, the Maryland Institute of Crop Ecology, and the New England School of Stringed Keyboard Instruments. Institutions of this kind are surely much less capital-intensive than is the typical college or university. At the same time, a nonaccredited institution is also likely to be almost exclusively dependent on tuition revenue and thus subject to closure if its clientele deserts it.

The next question of interest is the relationship between institutional age and exit. Can we confirm Arthur Stinchcombe's hypothesis that there exists a "liability of newness," with younger organizations most likely to exit because they have not developed the strong constituencies and stable bases of support common to older organizations?[19]

For six of the eight fields included in this analysis (all except dance and ballet), very old organizations—those with ruling years prior to 1966—are less likely to exit than those formed in more recent years (Table 6.3). Many of the organizations in the oldest category have sizable assets, including endowments, that provide financial security and stability. This finding is consistent with the results of a study of institutional mortality in the Minneapolis–St.Paul area, which found that organizations ceasing to function between 1980 and 1988 were younger on average than the surviving organizations within the sample.[20]

In four fields—theater, ballet, opera, and job training—the exit prob-

Table 6.3.   Age-Specific Exit Rates by Field.

Field	Exit Rate by Ruling-Year Cohort (%)				
	Pre-1966	1966–1970	1971–1975	1976–1980	Post-1980
Theater	11.9	20.2	28.4	30.6	14.8
Opera	18.6	27.9	25.0	33.3	15.2
Dance	35.7	29.8	34.9	29.6	13.8
Ballet	25.0	23.3	27.3	36.8	18.4
Museums	5.6	16.1	15.5	15.9	6.5
Historical societies	5.7	10.0	9.2	9.4	4.8
Higher education	11.8	32.9	34.6	34.6	21.0
Job training	27.1	30.3	32.2	35.2	16.5

Source: Business Master File, October 1991, active and inactive, independent only. See also Appendix G, Table G.6-1.

Figure 6.1. Age-Specific Exit Rates, Theaters and Historical Societies.

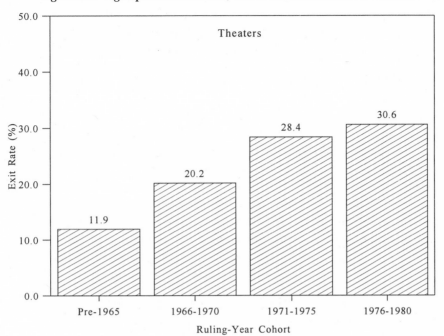

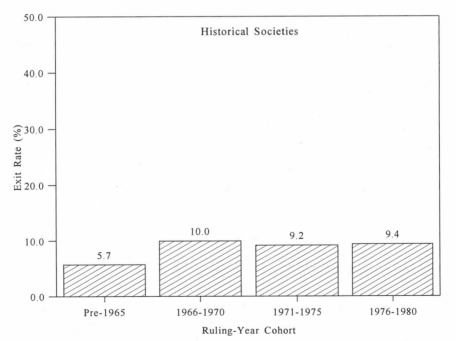

Source: Business Master File, October 1991, active and inactive, independent only.

abilities are highest among the very young organizations, which suggests that organizations in these fields are most fragile in their early years. Museums and historical societies illustrate a second regime: exit probabilities are essentially the same among organizations with ruling years between 1966 and 1990, while older organizations show a decidedly lower exit rate. (These two regimes are illustrated in Figure 6.1, which shows the patterns in the two fields with the most organizations: theaters, and historical societies.) The field of dance is the one anomalous case, with relatively high exit rates among all ruling-year cohorts and no discernible trend.

A final hypothesis which we had hoped to test empirically with these data is that large organizations are less likely to close than small organizations. Unfortunately, this proposition is difficult to address empirically, since an institution's financial scale is measured only at one point in time in these data, by the assets and revenues shown on its most recent tax return. A further complication is the fact that an institution may shrink (for example, by spending down endowments or selling assets) before filing a closing return with the IRS. We have no way of knowing whether an institution that exits has always been small, was at one time large but "ate through" its assets before reaching the decision to close, or was of substantial size when the decision to close was made and subsequently transferred its assets to another institution before a final filing was made with the IRS.

These difficulties prevent us from pursuing this line of inquiry, but we hope that others will be interested in exploring this question, as well as other facets of institutional life cycles. A valuable by-product of our analysis of the inactive part of the BMF is a list of entities that closed within each of the fields under investigation here. It would be useful to study what actually happened to these organizations, and whether there are behavioral—and policy—conclusions to be drawn.

Notes

1. There are, however, studies of closures within specific nonprofit sectors, such as higher education. One particularly valuable study is O'Neill and Barnett (1980). In addition, Bielefeld (1993) has looked at the frequency of closures in the St. Paul–Minneapolis metropolitan area. There have also been case studies, such as the discussion of the closing of the Oakland Symphony.
2. The theoretical, economic explanation of "company failure" is that firms which are inefficient, using obsolete technologies or producing goods in excess supply, will leave the market when they cannot cover average costs over the long run (Meeks, 1992, pp. 410–411).
3. Bowen (1994, p. 23).
4. Oleck (1992, p. 1155).
5. See Appendix 2 in O'Neill and Barnett (1980) for a state-by-state summary of the required processes for nonprofit dissolution.

6. Kim (1992, p. 768).

7. The disposition of assets is covered by the legal doctrine of *cy pres*, which holds that "the intention of the donor should govern, as near as possible, when literal effect cannot be given to it" (Oleck, 1992, p. 1192). The functional process of disposition of assets differs from state to state. In cases where state statutes are similar to the Model Non-Profit Corporation Act, trustees of an institution may make decisions about the disposition of assets. In other cases, the *cy pres* determination is made by the court, rather than by the board of directors. See O'Neill and Barnett (1980, pp. 46–47) for further discussion.

8. See O'Neill and Bartlett (1980) for a general discussion of merger and dissolution experiences in higher education. The Wilson College case is a particularly interesting example of how hard it can be to close an institution of higher education.

9. Sterne (1989). Sterne also notes, along with others, that mergers in the nonprofit sector frequently occur when one of the two organizations is in a dire financial condition. Among health care corporations, some institutions have attempted to change the corporate structure from nonprofit to for-profit in order to take advantage of equity financing options available in the latter structure (Shields, Dunn, and Stern, 1991).

10. Singer and Yankey (1991, p. 358). See also the references cited in this article.

11. Hansmann (1986, pp. 79–80) provides a strong argument that the absence of a profit motive leads to slower response among nonprofits to changes in demand. We suspect, however, that nonprofits which depend heavily on government contracts and grants are both more adaptable and more likely to cease operations than the kinds of nonprofits which are the focus of this study.

12. See Elizabeth Hudnut Clarkson's response to the Beeman Report in Beeman (1979) for a further description of the Wilson College case.

13. See Bowen (1994, pp. 165–166) for a further description of the University of Bridgeport's decision to accept support from Sun Myung Moon, and the ensuing lawsuits.

14. Calculated from data in Table 845 of U.S. Bureau of the Census (1992, p. 530). The underlying data are from Dun & Bradstreet (1991).

15. Another "inactive" incarnation of nonprofits occurs when public charities "lapse" into the status of private foundations. There were almost 9,000 lapsed public charities in the BMF in October 1991.

16. Voluntary liquidations are infrequent among large corporations, at least in part because there are substantial tax advantages to mergers as a form of corporate liquidation. Kim and Schatzberg (1987) note that over a period of about twenty-five years there were fewer than one hundred voluntary liquidations among NYSE and AMEX corporations.

17. Calculated from Table 853 in U.S. Bureau of the Census (1992, p. 534).
18. National Institute of Independent Colleges and Universities (1980, 1983, 1984), and unpublished data made available to us.
19. Stinchcombe (1965). See also Singh, Tucker, and House (1986) for a discussion of the liability of newness in a population of voluntary social service organizations.
20. Bielefeld (1993).

PART THREE

Institutional Characteristics: Comparisons of Selected Fields

SEVEN

Field of
Activity and Size

I n the preceding part of this book, we described overall patterns of growth in the numbers of various kinds of charitable institutions which populate the nonprofit sector. We looked at organizational births and deaths—making comparisons across fields, historical periods, and geographic regions—but we paid little attention to the internal characteristics of these entities.

Our focus now shifts, and in the next three chapters we examine relationships among fields of activity (or organizational type), size (measured by annual receipts or expenditures), revenue profiles (the relative importance of earned income, private support of various kinds, and governmental support), and age (ruling year or establishment date). Then, in the final chapter, we examine these same relationships over time, drawing on new data we have collected from a sample of individual organizations.

Central Questions and Conceptual Framework

Among the questions we hope to answer in this part of the study are the following:

- How—and why—does the type of organization (art museum versus theater versus university, for example) affect the typical size of entities in various fields? Does normal size vary appreciably by field of activity? How extensive is the range in size within a given field?
- Do different types of nonprofits have distinctly different revenue profiles? How closely can these patterns be related to the kinds of outputs

they produce? Are some sets of organizations heavily dependent on single revenue sources?

- Do revenue profiles in turn affect size? For example, to what extent does the ability of an organization to grow beyond a certain scale depend on the amount of income it can earn, relative to its private contributions, investment income, and governmental grants?
- How does the age of an organization affect its size and revenue profile?

In addressing these questions, we work within a simple conceptual framework, which is outlined schematically in Figure 7.1. The arrows indicate the main causal links; the numbers are for reference purposes only.

Field of activity (top box on the left-hand side of the figure) drives all else, mainly because the mission of the institution has so much to do with defining outputs or products. A university, for example, is committed to providing both graduate and undergraduate education and to advancing knowledge by carrying out research. Selective liberal arts colleges have narrower missions, focusing on the general education of undergraduates. Museums offer opportunities for individuals to see objects and exhibits. They also provide, in many cases, educational programs, some highly structured and some informal. Theaters obviously give performances and, in some cases, provide training opportunities for aspiring actors and directors. Historical societies may have active outreach programs, directed at both scholars and the public at large, or they may be concerned mainly with preserving objects and records.

Together, the mission of the institution and the products which it offers have a major impact on the necessary size of the organization (arrow 1 in the figure). Universities and hospitals are much more capital-intensive and require larger infrastructures than, for example, modern-dance troupes; therefore, they must have larger budgets in order to function at some acceptable level of quality. The level of fixed costs, defined appropriately, is the major determinant of both a normal size and a minimum scale of operations.

An organization's mission and the products which it provides also have a major impact on its revenue profile (arrow 2), primarily because it is much easier to charge for some products and services than for others. The "exclusion principle," in the lexicon of economists, is directly relevant: it is possible to charge only for those services from which potential purchasers can be excluded if they do not pay. Private colleges and universities charge tuition to their students, and theaters sell tickets, thereby generating substantial earned income. Certain types of independent libraries and historical societies, however, have more difficulty covering substantial parts of their costs by charging fees, since some of the most essential services which they render, including the preservation of documents, are not readily sold to individual buyers.

The funding profile of an enterprise in turn can have a strong influence on its size and level of activity, and vice versa (arrow 3). Being able to command a substantial amount of earned income is the *sine qua non* of large size in most but not all sectors of the nonprofit world.

Figure 7.1. Relationships Among Institutional Characteristics.

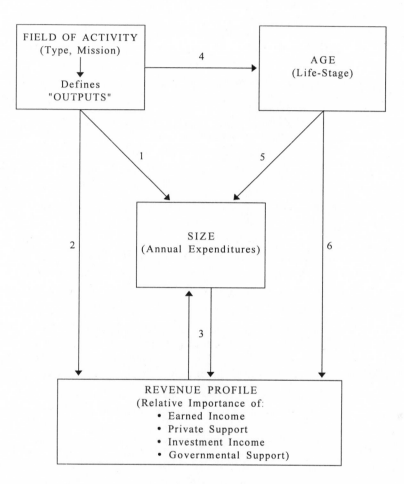

The age distribution of organizations also varies by field (arrow 4) because some fields were established much earlier than others, and exit rates differ by field. Higher education and civil rights are polar opposites in this regard, as discussed in Chapter Five.

Age in turn influences size (arrow 5), at least up to some point; that is, institutions go through life cycles, and we would expect young institutions to be smaller than old institutions, other things being equal. It is also true, however, that once an institution becomes mature, the correlation between age and further growth in size may weaken appreciably or even disappear altogether.

Age per se also can be expected to influence an organization's revenue profile (arrow 6), especially via the potential amount of investment income and donations available. Older colleges, for example, have had much more opportunity to accumulate endowments than have their more recently established counterparts.

The sequencing of the numbers in Figure 7.1 indicates how the discussion of these interrelationships is presented. In this chapter, we concentrate on the effects of field of activity on size (arrow 1). We turn in Chapter Eight to the relationship between field of activity and revenue profile, recognizing the feedback to size (arrows 2 and 3). Finally, in Chapter Nine, we add the age of the institution to the analysis (arrows 4, 5, and 6).

There are any number of nonprofit sectors which might be studied with these relationships in mind, but we have chosen to limit this discussion to selected fields within the broad areas of arts/culture and higher education. More specifically, we focus on the performing arts, with opera, orchestra, ballet, dance, and theater considered separately; museums, with art museums, natural history museums, science museums, and "other" museums considered separately; historical societies; and higher education, with Research/Doctorate universities, Comprehensive I universities, Liberal Arts I colleges, and "Other Four-Year" institutions considered separately (see Appendix D for definitions of the higher education categories, which are based on the Carnegie Classification system). All told, we examine fourteen fields, which is enough to permit the testing of simple hypotheses concerning the relationships among field of activity, scale, funding profile, and age.

The basic source of financial data is IRS Form 990, which all charitable nonprofits above a certain size (all positive filers) must complete and submit to the IRS each year. A very limited number of entries from this form are then recorded in the Business Master File (BMF)—most notably "gross receipts," which, as explained below, we often use as a rough proxy for the size of an organization. Much more detailed financial information is available for a sample of entities from the Statistics of Income Division (SOI) of the Internal Revenue Service, which is described in Appendix E. In the case of museums, we have been able to obtain additional information directly from the American Association of Museums (AAM). Similarly, the American Symphony Orchestra League (ASOL) has conducted a member survey, which has been useful.

Field of Activity as a Determinant of Size

Concepts and Measurements

We define size in terms of an organization's total annual revenues or expenditures—that is, its annual operating budget, which we regard as the best available indicator of the level of current activities. Assets is the other measure frequently used, but it does not seem to us to be nearly as useful. The stated value of assets depends on a range of factors, including the age of the organization and accounting conventions, which in turn reflect varied methods of valuing fixed assets and marketable securities. The relationship between assets and operating budgets also varies widely, depending on, among other things, the capital-intensiveness of the enterprise in question.

The measure closest to total revenue that is available in the BMF is "gross receipts," and we generally use this measure of current activity as our proxy for size. Gross receipts is by no means a perfect measure for our purposes, however, primarily because this measure is *so* "gross." The problem with the "gross receipts" line in the BMF is that it fails to exclude any of the categories of expense which are normally netted out in determining total revenue, such as the costs of goods and assets sold during the year (including marketable securities). Organizations with large endowments are particularly affected because money managers routinely buy and sell securities. The use of gross figures can have staggering consequences. To cite one example, the Metropolitan Museum of Art sold $568 million worth of marketable securities in 1987, all of which was included in its gross receipts in the BMF. But the Met had purchased the same securities for $554 million, and so the net proceeds associated with these transactions amounted to only $14 million.

The failure to net out substantial items of this kind is the main reason why the gross receipts of a large, heavily endowed organization is often a highly unreliable indicator of its true size. As a partial corrective, we use medians rather than means throughout this analysis, and we consider organizations at the 95th percentile as more representative of the size of truly large organizations in each field than those organizations that happen to have the largest gross receipts in any particular year. For a subset of institutions, we were able to minimize the problem in a more direct way by substituting total revenue figures from the SOI database for the gross receipts figures reported in the BMF. Total revenue in the SOI database includes only *net* proceeds and thus is not distorted by the turnover of investment portfolios.* Finally, when we need to know the absolute size of one of the very largest organizations, we use other data—usually either current expenditures or operating revenue, taken directly from the organization's most recent financial statement.

Another problem affecting both gross receipts and total revenues is that infusions of capital funds, which may be large in any one year and which are often unrelated to the operating condition of the organization, are lumped together with current revenues. Examples of capital contributions included in "total revenue" are a capital gift for a new building, a bequest in-

---

*Since the SOI sample (described in detail in Appendix E) includes all of the largest organizations, this "fix" largely solves the problem at hand. Combining the SOI and BMF databases does introduce one other inconsistency, however, in that the SOI data are for 1987 and 1988, whereas the BMF data are for the fall of 1991. But this is not a significant problem in the present context, since we are interested here only in the general relationship between field of activity and size. We do not believe that any of the key comparisons made in the text are affected by this mixing of dates.

tended to set up an endowed fund, or realized capital gains on permanently restricted endowments.[*]

Putting to one side these measurement problems (which can be handled, once they are understood), there is, we believe, a roughly predictable relationship between field of activity and normal size, based on differences among sectors in typical levels of fixed costs. For example, a university has to have a considerable infrastructure, some of it (like libraries and laboratories) quite capital-intensive, in order to operate. In addition, the core administrative and general expenses involved in running such an institution are much greater than the comparable overhead expenses involved in operating most dance companies and historical societies. Hospitals are another set of entities with high fixed costs.[1]

Of course, we would also expect to find a considerable range of levels of activity around whatever norm may characterize a particular field of activity; that is, there will be larger and smaller versions of any prototype institution, and another interesting question is the extent of such ranges. What is the characteristic difference in size between the typical organization in a field (located at the median of the size distribution) and smaller organizations (those located, for example, at the 25th percentile of the size distribution)? At the other end of the spectrum, is there any limit to how large an organization in a given field can become? These questions are empirical, although it is also possible to suggest reasons for some of the patterns which we observe.

Arts/Culture

Within arts/culture, we look first at the normal or median levels of receipts for various types of entities (see the middle panel of Figure 7.2).[2] The historical societies have the lowest median level of gross receipts ($82,000 in 1991) in arts/culture. Typical of organizations found near the middle of the historical societies' size distribution are Aurora Colony Historical Society, in Oregon (which collects and exhibits artifacts made or used by members of Aurora Colony, a nineteenth-century communal society), and Wailla-Knik Willow Creek Historical Society, in Alaska (which is home to, among other things, the Sled Dog Mushers' Hall of Fame). The low median level of gross receipts for historical societies suggests that it is possible to operate these societies on a very moderate scale.[3]

---

[*]The presence of these capital flows is the reason why we make no attempt to analyze deficits, surpluses, or profits. Such concepts are plainly very important, but the data on Form 990 do not allow them to be defined in a meaningful way. Treating the difference between "total revenues" and "total expenses" as "profit" leads to absurd results, such as the assertion that in 1991 the University of Pennsylvania "made $0.11 in profit for each $1.00 it took in— $153 million profit on revenues of $1.3 billion" (Gaul and Borowski, 1993, p. 15).

Figure 7.2. Size of Arts/Culture Organizations by Field, 1991.

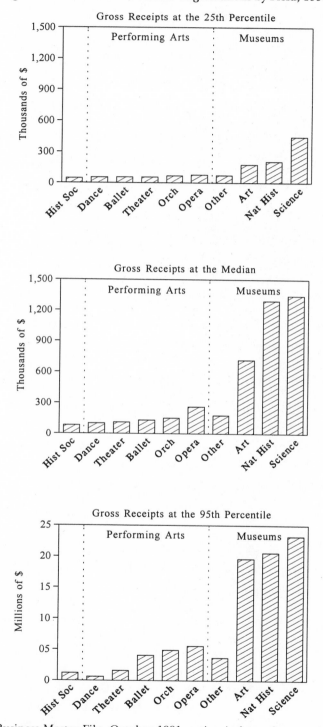

Source: Business Master File, October 1991, active, independent, positive filers only. See also Appendix G, Table G.7-1.

The median level of receipts then drifts up modestly as we consider specific fields within the performing arts, which display a hierarchy of their own (see again the middle panel of Figure 7.2). Dance and theater have lower medians than ballet or orchestra. Opera is at the high end of the performing arts' size distribution, with median receipts of just over $260,000 per year, more than double the median for theater. This rank-ordering is consistent with the characteristics of the various fields. In general, lower levels of fixed investment (and less complex infrastructures) are required to operate a dance company or a theater than a ballet company or a symphony orchestra. Opera is the most expensive of the performing arts, since it usually combines elements of all the other art forms.

As a group, museums have appreciably larger median receipts than the performing arts. Science and natural history museums have median receipts of about $1.3 million—approximately ten times the medians characteristic of the performing arts. We suspect that these two types of museums have the highest medians because, generally, they are the most capital-intensive. The Science Museum of Connecticut is a typical midsized science museum. In addition to standard exhibit areas, this museum has a planetarium, a nature center, a marine tank, a hands-on discovery room, a live-animal center, a nursery school, and a computer laboratory. The mid-sized natural history museums probably share many of these characteristics. The typical art museum, by contrast, is about half as large as the corresponding science and natural history museums, with gross receipts (or revenues) of about $700,000—which is still about five times larger than the median performing arts organization.

The "other museum" category includes an enormous range of activities and contains (as we show below) some very large entities. But the category also includes many smaller museums, such as the American Merchant Marine Museum, in Kings Point, New York, and the Museum of Early Trades and Crafts, in Madison, New Jersey, which fall near the middle of the size distribution. Indeed, because the "other museum" category is so open-ended as to type of collection, the activities of these museums are often more specialized and therefore more modest in size than the activities of full-fledged art or science museums. Even so, the "other museum" category has a median level of gross receipts that is higher than the median for any performing arts field except opera.[4]

Much the same pattern holds when we move down the size scale and compare the annual receipts of organizations located at the 25th percentile of their respective size distributions (see the top panel of Figure 7.2). (We examine the gross receipts of organizations at the 25th percentile of the size distribution rather than at a lower percentile because of the inevitable bunching that occurs near the minimum filing cutoff of $25,000 of gross receipts—which is, by definition, the same for all fields.) It is significant that the rank-ordering of fields at the 25th percentile is almost the same as the rank-ordering at the median (with ballet and theater trading places). There is also a considerable convergence of values: the range of $45,000 to $75,000 now captures all of the arts/culture fields except the three sets of museums with broadly defined objectives. Thus the annual running costs of small organizations are closer together within arts/culture than one might have anticipated (with opera, for example, only about $20,000 higher than theater).

There is much less congruence among the small museums under consideration here. The science museums at the 25th percentile, with gross receipts of nearly $500,000, are separated from all of the other categories, including the natural history museums. At this small end of the distribution, the natural history and art museums are close together in size, with gross receipts in the range of $175,000 to $200,000. The "other museums" at the 25th percentile are smaller yet and operate at about the same scale as the performing arts organizations (with roughly $70,000 of gross receipts). We interpret these results as reinforcing the central point made above—namely, that because of technical requirements, science museums are confronted with higher budgetary thresholds than are other kinds of museums. We suspect that natural history museums have now left the company of the science museums and joined the art museums because it is easier for a natural history museum than for a science museum to operate with a minimal staff and infrastructure. Visitors can simply look at art objects or specimens, whereas science exhibits are more likely to require both higher levels of maintenance and greater hands-on efforts to explain them.

The much larger organizations, operating at the 95th percentile within each of their respective fields, are depicted in the bottom panel of Figure 7.2, which has millions, not thousands, of dollars on its vertical scale. Once again, the ordering is essentially the same, with art, natural history, and science museums reporting far higher total revenues than historical societies or any of the performing arts fields. In fact, the gaps between the fields are appreciably greater than before, with the differences between fields of activity now often several millions of dollars, rather than thousands of dollars.

Particularly interesting is the rather close clustering of the three main types of museums, with total revenues for organizations at the 95th percentile ranging from $20 to $21 million (art museums and natural history museums) to $23 million (science museums). What explains the fact that the art museums have, as it were, caught up with the natural history and science museums? To anticipate an observation we make below in discussing very large organizations in all fields, we believe that at the top of the size distribution what matters most is not the *requirements* of a field but rather the *opportunities* open to particular organizations to grow. Art museums can and do attract very generous patrons and are no more constrained in terms of growth than science and natural history museums are.

Higher Education

Higher education is a useful counterpoint to arts/culture.* The institutions in this field are much larger than entities in the arts/culture fields, as we thought they would be, given the heavy investments of various kinds which must be made if a college or a university is to function effectively. All of the vertical scales in Figure 7.3 for higher education are in millions of dollars.

The rank-ordering of the sectors in higher education is exactly the same at each of the three points on the size distribution (25th percentile, median, and 95th percentile) and exactly what one would have predicted, given the characteristics of the various types of institutions. Median annual expenditures for the mid-sized Research/Doctorate universities (such as Case Western Reserve University and Northeastern University) exceed $200 million and dwarf the medians for the other three sets of educational institutions shown here. We are reminded again of the high costs associated with doctoral education and research, especially scientific research.

The next-highest median, $30.6 million, is for the Comprehensive I institutions (such as Mercy College, in Dobbs Ferry, New York, and John B. Stetson University, in Delard, Florida), which generally offer graduate education through the master's degree, as well as many specialized undergraduate programs. The Liberal Arts I colleges operating at the median of their own size distribution, such as Whitman College, in Walla Walla, Washington, and Hartwick College, in Oneonta, New York, are surprisingly close in scale to the Comprehensive I institutions, given their more restricted focus on undergraduate education, primarily in the arts and sciences. One explanation for the relatively high levels of expenditures of these liberal arts colleges—and for the large difference between their median and the median for "Other Four-Year" institutions—is the relative age, wealth, and prestige of many of these institutions (discussed further in Chapters Nine and Ten). Another explanation is the residential character of many Liberal Arts I colleges.

The median for the "Other Four-Year" institutions (such as Trinity College, in Washington, D.C., and the University of Mary Hardin-Baylor, in Bel-

---

* The universe of nonprofit institutions included in our discussion of higher education differs from that for arts/culture in that it is taken entirely from the SOI sample (described in Appendix E), not from the BMF itself, and includes only accredited institutions which were also listed in the *Higher Education Directory*. Using only the SOI sample is feasible in the case of higher education because even the smallest accredited institutions are large enough to be included in the SOI sample (which is not the case for most other fields). Using the SOI sample has the major advantage of allowing us to use total expenditures, rather than gross receipts, as our measure of size for all institutions. The disadvantages are that these data are for an earlier year (1988) and that we miss a relatively small number of accredited institutions that are in the BMF (about 15 percent in each of the sectors of higher education, except "Other Four-Year," where we miss about 30 percent). By defining our universe to exclude nonaccredited institutions, we exaggerate somewhat the differences in typical size between the fields of higher education and arts/culture. The basic patterns described below, however, would still hold, no matter how the universes were defined.

Figure 7.3. Size of Higher Education Institutions by Field.

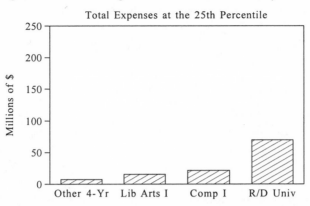

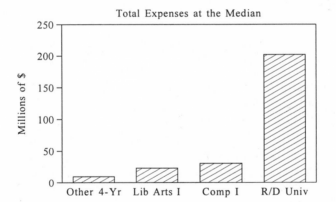

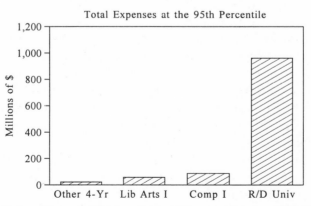

Source: Statistics of Income Division, Internal Revenue Service, 1987/1988. See also Appendix G, Table G.7-1.

ton, Texas) is much lower than the median for any of the other categories in higher education. Some perspective is gained, however, by noting that this median is nonetheless more than ten times higher than the median for any of the arts/culture fields. Some quite small institutions can function successfully in all of the arts/culture fields, but it is much harder for accredited institutions of higher education to operate below some minimum scale.

Strong evidence in support of this claim is provided by the relatively high levels of expenditures incurred by "Other Four-Year" institutions operating at the 25th percentile of the size distribution (see the top panel of Figure 7.3). The minimum annual running costs in higher education are much higher across the board than they are for historical societies, museums, or performing arts organizations. In higher education, expenditures of the relatively small institutions at the 25th percentile of the size distribution tend to be much closer to the expenditures of the mid-sized institutions at the 50th percentile than is the case in arts/culture. (The Research/Doctorate universities are something of an anomaly in this regard because of the role played by sponsored research, as discussed below and in Chapter Eight.)

Very Large Organizations

The relatively large size of many colleges and universities is evident from the bottom panel of Figure 7.3, which indicates that annual expenditures at the largest Research/Doctorate universities were at roughly the $1 billion level. The 95th percentile values are lower elsewhere in higher education, but they are still substantial: nearly $90 million among the Comprehensive I institutions, almost $60 million per year in the Liberal Arts I sector, and over $20 million among the "Other Four-Year" institutions. Within arts/culture, only some of the museums at the 95th percentile have budgets near $20 million (compare the bottom panel of Figure 7.2).

The more general and more important point is that in almost all of these fields, unusual opportunities for growth and expansion have been seized by key institutions. One way to demonstrate this proposition is by comparing gross receipts (or, in the case of higher education, total expenditures) at different points along the size distribution. In opera, orchestra, and ballet, there are dramatic differences between institutions at the 75th percentile and those at the 95th percentile. (See the top panel of Figure 7.4 for graphic depictions of how steeply gross receipts rise as we move toward the top of the size distributions within these fields.) The gradients are less steep for theater and dance but are still far from negligible. The category of Research/Doctorate universities once again constitutes a case in itself, with quite steady increases over each interval along the size distribution; otherwise, higher education is notable for the lack of steep gradients (see the bottom panel of Figure 7.4).

In thinking about very large organizations, there is no substitute for looking at identifiable institutions. Accordingly, we compared the largest single organization of each type (using gross receipts, or 1991 operating rev-

Figure 7.4. Range of Institutional Sizes by Field.

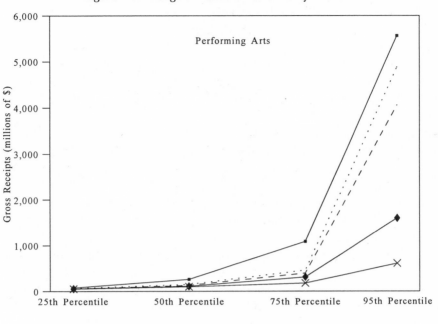

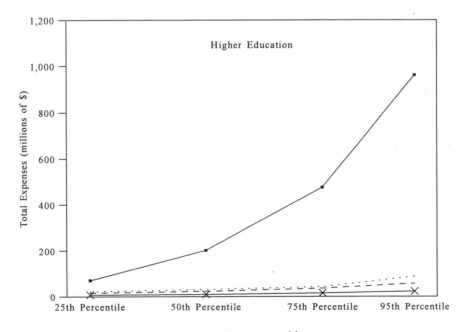

Sources: Performing arts—Business Master File, October 1991, active, independent, positive filers only; higher education—Statistics of Income Division, Internal Revenue Service, 1987/1988. See also Appendix G, Table G.7-1.

enues when necessary, with the corresponding organization at the 95th percentile. The relationships between size at the very top and size at the 95th percentile among the different fields are illuminating.

In many of the sectors of higher education and in the world of museums the maximum values and the values at the 95th percentile are roughly similar. In these fields, there appears to be some kind of collective upper boundary on size—a level which has been reached by a reasonable number of institutions of the same type. Indeed, in the case of the Research/Doctorate universities, there is such a bunching of values at the top of the size distribution that it is more or less accidental which particular private university records the highest level of expenditures at any one point in time. The University of Pennsylvania enjoys that distinction in this database, but the institution at the 95th percentile, the Massachusetts Institute of Technology, reported expenditures only about 10 percent lower than those reported by the University of Pennsylvania.

What is most interesting is not which institution is largest but rather how large "large" is—and how closely bunched in size the largest private universities are. The largest gaps in expenditures are in the "other museum" and "Other Four-Year" fields, which is not surprising, given the broad range of organizations included in these categories. Still, Gallaudet University (the largest "Other Four-Year" institution, with $82.8 million in total expenses) is not even four times larger than Pacific Union College, in Angwin, California (an institution at the 95th percentile, which had $22.8 million in total expenses). Similarly, the Winterthur Museum, in Wilmington, Delaware, is about four times larger than its counterpart at the 95th percentile, the Maritime Center, at Norfolk, Connecticut.

By contrast, in the performing arts, and among historical societies, the distances between the highest value and the value at the 95th percentile are much greater—so large, in many cases, that they remind us of why it is important to think in terms of medians, not means, and of why we regard the 95th percentile value as a better indicator of the regular top of the size distribution than the receipts or expenditures of the largest single institution in a field.

The New York Metropolitan Opera, which had a budget of about $110 million in 1991, is more than fifteen times larger, in operating revenues, than the corresponding institutions at the 95th percentile of the field (such as the San Diego Opera). The corresponding multiples are high elsewhere in the performing arts, although not usually so high. For instance, the New York Shakespeare Festival had receipts that were eight times greater than the receipts of the comparable institution at the 95th percentile (Williamstown Theater, in Williamstown, Massachusetts). Similarly, New York City Ballet, which had receipts of almost $31.5 million, was nearly eight times bigger than its 95th percentile counterpart, Miami City Ballet, which had gross receipts of $4.1 million.

These extremely skewed size distributions cannot be explained by cost structures. Rather, they indicate that in sectors such as the performing arts, in which it is possible for strong institutions to operate at smaller scales, it is also possible for certain institutions in special circumstances to expand dramatically beyond the scale that is usually characteristic of their field. The factors which make this possible have much to do with history and geographic location. For example, most of the very largest arts/culture institutions are in New York City.

We hasten to add, before ending this discussion, that we are not rendering any judgment as to when, if at all, "very large" becomes *too* large. The largest institutions play exceedingly important roles in the cultural life of the nation, with influences that extend far beyond their own cities and regions. Their exceptional size enables them to do certain things which smaller institutions simply cannot do. Very large historical societies not only have much bigger collections than their smaller counterparts but also often have considerable exhibit space and sponsor extensive educational programs. For example, the Connecticut Historical Society, one of the "very large" historical societies, has nine exhibition galleries and offers guided tours, lectures, gallery talks, slide shows, traveling exhibits, family programs, workshops, educational outreach programs, and curricular materials.

Smaller institutions of high quality have other advantages, most notably flexibility and relative simplicity. The distinctive situations of very large versus small orchestras illustrate these different kinds of advantages. Very large orchestras generally feature highly paid conductors and soloists. In order to support these well-compensated stars, the repertoires of very large orchestras must appeal to a broad audience, and the orchestras must negotiate complicated union, recording, and broadcasting contracts. Smaller orchestras face very different financial realities: while they do not have the international reach of the largest symphonies and cannot compete for the most highly regarded conductors, soloists, or graduates of conservatories, they do have a less pressured life-style. They experience neither the highs nor the lows common to life among the largest orchestras, and some people believe that they are better able to remain artistically rather than financially driven.

This discussion concludes our analysis of the effects of field of activity on size. We turn in Chapter Eight to the relationship between field and revenue profile.

Notes

1. The correct division of costs between the fixed and variable categories is a highly complex subject, which we do not pursue in any detail. Much depends on time horizons and on the nature of various contractual and programmatic commitments. For example, once a college or university

has decided upon the curriculum it will offer, it has to make a "fixed" outlay on core teaching personnel in the relevant fields. Additional outlays (marginal or incremental expenses) will then have to be made, although they are often not very substantial, when (if) enrollment rises above the threshold level. If higher levels of enrollment are to be sustained, however, it may be necessary to make still larger core investments (for example, in tenured faculty, library collections, and laboratories).

2.   The NTEE categories were the basis for the selection of organizations, but we did some "weeding" to remove entities that were obviously misclassified. See Appendix D for the application of this approach in arts/culture. The organizations included in this analysis are all the independent positive filers that belong to this "weeded" BMF universe.

3.   The ability of historical organizations to operate at a modest scale is confirmed by the 1989 National Museum Survey (American Association of Museums, 1992). Over 90 percent of all nonprofit historical museums and historical sites included in this survey were classified as "small" (under $350,000 in annual operating expenses). Historical organizations had by far the highest concentration of entities in the "small" category.

4.   The patterns for museums described in the last two paragraphs are confirmed by tabulations based on data for mean total revenues, obtained from the American Association of Museums 1989 survey. "General" museums (roughly corresponding to what we call "other" museums) are decidedly at the bottom of the size distribution, with mean revenues of $257,000. Next come art museums (mean revenues of $1,008,000). In this sample, science museums rank below museums of natural history, with mean revenues of $1,536,000 and $2,136,000, respectively, rather than the other way around. We suspect that this reversal is due to the presence of a few very large natural history museums (see the last part of this chapter) that have a large effect on the average when means rather than medians are calculated.

EIGHT

Revenue Profiles
by Field

I n seeking to understand various nonprofit organizations and how they differ from one another, a defining characteristic is their revenue profiles. By *revenue profiles*, we mean the percentages of total revenue coming from each principal source—earned income, governmental appropriations and grants, and private contributions, including both current gifts and returns on endowments.

Unlike for-profit entities, which earn all their revenue in one form or another, nonprofits obtain revenues in a wide variety of ways. While they too sell goods and services, they may also collect membership dues; ask for voluntary contributions from visitors; put on benefits; conduct regular fundraising drives, as well as capital campaigns targeted at individual donors, corporations, and foundations; compete for sponsored research support that is provided via grants or contracts; and seek governmental subventions from local, state, and federal entities. In effect, a nonprofit organization has a portfolio of revenue-generating activities which together are expected to yield enough revenue to permit it to carry out its basic mission.

General Patterns

One would expect the revenue profiles of nonprofit institutions to vary significantly according to field of activity (a causal relationship symbolized by arrow 2 on Figure 7.1). We have tested this proposition by using detailed data collected by the Statistics of Income (SOI) Division of the Internal Revenue Service. This database is described in detail in Appendix E. Unlike the Business Master File (BMF) database used in earlier chapters, which approximates the entire universe of nonprofit organizations, the SOI database is a relatively small sample of entities. In our fields, there are 82 performing arts organizations, 151 museums and historical societies, and 665 colleges and universities.

The great advantage of the SOI database is that it contains fairly complete financial information for each organization. (Recall that the only financial data in the BMF database are total assets and gross receipts.) However, the sampling design used to construct the SOI database constrained our analysis in some respects. Small organizations are underrepresented, which meant that there was a limited number of organizations in some of the fields we had selected. Thus we were forced to combine the science and natural history museum fields and to eliminate dance altogether. More generally, the characteristics of the SOI sample mean that too much importance should not be attached to fine distinctions. It is the general pattern of results which is important.[1]

The evidence demonstrates that the relationship between field of activity and revenue profile is indeed an exceedingly powerful one (see Figure 8.1). Higher education is seen to depend overwhelmingly on earned income (basically, tuition payments). Historical societies and museums are just as heavily dependent on private support (a combination of current gifts and investment returns on prior gifts). Performing arts organizations are the only genuinely mixed case: as a group, they depend almost equally on earned income and private support.

There are differences, of course, sometimes substantial ones, in revenue profiles among individual organizations of each type, as well as between related fields (art museums versus science museums and orchestras versus operas, to cite two examples). While some of these intrafield differences are highly instructive, we concentrate first on the broad patterns revealed by the SOI data and on the theoretical considerations which explain them.

The Role of Earned Income

The most fundamental dichotomy is between earned income and all other revenue sources. In general, the earned income share can be expected to be high when the product produced by the institution provides a direct private benefit; that is, someone can be excluded from enjoying the benefit if he or she does not pay for it. There are many applications, not included in this study, of this principle in nonprofit fields; day-care centers and nursing homes are clear examples.[2]

At the other end of the spectrum, we would expect earned income to be a small percentage of revenues in the case of organizations which produce outputs that are not readily divisible into units that can be sold to individuals. Such products are often called *public goods*. The characteristics of a public good have been described in layman's terms by Hansmann, as follows:

Figure 8.1. Average Revenue Shares by Field, 1987/1988.

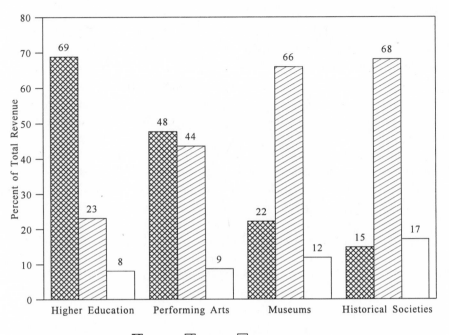

Source: Statistics of Income Division, Internal Revenue Service, 1987/1988. See Appendix G, Table G.8-1.

A public good, in the economists' sense, is a good that has two special attributes: first, it costs no more to provide the good to many persons than it does to provide it to one, because one person's enjoyment of the good does not interfere with the ability of others to enjoy it at the same time; second, once the good has been provided to one person there is no easy way to prevent others from consuming it as well [the exclusion principle]. Air pollution control, defense against nuclear attack, and radio broadcasts are common examples of public goods.[3]

Other things being equal, the greater the degree to which an organization's product has the attributes of a public good, the lower the likelihood that earned income will be a significant source of revenue.

Much of the discussion that follows applies these basic principles to the fields under discussion here. We also note special attributes of each field and other principles that help us to understand differences in revenue profiles.

First, however, it is necessary to be clear about what we mean by the term *earned income*. The line separating earned income from all other revenues can be surprisingly difficult to draw. For example, how should one treat membership dues? In the empirical work that follows, we have arbitrarily assigned half of dues to earned income and half to private contributions (see Appendix E). A more general problem is the treatment of governmental contracts. In the SOI database, governmental purchases of services are not usually counted as earned income, but rather are grouped with governmental grants under the single rubric *governmental support*.[4] These problems notwithstanding, it is possible to distinguish fairly readily between, for example, the revenue earned by a dance company from ticket sales and a foundation grant to the same troupe in support of its general operations. Recurring examples of earned income, as we use the term here, include college tuition, admission fees, ticket sales, sales of publications, service charges, and profits earned from a gift shop or a cafeteria.

There is a clear rank-ordering of fields, based on their degree of reliance on earned income (see Figure 8.2). Roughly 70 percent of the revenue received by the typical private college or university is reported as earned income (mostly tuition payments).[5] Next come the performing arts organizations, where roughly half of total revenue is typically earned income (predominantly ticket sales).[6] Museums and historical societies offer a sharp contrast: earned income is less than 20 percent of total revenue for the median museum. Science museums are more dependent on earned income than are other museums, but even in this case, median earned income is less than 40 percent of total revenue. An even smaller share, under 10 percent, of the revenue of the typical historical society can be classified as earned income.

As already suggested, this sharply differentiated pattern can be explained largely in terms of the nature of the output produced by each type of organization. To what extent do the missions of organizations in various fields of activity cause them to provide a product or a service for which there is a market? Is the output more like a public or a private good? How much output can be sold, at what price, consistent with the purposes of the organization?

Higher Education

At one extreme, colleges and universities offer a principal product—higher education—for which there is a strong demand. Moreover, it is easy to exclude nonpurchasers, since only tuition payers are permitted to matriculate. Many prospective students and their parents regard higher education as a necessity, and the evidence of high monetary returns on such investments is one justification (although certainly not the only one) for decisions by students and their families to spend substantial personal resources obtaining a

Figure 8.2. Median Earned-Income Share of Total Revenue by Field, 1987/1988.

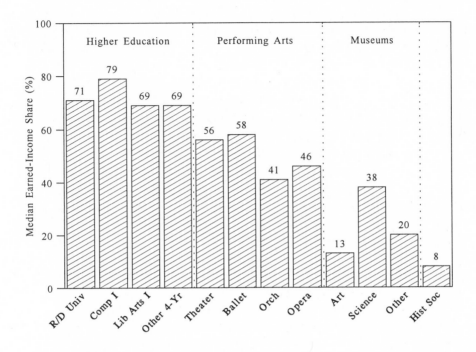

Source: Statistics of Income Division, Internal Revenue Service, 1987/1988. See Appendix G, Table G.8-2.

college education.[7] The private-good aspect of higher education is also reflected in the growing number of proprietary, profit-making enterprises that have been established in recent decades.

Earned income might be an even higher percentage of total revenue at private colleges and universities were it not for another market consideration: the existence of a strong set of *public* institutions of higher education, which compete for students as well as for faculty members and, increasingly, for private donations. Tuition is much lower in the public sector, especially for in-state students, and the capacity of private institutions to impose higher charges (and to collect the stated tuition from larger numbers of full-paying students) is constrained by the availability of places at excellent public institutions.

The existence of this dual structure reflects the fact that higher education has long been perceived as conferring benefits on society at large, as well as on those students who are its most direct beneficiaries. There is a national interest in having a well-educated population—the functioning of a democratic society and the self-reporting of taxes, for example, depend on a well-educated citizenry—and this interest can be said to transcend the purely personal interests of those who are educated. For these and other reasons, there is a national interest in encouraging broad access to higher education—in ensuring some reasonable degree of opportunity for all qualified students. We do not want to educate only those who can pay the full costs, which are generally much higher than tuition.

The fact that higher education is provided primarily through a combination of private nonprofit institutions and publicly controlled institutions, rather than through for-profit entities, also reflects other values. In particular, the quality and character of programs offered, as well as constituencies served, will differ according to whether the objective of the institution is to maximize profit or to serve a broader set of goals.

Historical Societies

At the other extreme from higher education are historical societies. It is impossible to imagine these organizations—especially those which exist primarily to collect and preserve historical documents—entertaining any thought of surviving on earned income. While scholars and others use their collections, it is unrealistic to expect users to defray any significant share of the costs of operating historical societies. Occasional sales of duplicate documents (or other weeding of the collections) can yield some revenue. Royalties are earned on some publications, and educational outreach can produce some income. But opportunities of this kind are plainly limited. The real product of historical societies is the preservation of the historical record for the benefit of future as well as present generations, and this product is not readily divisible into units which can be sold to individuals.

The revenue profiles for historical societies are fully consistent with this interpretation of their character and purposes. The earned-income share for the median organization was 8 percent in 1988. For three-quarters of the historical societies, earned income was 20 percent or less of total revenues, and the bottom quarter had earned-income shares of 4 percent or less (see Appendix G, Table G.8-2). Moreover, these figures probably exaggerate the importance of earned income within the full range of historical societies, since it is presumably especially hard for small entities (which are underrepresented in our sample) to charge fees and earn income.

Museums

In this regard, most museums are more like historical societies than like institutions of higher education. One of their principal functions is to collect and preserve objects, so that future generations will be able to enjoy and learn from great works of art, natural history exhibits, and a wide variety of specialized collections of almost every conceivable kind. Conservation is considered, appropriately, an important responsibility of major museums. At the same time, individuals are more inclined to pay in order to visit art galleries and exhibits than they are to pay in order to use collections of historical documents. Thus it is feasible to charge admission, and we saw in Figure 8.2 that the median earned-income share for museums was more than twice as high, overall, as the earned-income share for the typical historical society.[8] There is evidence that financial pressures are forcing more and more museums to charge admission. Museums, like libraries, used to be considered civic institutions, and they were open free of charge to the public. Then museums began requesting suggested donations, and now many museums have instituted mandatory charges.[9]

At the same time, there are real limitations on the ability of museums to finance their activities primarily through earned income. Costs, including especially the costs of new acquisitions, may exceed the revenue that can be collected from those willing to pay admission. More generally, even if it were possible to raise earned income by increasing admission charges, there are arguments against pushing this approach too hard. While those who are unwilling or unable to pay *can* be excluded from the privilege of viewing the collection, such a policy may not be desirable from a social point of view. The mission of most museums, after all, is to encourage people to see the exhibits—to educate, in a broad sense—and, in many situations, admitting another visitor neither imposes new costs on the museum nor prevents anyone else from enjoying the art.

The great popularity of some exhibits (such as the Matisse show at the Museum of Modern Art in New York in 1992) creates quite different issues that also limit the degree to which museums can rely on earned income. When demand is so strong that space simply must be rationed, another consideration comes to the fore: equity. Nonprofits differ from for-profit entities in that they often care—and society often cares—about the set of individuals who benefit most directly from their products or services. Car dealers cheerfully sell to the highest bidder, and no one objects. But universities would be criticized severely if they were to auction off places in the entering class, and boards of trustees of museums would be reluctant to set admission charges at such a high level that only the affluent could afford admission. The tax-exempt status of nonprofits implies an obligation to serve the general welfare—in this instance, by offering individuals at many income levels ready access to educational and cultural institutions.

There is also at least one major distinction to draw among types of museums. It is illustrated by the contrast between art museums and science museums, and then by the further contrast between natural history museums and museums devoted more exclusively to science and technology. We have seen that art museums, as a group, tend to rely much less heavily on earned income than do science museums; the median share of earned income, as shown on Figure 8.2, is 13 percent for art museums, as compared to 38 percent for science museums. The explanation of this difference has partly to do with the greater capacity of art museums to attract private support, because of a combination of the affluence of patrons and the social status often associated with contributing to an art museum. Another part of the explanation, we suspect, has to do with the broader appeal of many science museums to a fee-paying clientele.

Why would science museums be in a relatively good position to attract earned income? The programs of many science museums contain larger educational components. As a consequence, they may be able to appeal to a broader public. Moreover, potential visitors, especially those concerned with preparing their children to live in a science- and technology-oriented world, may be willing to pay more for access to science museums. In Philadelphia, for example, adults pay $8.50 and children pay $4.00 to visit the Franklin Institute Science Museum, but they pay only $6.00 and $3.00, respectively, to visit the Philadelphia Museum of Art. In addition, some of the programs offered by science museums border on entertainment, which is also something for which people are used to paying. For example, it is common for visitors to pay $5.00 to view IMAX films at science museums.

More generally, there may be an important difference between "collecting" and "noncollecting" museums, with collecting museums having a larger public-good component and noncollecting a larger private-good component.[10] The difference between the earned-income share of natural history museums and science-technology museums is indicative. When we examined separately those museums in our sample that could be clearly classified as either science or natural history museums, we found that the nine natural history museums had an earned-income share of 36 percent, whereas the corresponding share for the seven science-technology museums was 55 percent. The American Association of Museums reported a similar difference. For all nonprofit science museums in their survey, earned income was 59 percent of total income; for natural history museums, earned income was 43 percent of total income.[11]

In terms of the attributes just discussed, natural history museums have more in common with art museums than do science-technology museums. The contrast between two institutions in Chicago is instructive. The Field Museum of Natural History, with an earned-income share of 20 percent, has collections in anatomy, anthropology, archaeology, botany, entomology, ethnology, geology, mineralogy, paleontology, and zoology—all the "ologies." The Museum of Science and Industry, with an earned-income share of 38 percent, contains the Curiosity Place (for children), Delivering the Mail, Explorations of the Human Brain, Sante Fe Model Railway, Calculating to Computing, the Energy Lab, Food for Life, the Circus, the Coal Mine, Colleen Moore's Fairy Castle, Managing Urban Wastes, the U-505 Submarine, and other attractions, including an Omnimax theater. In short, the marketability of the exhibits and programs of various types of museums differs significantly, and their earned-income shares vary accordingly.

Performing Arts

The factors affecting earned income within the last of our major sectors, the performing arts, are in many ways the most intriguing. We have seen that revenue in the performing arts sector is split almost equally between earned income and private support (Figure 8.1). From the perspective of museums and historical societies, the earned-income share is a high percentage, but it is low relative to higher education. Overall, less than one-quarter of the performing arts organizations in our sample have earned income equal to as much as 60 percent of total revenue (see the 75th percentile column of Appendix G, Table G.8-2).

The main product of performing arts entities—performances—can be enjoyed directly by those who attend performances, and potential attendees can be excluded if they do not buy tickets. The private benefits are clear. The interesting question is not why the median earned-income share is as high as 50 or 60 percent, but rather why it is not appreciably higher—at least as high, for example, as the median earned-income share in higher education. On first blush, at least, it is hard to argue that the public benefits of the performing arts are greater than those associated with higher education.

At least part of the answer to this puzzle is due to the combination of two factors: a cost structure for the performing arts characterized by fixed costs (rehearsals, sets, costumes, performance space, and so on), which are high relative to the marginal costs associated with an extra performance; and less robust demand than one finds for higher education. As an almost invariant rule, no ticket price for high-culture performing arts events will generate enough earned income to cover fixed costs; demand is not that inelastic. If earned income were not supplemented by other sources of support—and supplemented substantially, our data suggest—performing arts organizations would not exist in anything like their present form. The obvious contrast is with movies and the Broadway stage, which have broader popular appeal and are therefore able to spread their fixed costs over enough attendees to manage financially without subventions.[12]

In and of itself, being impecunious is hardly sufficient justification for continuing existence. The philistine is surely entitled to argue that those who want to see performances ought to cover their costs. Why should others pay? The interesting question is how performing arts organizations have been able to attract enough other revenue to fill the sizable "income gap" created by their apparently limited capacity to generate earned income. This question leads directly to a broader examination of the roles of private and governmental sources of support throughout the nonprofit fields being considered here.

Private and Governmental Contributions:
The Special Case of the Performing Arts

By definition—it is a tautology—the share of revenues coming from private and governmental sources combined must be high when the share coming from earned income is low.* Thus private and governmental sources together account for about 80 percent of all revenues for historical societies and museums. Conversely, private and governmental shares, taken together, are lowest (about 30 percent, typically) in higher education. The performing arts are the middle case (see Figure 8.1).

In general, the logic explaining this pattern is precisely the opposite of the logic used in explaining the variations in earned income. Organizations such as historical societies, which provide products that have a considerable public-good flavor, should be expected to depend more heavily on private and governmental contributions than on earned income. In one way, a historical society may be viewed as analogous to the spotted owl: one may want to preserve it for future generations, even though one may not expect to see it oneself.

The performing arts represent a more complex case. Superficially, at least, these organizations might be thought to offer products with the least public-good content of all the fields of activity considered here, and yet they receive a larger share of their revenue from private and governmental sources than institutions of higher education do. Why?

As Hansmann has pointed out, at least part of donative financing in the performing arts can be regarded as a form of "voluntary price discrimination."[13] Certain individuals who are highly committed to the opera, for example, would be willing to pay a much higher price than the one stated on the ticket. Rather than attempt to identify all such individuals and actually charge them a higher price—a practical impossibility for many reasons, including the transferability of tickets—the arts organization may in effect ask these individuals to contribute voluntarily in the form of donations. The presumption is that there are patrons who care deeply about the enterprise and are willing to pay more through donations—perhaps appreciably more—than the official ticket price. They know that, without their support and the support of people like them, there is no hope for the organization. Voluntary price discrimination is one way of resolving the dilemma faced by the arts organizations and their potential supporters. In addition to "looking better" than overt price discrimination, this solution confers a tax benefit on the donor.

A similar principle may help explain at least part of the flow of private donations to museums and historical societies, especially when wealthy pa-

---

*Private income includes investment income as well as private contributions. Investment income is dealt with as a separate source of income in Chapter Nine.

trons are strongly committed to particular institutions. An analogous kind of behavior is also observed at the most selective private colleges and universities, where some individuals and families are prepared to pay much more than the tuition cost, either when they are still in school or, more frequently, at some later date when they have become alumni and (everyone hopes) have prospered. Thus Hansmann has suggested that donations by alumni to colleges may represent repayment of implicit loans.[14]

Putting voluntary price discrimination to one side, there are additional reasons—related more clearly to the broad public interest in aspects of the output of performing arts organizations—which also help to explain the willingness of private and governmental sponsors to provide roughly half the revenues of these institutions. Individuals, corporations, and foundations have been willing to contribute out of the simple belief that the arts and culture are intrinsically good for society and should be preserved for future generations; that opportunities to see performances should be made available to those who could not afford to pay top prices, including young audiences; that the presence of a highly regarded performing arts organization confers tangible benefits of many kinds on the city or region in which the arts organization exists; and that performing arts organizations serve broadly educative roles in our society. These same public-good arguments have been the justification for support provided through local, state, and federal programs. And, of course, they have been the basis for extensive state support of the arts in other countries.[15]

Governmental Support

Governmental support as a share of all nonearned income for each of our fields is shown in Figure 8.3. (These shares are independent of earned-income levels; they merely tell us how the nonearned portion of revenues is divided between public and private support.) In general, higher education receives the largest share of its nonearned revenues from the government, followed by museums and then by the performing arts. There are notable exceptions to this pattern, however. In particular, governmental revenues comprise only 13 percent of the unearned revenues for art museums and Liberal Arts I colleges. These small percentages and the modest governmental shares in the performing arts fields are highly consistent with what one would have expected on the basis of voluntary price discrimination; in these fields, private support is relatively high.

The Research/Doctorate universities might appear to be an exception, since they show the highest governmental share of any set of institutions, even though they, like the Liberal Arts I colleges, have wealthy alumni who identify strongly with them and give generously. However, their higher governmental support is deceptive in that it is due to another phenomenon, very different and entirely unrelated—namely, the presence on their finan-

Figure 8.3. Average Governmental Share of Nonearned Income by Field, 1987/1988.

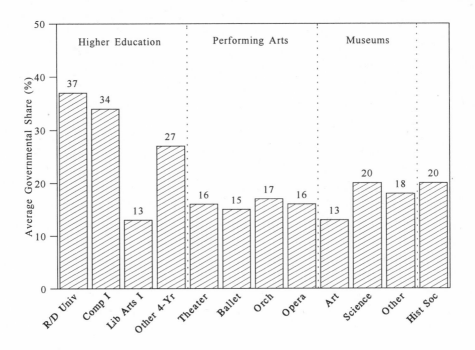

Source: Statistics of Income Division, Internal Revenue Service, 1987/1988.

cial statements of extremely large amounts of governmental funding for sponsored research. We suspect strongly (although we have found no easy way to test this proposition) that if federally sponsored research money were excluded from the governmental total, the governmental share of nonearned revenue for Research/Doctorate universities would be very close to the share for Liberal Arts I colleges.

It is important to note that there are also wide ranges of governmental support within nonprofit fields. Governmental support varies significantly by state and by city, as a consequence of differences in both resources and attitudes toward the arts and other nonprofit entities. To cite just a few examples from among the individual organizations included in the SOI sample, the Baltimore Symphony Orchestra and the Baltimore Museum of Art rank high in governmental share of unearned revenues (31 percent and 55 percent, respectively). Similarly, the strong financial support provided by the New Jersey Arts Council to many organizations was reflected in the corresponding governmental shares of the New Jersey Symphony (58 percent) and the Crossroads Theater (71 percent). We see too that certain states, usually in the midwest, have elected to support their historical societies generously and that these organizations serve broader purposes. For example, the Minnesota and Ohio Historical Societies received more than three-quarters of their unearned revenues from governmental sources (77 percent and 91 percent, respectively).

The federal government also supports a wide variety of nonprofit entities for a broad array of programmatic reasons. Unfortunately, the SOI data do not permit us to distinguish federal funding from that provided by state and local authorities. Nonetheless, it is possible to make some conjectures concerning the federal role in determining the revenue profiles of certain components of one nonprofit sector: higher education.

We surmise that broad-based governmental support (excluding sponsored research) for nonprofit institutions of higher education of all types is largely a function of student aid programs. Government-supported student financial aid is a good example of a programmatic initiative which does not loom large in the overall revenue profiles of institutions (amounting, we would guess, to less than 5 percent of total revenues, in most cases)[16] but which has major consequences for the provision of one type of public good—namely, increased access to private institutions by students from less affluent families, particularly minority students.

The federal government has also provided special support for historically black colleges and universities. For example, according to SOI data, the governmental share of unearned revenues at Howard University was 86 percent in 1988. Similarly, it was 61 percent at Tuskegee University. The federal government has also taken a special interest in Gallaudet University, which is well known for its efforts on behalf of hearing-impaired students. In 1988, Gallaudet had the largest governmental share of unearned revenue of any college or university in our sample—93 percent.

We note again the highly specialized nature of another form of governmental support concentrated at the federal level: sponsored research. Sponsored research funding goes to particular investigators and projects, and not to institutions per se. Still, it can dominate budgetary totals. For example, it is the concentration of highly rated projects at the Massachusetts Institute of Technology (M.I.T.) and Johns Hopkins, not the universities themselves or other forms of governmental assistance to them, that has led to such a significant governmental share of unearned revenue at these institutions (82 percent at M.I.T. and 78 percent at Johns Hopkins in 1988).

Finally, it must be pointed out that the nonprofit organizations included in our sample, considered as a group, are highly atypical of all nonprofits with regard to governmental funding. With the few exceptions already noted, our organizations are much more dependent on both earned income and private donations (including investment income attributable overwhelmingly to prior donations) than they are on governmental funding.

In sharp contrast, for many other types of nonprofit service providers, government is a much more important source of revenue than all private giving combined.[17] In certain fields—for instance, mental health, housing and community development, legal services, and social services—the governmental share of total revenues is well over 50 percent. It has been argued that the nonprofit sector is often the preferred provider of such services and operates effectively in partnership with governmental funders, which choose to subsidize the private sector's provision of certain services instead of providing them directly.[18] The broad sectors of health and social welfare are very different from those parts of the universe of charitable nonprofits with which we are primarily concerned in this study.

Each sector—really each field within each broad sector—operates on the basis of a set of objectives, revenue profiles, and operating characteristics of its own. In sum, field of activity does drive revenue profiles. While specific patterns will vary, the basic principles apply regardless of field. The most important consideration is the nature of the output: Can it be sold to individuals, or is it more like a public good?

Diversification of Revenue Sources

In this, the final section of the chapter, we investigate a somewhat different question: How diversified are the revenue sources for our sets of nonprofit organizations? This question is important for two reasons. First, an organization that has a diversified portfolio of revenue sources is likely to be more stable financially, other things being equal, than an organization that is heavily dependent on a single source of revenue. Second, an organization that depends overwhelmingly on one source of revenue may be more subject to challenges to its autonomy and may enjoy less freedom of action than a comparable organization that has access to a multiplicity of revenue sources. Of course, much depends on whether there are few or many providers (donors) within each revenue category, as well as on the attitudes and philosophies of the major sponsors.

Defining and measuring the diversification of revenue sources in an operational way is far from an easy task. We do not have the information on individual donors and grantmakers which would be needed to study this question at that level of detail. All that we can do is assemble aggregate data on major categories of revenue. Our approach is to distinguish what we call *hybrid* revenue profiles, which indicate that an organization relies on more than a single major source of revenue, from *primary* revenue profiles, which indicate that a single source of revenue dominates all others. Any boundary between these two broad categories is bound to be somewhat arbitrary.

In the end, after experimenting with several alternative approaches, we selected a strict definition. We consider an organization to have a primary revenue profile only if its largest source of revenue accounts for more than

50 percent of total revenue *and* if this primary revenue source accounts for more than twice the amount provided by the next most important source. We then classify organizations with a primary source into those that depend primarily on earned income, private contributions, investment income, and governmental support.[19]

Any organization that fails to meet this two-pronged test is considered to have a hybrid revenue profile. Thus, for example, an organization which received 55 percent of its revenue from private contributions and no more than 22.5 percent from any other source would be said to have a primary revenue profile—in this case, to be dependent primarily on private contributions. An organization which received 50 percent of its revenues from private contributions but also received, for example, 30 percent from earned income would be classified as a hybrid, as would organizations that had revenues divided about equally among three or four sources.

Generally speaking, there are relatively more organizations with hybrid revenue profiles in the performing arts than there are elsewhere in the universe under consideration here (see Table 8.1). Roughly two-thirds (65 percent) of all performing arts entities are hybrids, as contrasted with about half of all museums and historical societies. Opera is the field that has been the most successful in diversifying its revenue sources, with 78 percent of its members classified as hybrids; theater has the lowest percentage of hybrids among the performing arts fields. Science museums also stand out, with 74 percent of their members in the hybrid category, as contrasted with only 43 percent of art museums.

As one would expect, those performing arts entities which have primary rather than hybrid revenue profiles are most frequently dependent on earned income and less frequently dependent on private contributions. Science museums are like the performing arts in this regard. In contrast, art museums, other museums, and historical societies with primary revenue profiles are more likely to be dependent on private contributions.

Over one-fifth of all historical societies are heavily dependent on investment income, as are 8 percent of all art museums, but the implications of dependence are obviously quite different in the case of this revenue source, since a nonprofit with a large endowment is less subject to withdrawal of external support than is a nonprofit dependent on any other revenue source. However, financial markets can display their own kind of volatility. Institutions which are able to cover a large proportion of their costs with endowment income are also subject to another kind of danger: they may perceive themselves as too independent and lose touch with the public which they are meant to serve (as is alleged to have happened to Colonial Williamsburg at an early stage in its development).

Very few organizations in our sample are primarily dependent on governmental support. But even organizations that do not meet the stringent test of primary dependence—receiving more than twice the support from

Table 8.1 Diversification of Revenue Sources by Field, 1987/1988.

| | | | Percent of Organizations | | | |
| | | Without a Primary Source (Hybrid) | With a Primary Source | | | |
Field	Number of Organizations		Earned	Contributed	Investment	Governmental
Performing arts						
Ballet	8	63	25	13	0	0
Opera	9	78	11	11	0	0
Orchestra	40	70	20	10	0	0
Theater	25	52	32	16	0	0
All performing arts	82	65	23	12	0	0
Museums/historical societies						
Art museums	63	43	0	49	8	0
Science museums	19	74	26	0	0	0
Other museums	35	46	6	43	0	6
All museums	117	49	6	39	4	2
Historical societies	34	56	3	15	21	6

Source: Statistics of Income Division, Internal Revenue Service, 1987/1988.

government as they do from any other source—can still be at risk. Given the speed with which fiscal crises can engulf states and municipalities, and the speed with which legislative priorities can change, governmental funding is sometimes the riskiest revenue source of all.

The effects of the sharp and rather sudden reductions in funding provided by arts councils and other governmental funders illustrate this point dramatically. Most recently, the Los Angeles County Museum of Art went through an exceedingly traumatic period, in part because of a drastic change in the support provided by the county. When Los Angeles prospered, in the 1980s, the museum prospered with it, receiving about half of its support from the county. Then, when recession and riots hit Los Angeles, the museum experienced sharp funding cuts, since the county was unable to live up to the terms of its contract with the museum.[20] Experiences elsewhere—in Michigan and New Jersey, for example—provide other case studies. The lasting lesson may be about how hard it is for any nonprofit organization that is doing well, with governmental help, to anticipate a sudden shift in circumstances and be able to make the necessary adjustments smoothly.

In other parts of the nonprofit universe, however, governmental funding is considered a relatively stable and reliable source of revenue. Kirsten Grønbjerg, for example, in her studies of nonprofit organizations in Illinois, found that social service agencies tend to enjoy stable public funding and to encounter much greater volatility in private donations because "their donations usually do not involve ongoing and reciprocal relationships, but their government grants do."[21]

So far in our discussion of field of activity, size, and revenue profiles, we have abstracted from the age of organizations. The next chapter adds this dimension to our analysis and prepares the way for the final chapter in this part of the book—an examination of trends in expenditures and revenue profiles for a selected group of individual organizations.

Notes

1. We did not attempt to test the statistical significance of the results presented in this chapter. Less-than-random methods of selecting organizations and small sample sizes would make interpretation of significance tests difficult.
2. Indeed, there has been much discussion of why nonprofit entities are needed at all in such fields as day care and nursing homes, especially since profit-making entities exist in large numbers alongside the nonprofits (Weisbrod, 1988, pp. 142–159). Several authors have argued persuasively that the reason is what they call "contract failure." As Hansmann puts it, "This theory suggests, in essence, that nonprofits arise

where ordinary contractual mechanisms do not provide consumers with adequate means to police providers" (1987, p. 29). See Ben-Ner (1986) and Krashinsky (1986) for other theories concerning the unique roles of nonprofit organizations.

3. Hansmann (1987, p. 29). The classic citation is Samuelson (1954).

4. There is also a more abstract definitional problem. It can be argued that an individual donor who makes an unrestricted contribution—for example, to a social service agency which assists the homeless—is in effect paying the agency to do something which the donor wishes to have done but cannot accomplish in an equally effective way through some other means. As Hansmann puts it, "A donor is, in an important sense, a purchaser of services" (1987, p. 30).

5. Accounting conventions lead to overstatements of the true percentage of total revenues (or total expenditures) that institutions of higher education derive from earned income. For one thing, many private educational institutions discount tuition in order to meet enrollment targets (by providing "scholarships" not designed to serve purely educational objectives), and yet it is the gross tuition revenue which is counted here. (By no means all scholarship aid should be regarded as discounts, however. Many institutions invest considerable sums of money in scholarship programs because of their interest in enrolling a more diverse and better-qualified student body than could be enrolled otherwise. In these situations, the gross tuition revenue should be included; see Bowen and Breneman, 1993.) For another, the tendency to exclude many capital costs from the financial statements of colleges and universities, especially when buildings or other assets have been donated, overstates the share of total revenues, or total expenditures, provided by earned income (Winston, 1993).

6. It is the overall pattern for the performing arts that is significant. The small number of ballet (8) and opera (9) companies makes it inadvisable to put great weight on the finer-grained distinctions.

7. Murphy and Welch (1989).

8. The boundary between historical societies and museums is far from firmly delineated, and those historical associations that have collections of interest to the general public have at least the possibility of obtaining earned income above the median level. For example, The New-York Historical Society, which is hoping to recover from the brink of financial collapse, is betting heavily on its ability to attract a larger number of paying visitors to see its Audubons, as well as its unique collection of photographs, architectural drawings, and other objects of general interest, including Tiffany glass.

9. See Herrick, Leven, Remes, and Frey (1992, p. 30) for recent information on admission fees.

10. The distinction between collecting and noncollecting institutions is made by the American Association of Museums (1992, p. 1).

11. We calculated the museum earned-income percentages on the basis of special tabulations provided by the American Association of Museums from its *Data Report from the 1989 National Museum Survey*. Tabulations in the published report do not distinguish between public and private museums.

12. For a good, succinct discussion of the need for performing arts organizations to supplement their earned income, see Hansmann (1987, pp. 35–36). For an earlier treatment, see Baumol and Bowen (1962). For a more recent reference, see Heilbrun and Gray (1993).

13. Hansmann (1987, p. 35).

14. Hansmann (1987, p. 36).

15. For an earlier, extended discussion of the rationale for public support (and, by implication, for contributions by corporations, foundations, and other private donors), see Baumol and Bowen (1962, pp. 369–386).

16. It should be noted, moreover, that our measure of governmental support of student aid does not include subventions paid directly to students as grants or subsidized loans.

17. The importance of governmental support to the nonprofit sector may have been noted first by the Filer Commission, in 1976. More recently, Salamon (1987) has been the most active—and effective—proponent of this proposition. See also the results of case studies conducted by Grønbjerg (1991) and by McMurtry, Netting, and Kettner (1991).

18. See Salamon (1987, especially Tables 6.5 and 6.6 on p. 105 and the accompanying discussion). Salamon sums up as follows: "The voluntary sector's weaknesses correspond well with government's strengths, and vice versa. Potentially, at least, government is in a position to generate a more reliable stream of resources, to set priorities on the basis of a democratic political process instead of the wishes of the wealthy, to offset part of the paternalism of the charitable system by making access to care a right instead of a privilege, and to improve the quality of care by instituting quality-control standards. By the same token, however, voluntary organizations can personalize the provision of services, operate on a smaller scale than government bureaucracies, reduce the scale of public institutions needed, adjust care to the needs of clients rather than to the structure of government agencies, and permit a degree of competition among service providers" (p. 113).

19. Needless to say, there are many formulae that could be used to measure diversification of revenue sources. One reviewer of a draft of this manuscript proposed a heterogeneity index, defined as the sum of the squares of the percentages of revenue obtained from each source. This index would approach 1 if a single source of revenue were dominant, and it would take on a lower value if many sources were more or less equally important. We experimented with a more complex version of the same basic idea but became convinced that the general pattern of the results was not significantly affected by the choice of the measure.

More refined measures probably require more detailed data to make a real difference.

20. Kimmelman (1993b, pp. C17, C20).

21. Grønbjerg (1993, p. 32). See also Grønbjerg (1991), Reiner (1989), and Bielefeld (1992) for further discussion of the reciprocal relationships between some nonprofits and governmental funders and discussion of how nonprofit organizations are able to exploit these relationships to ensure continued funding. Pfeffer and Leong (1979) and Provan, Beyer, and Kruytbasch (1980) have also studied how "power/dependency" relationships affect United Fund and United Way allocations.

NINE

Life Cycles:
Age and Size

The age of an organization—where it is in its own life cycle—affects both its size and its revenue profile (see arrows 5 and 6 in Figure 7.1). Moreover, as we saw in Chapter Six, age can correlate with size simply because relatively few old (and large) organizations die off, whereas the mortality rate among new (small) entities can be quite high. Size in turn is itself related to an organization's revenue profile (arrow 3 in Figure 7.1). All these age-size relationships interact in turn with field of activity, since some fields are younger than others—that is, higher proportions of their surviving organizations have been formed recently (arrow 4 in Figure 7.1). We begin this chapter by noting the degree to which the age distributions of organizations vary by field of activity, and then we explore the relationships between age and size, as well as the relationships among age, size, and revenue profiles. The data in the first two sections are from the Business Master File (BMF). The data source for the remainder of the chapter is the Statistics of Income (SOI) sample.

Field of Activity and Age

Within the arts/culture sector, natural history museums constitute by far the oldest field, followed by art museums, historical societies, and science museums (Table 9.1). The median age of natural history museums, based on ruling year, is thirty-three, and nearly 60 percent of all the entities in this field are over twenty-five years old. Art museums, science museums, and historical societies are all of roughly the same vintage, with median ages ranging from twenty to twenty-five years, and with more than 40 percent of their constituent

147

Table 9.1. Age Distribution by Field, 1991.

Field	Number of Organizations	Age Distribution (percent)			Median Age (years)
		Less than 10 Years	10 to 25 Years	Over 25 Years	
Museums/historical societies					
Science museums	46	26.1	30.4	43.5	20
Art museums	266	15.8	36.1	48.1	25
Natural history museums	31	9.7	32.3	58.1	33
Other museums	814	36.5	42.3	21.3	13
Historical societies	829	11.9	46.2	41.9	23
Performing arts					
Opera	222	20.7	55.9	23.4	15
Orchestra	641	20.9	37.9	41.2	22
Ballet	243	28.8	58.4	12.8	15
Theater	1,524	36.9	45.4	17.7	13
Dance	280	45.7	52.1	2.1	11

Source: Business Master File, October 1991, active, independent, positive filers only.
Note: Ruling year was not available for 63 organizations.

organizations over twenty-five years old. It is noteworthy, however, that one of these fields—science museums—also has a large component of young organizations; indeed, over a quarter of its entities are less than ten years old.

The broad category of "other museums," with a median age of just thirteen years, is young overall. More than a third of its organizations are less than ten years old. This very different age distribution is consistent with the comments on specialization made earlier, in our discussion of the evolution of the civil rights field (Chapter Five). In the museum fields, as well as in civil rights, there is evidence of a growing tendency in recent years to form entities designed to serve specialized purposes. Examples include the Pacific Northwest Truck Museum, the Offshore Rig Museum, the World Kite Museum and Hall of Fame, and the Dog Museum.

In general, the performing arts sector is appreciably younger than museums and historical societies. Only one of its component fields, orchestra, has either a median age over twenty or a large population of long-established entities. We expected dance to be at the other extreme of the age distribution, and so it is. Only 2.1 percent of the dance organizations are more than twenty-five years old, and nearly half are less than ten years old.

We do not show age data for higher education because the years of establishment of colleges and universities of various types were discussed at length in Chapter Five, and there is no need to repeat that commentary here. It is worth recalling, however, that institutions of higher education are generally much older than other types of nonprofits (except some churches). For example, the median age for Comprehensive I institutions is 100 years, and the median for Liberal Arts I colleges is 135 years.

In interpreting the meaning of the relationship between field of activity and age, alternative hypotheses deserve consideration. The most obvious interpretation assumes that young average age implies that the field itself has been populated only recently; organizations have not had time to grow old. It is also possible, however, that young average age is mainly a result of a short lifespan for the typical entity. Museums of a highly specialized kind, for example, may be easy to start but hard to sustain. Pursuing biological analogues, one thinks of short-lived insects as contrasted with long-lived turtles.

Some conjectures are easy to make. We can be quite sure, for example, that old average age for liberal arts colleges is the product of both early dates of formation and of long lifespans. But, without more detailed data than we possess on exit rates and typical life histories, it is impossible to parse out the relative importance of these two effects. We believe this line of analysis is well worth pursuing.

Organizational Life Cycles

The relative size of an organization within its field (as measured by annual receipts or expenditures) is a function of its current "life stage."[1] Another analogy to biological life is useful: When an organization is in its infancy, it is generally small, relative to other organizations in its field. As time passes, it grows, eventually reaching maturity. Just as different species grow at different rates in the natural world, so too do different types of organizations mature at different rates. Not only are gestation periods unequal, but what it means to be mature also varies among both species and organizations. Some species, such as humans, reach a stage beyond which they stop growing altogether. Other species, such as trees, lobsters, and (almost alone among mammals) elephants, continue to grow throughout their lives, albeit often at a slower rate as they age. In theory, organizations can live forever and can continue to grow for an indefinite number of years, but they often experience declining rates of growth as they age.

In order to examine more closely the life cycles of organizations, we classified all entities within each field as *small* if they fell within the bottom quartile of their own size distribution, as *medium-sized* if they fell within the middle two quartiles, or as *large* if they were in the top quartile of the size distribution for the field. Then we calculated the relative numbers of small, medium-sized, and large organizations in each field, with ruling years in each decade. (Our data extend through the 1980s, and we have also assigned the 1990 and 1991 ruling years to this decade.)

Arts/Culture

The results of this exercise for the museum and performing arts sectors are shown in Figure 9.1. (It was necessary to aggregate some fields in order to

Figure 9.1. Age-Size Distribution by Ruling Year, Museums and Performing Arts.

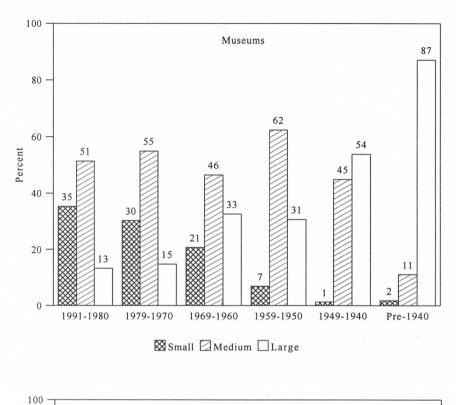

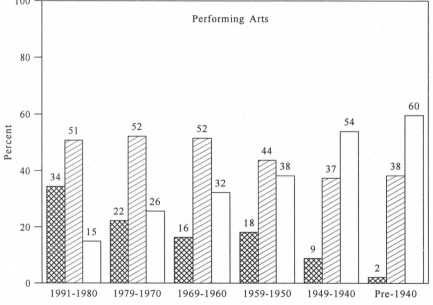

Source: Business Master File, October 1991, active, independent, positive filers only. See also Appendix G, Table G.9-1.

have enough institutions born in each decade. There are not enough science museums or dance companies alone, for example, to permit this type of decade-by-decade analysis.) As our biological analogy would lead us to predict, there is an overarching pattern: in both the museum and performing arts sectors, the percentage of small entities declines quite steadily as age increases (as we move from recent ruling years to more distant ruling years); conversely, the percentage of large organizations rises with age.

A second similarity worth special mention concerns the frequency with which very young organizations are also small. In both the museum and performing arts sectors, just over one-third of the members of the youngest cohort (the group of organizations with ruling years in the 1980s and early 1990s) are classified as small. We are surprised that these percentages (35 percent and 34 percent, to be precise) are not even higher, given our expectations about size during infancy. Moreover, fully 15 percent of performing arts organizations in this youngest cohort, and 13 percent of the youngest museums, are classified as large. It is evident that some of these organizations were either born large (which seems especially likely in the museum sector) or grew rapidly during the first decade of life (which seems more likely in the performing arts).

The age-size relationships for the museum and performing arts sectors continue to resemble each other as we shift our attention to the "middle aged" cohorts (those with ruling years in the 1970s, 1960s, and 1950s). But there are also some interesting differences spanning these decades. In general, performing arts organizations appear to grow faster and to reach some form of maturity sooner. Among those entities in the second decade of life (with ruling years in the 1970s), the fraction of large organizations is nearly twice as high for the performing arts as it is for museums (26 percent, as compared with 15 percent). In the third decade of organizational life, the corresponding fractions of large organizations are about the same in the two sectors (32 percent and 33 percent). Then, in the fourth decade, the share of large organizations is again higher in the performing arts than in the museum sector (38 percent versus 31 percent).

We think that this rather subtle difference in the slopes of the age-size relationships for these two sectors is a reflection of differences in characteristic assets and in the respective rates at which different kinds of asset bases are built. The main assets for performing arts entities are their artistic personnel. If these personnel are exceptionally talented, they can attract a considerable following fairly quickly, and their organizations can become large in a relatively short time. After all, in the performing arts, size is mainly a function of the organization's ability to attract audiences.

The principal assets of museums are their collections, which tend to grow more incrementally and inexorably. Even if a museum establishes its reputation fairly early in its lifetime (which is probably more difficult in this sector than in the performing arts), it will often take time to attract additional pictures or other objects and to build space for collections and exhibits. The natural pace of growth is likely to be slower and maturity to be farther in the future. There are exceptions to this generalization, however. The Getty is an example of a museum that was "born large," as a consequence of the endowment and institutionalization of a large private collection. This is a second, less prevalent, model of entry into the museum field.

The consequences of the basic difference in the nature of the principal assets of entities in the museum and performing arts sectors are seen even more dramatically when we compare "old age" cohorts (those with pre-1940 ruling years). At this stage of organizational life, there are almost no small organizations in either of these sectors (2 percent, in both cases). In the case of museums, there are also very few medium-sized entities; 87 percent of all old entities in the museum fields are large. In the performing arts, however, while the large entities again comprise the biggest single group within the old-age cohort, they are just 60 percent of the total; 38 percent of the old entities in this sector are medium-sized.

Some performing arts entities apparently achieve a certain scale and then continue to operate more or less at that scale, relative to other organizations in their field. This tendency may be partly a consequence of the ephemeral nature of the main assets of performing arts entities. Individual performers and artistic directors come and go; therefore, their institutions must continually rejuvenate themselves artistically. Museums, by contrast, do not have to worry about having their initial assets disappear. They are able to amass assets by holding on to what they acquired in earlier days while simultaneously continuing to collect. In short, museums are more like trees than like humans. They continue to grow even in old age, and the oldest representatives of the species are almost sure to be large in relation to their younger counterparts.

The last set of entities within arts/culture, the historical societies, is pictured in Figure 9.2. Its age-size relationship reinforces the general comments already made. As one would expect, historical societies bear a closer resemblance to museums than to the performing arts. At the same time, age-size relationships in this sector differ from those for museums at both ends of the life cycle.

The youngest cohort of historical societies contains fewer large organizations (just 8 percent) than either performing arts or museums. The explanation, we believe, is that few historical societies start out as large entities. Historical societies are also less likely than performing arts entities to grow rapidly at a young age.

The oldest cohort of historical societies, while also dominated by large entities (77 percent), has an appreciably larger share of small entities (7 percent) than either performing arts or museums. A historical society focused on a definite period, region, or event, especially if it has a more or less fixed collection, has an easier time remaining small than does the typical museum.

Figure 9.2. Age-Size Distribution by Ruling Year, Historical Societies.

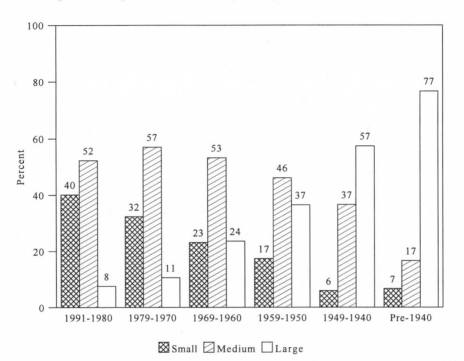

Source: Business Master File, October 1991, active, independent, positive filers only.
See also Appendix G, Table G.9-1.

Small historical societies may also be more stable than small performing arts organizations, since most performing arts entities that failed to grow fast enough by middle age to move out of the small end of the size distribution are likely to have died off altogether before reaching the sixth or seventh decade of life.

Higher Education

The age-size relationships for specific sectors of higher education are governed in many respects by the same principles applicable to arts/culture, but the way in which these institutions are classified affects the patterns revealed by the data. Institutions of higher education are susceptible to mutation. They can, under certain circumstances, transform themselves into another (generally more prestigious) type of educational institution.

In general, age confers status on educational institutions. Over time, a college or a university is likely to acquire assets (libraries, buildings, endowments) that are, like the assets of museums, long-lasting. In addition, educational institutions have another asset which is helped by aging: pools of alumni who can testify on the institution's behalf, who achieve prominence, and who, along with successive generations of distinguished faculty, confer prestige on the institution. Many older institutions also benefit from traditions and perceptions established decades ago. For example, Johns Hopkins will always be associated with the start of American doctoral education, in its modern form.

All of the above factors combine to cause reputation and size to correlate with age. It is not surprising, therefore, that the patterns of age-size relationships, by cohort, are even more pronounced in much of higher education than they are in arts/culture. In the case of the private Research/Doctorate universities, for example, no large institution had a founding year subsequent to the 1890–1913 period, and almost all of the large institutions are older yet, having been established in the seventeenth, eighteenth, and nineteenth centuries (see the top panel of Figure 9.3). Conversely, only 8 percent of the very old Research/Doctorate universities are small, as contrasted with 80 percent of the younger universities in the cohort founded after World War II.

The contrast with the Comprehensive I institutions (bottom panel of Figure 9.3) is striking: some correlation between size and age of establishment is evident here as well, but it is far weaker. At least part of the explanation has to do with the mutation phenomenon alluded to at the start of this section. Some of the large, well-known Research/Doctorate universities of today would have been classified as Comprehensive institutions earlier in their life cycles. In short, some of the most successful members of the comprehensive university sector in an earlier day were transformed (transformed themselves, really) into another kind of institution and left the sector altogether.

The significance of institutional migrations of this kind is even more evident when we compare two other sectors: Liberal Arts I colleges and Other Four-Year institutions (Figure 9.4). The age-size pattern for the Liberal Arts I colleges resembles the corresponding pattern for Research/Doctorate universities, with almost all the large institutions having been founded in the nineteenth century or earlier. By contrast, the Other Four-Year group, which comprises Comprehensive II institutions and Liberal Arts II colleges, shows almost no correlation between age and size. The key to understanding this dramatic difference in patterns is recognizing that Other Four-Year institutions naturally shift groups as a function of changes in either size or standing. Comprehensive II institutions that grow beyond 2,500 students are automatically reclassified as Comprehensive I institutions, and Liberal Arts II colleges that become more selective are typically reclassified as Liberal Arts I colleges.

Similar kinds of institutional migrations no doubt occur within the arts/culture fields, but the lack of "within-field" categories makes it impossible for us to measure them. Therefore, it is hardly surprising that no age-size

Figure 9.3. Age-Size Distribution by Date of Establishment, Research/Doctorate Universities and Comprehensive I Institutions.

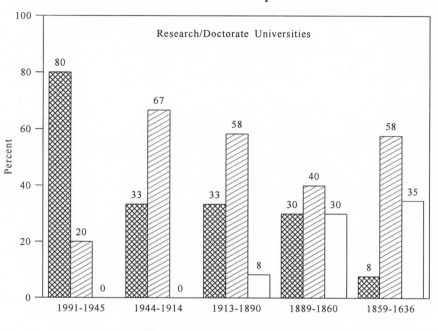

Research/Doctorate Universities

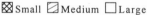
Small Medium Large

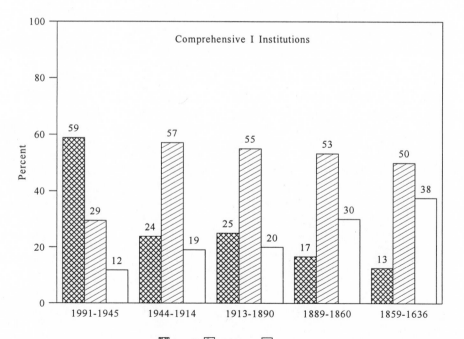

Comprehensive I Institutions

Small Medium Large

Source: Statistics of Income Division, Internal Revenue Service, 1987/1988. See also Appendix G, Table G.9-2.

**Figure 9.4.   Age-Size Distribution by Date of Establishment,
Liberal Arts I Colleges and Other Four-Year Institutions**

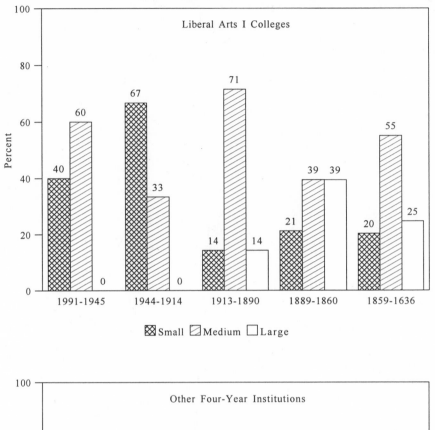

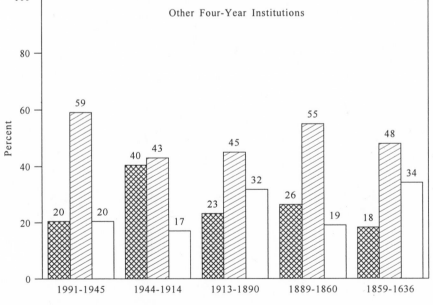

Source: Statistics of Income Division, Internal Revenue Service, 1987/1988. See also Appendix G, Table G.9-2.

patterns similar to those for Other Four-Year institutions appear in the data for arts/culture institutions. If, for example, we had worked with separate categories for "metropolitan" orchestras and "major" orchestras, we would probably have found migrations over time from one category to the other, as well as an age-size relationship for metropolitan orchestras more like the one for Other Four-Year institutions.

Size and Revenue Profile

This section consists of an analysis of the relationship between the size of an organization and its revenue profile. Size is itself a function of age, and since age also affects revenue profiles independently (see Figure 7.1), we first tried to examine simultaneously the effects on revenue profiles of these two variables. In an effort to tease out the effects of age and size, we constructed a number of multiple-regression models, but the results were so disappointing that we cannot justify reporting them in any detail. The correlation between age and size makes these two effects difficult to disentangle.[2]

It is possible to conclude, however, that the association between size and revenue profile is more consequential than the relationship between age and revenue profile. The relationship between age and revenue profile is also of some interest, however, especially when we are seeking to explain variations in investment income, and we report those results in the last section of this chapter.

We expected to find that earned-income shares would correlate positively with size, as measured by total expenditures. Our presumption was that earned income is less subject to upper limits than private contributions and governmental support, and that large organizations would therefore be more dependent on earned income than small organizations are. This general line of argument is supported by the SOI data, but the relationship between earned-income shares and organizational size is somewhat weaker than we expected it to be.

For the performing arts, the simple correlation between the earned-income share and total expenditures is +0.31, which, while statistically significant at the 95 percent level of confidence, is not a high correlation. (The partial correlation coefficient, holding age constant, is also significant.) Both the general shape of the relationship and the looseness of fit are best illustrated through the use of a scattergram (see the top panel of Figure 9.5).

It is clear that the range of earned-income shares within the performing arts is considerable at most levels of total expenditure. It is also evident that the range is widest among the smallest entities, where earned-income shares vary all the way from about 10 percent to over 90 percent. The floor under the earned-income share then begins to rise with size. Among the performing arts organizations in this sample with expenditures between $5 and $10 million, earned income is never appreciably less than 30 percent of total expenditures. From the $20 million level of expenditures on up, the earned-

Figure 9.5.   Earned-Income Share of Total Revenue by Size of Organization, Performing Arts and Art Museums, 1987/1988.

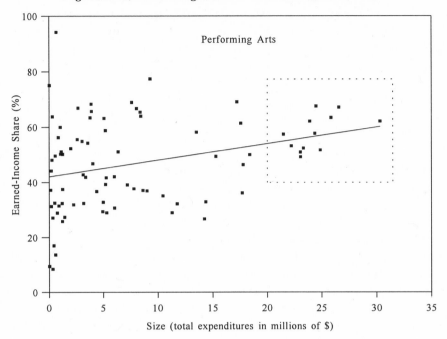

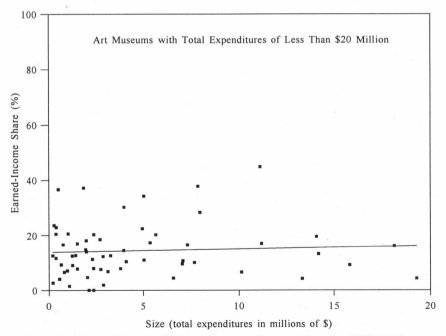

Source: Statistics of Income Division, Internal Revenue Service, 1987/1988.

income share is never below 45 percent (see the box outlined in Figure 9.5). A study carried out by the American Symphony Orchestra League (ASOL) reports similar findings: earned income was 34 percent of total revenues for the smallest orchestras (those with budgets between $21,000 and $631,000), whereas it was 45 percent of total revenues for the largest orchestras (those with budgets between $8.5 million and $38.7 million).[3]

Art museums reveal a rather different pattern, perhaps because the charging of admission is less common and, to this day, more controversial. At the very top end of the size distribution, however, the data are consistent with the results for the performing arts. Here again, we find that earned income is especially important for the largest entities. All three of the art museums in the SOI sample with total expenditures over $20 million had earned-income shares of 40 to 50 percent, whereas the average for all art museums was around 15 percent (see Appendix G, Table G.8-1). But when we look only at art museums in the SOI sample with expenditures below $20 million, we find essentially no correlation between size and earned-income share (bottom panel of Figure 9.5).

Fortunately, we were able to obtain special tabulations from the American Association of Museums' 1989 national museum survey, which, because of the stratification of the sample, permits closer analysis of the relationship between size and earned-income share. Earned income, as a percentage of total revenues, rises steadily, from 10 percent for small art museums (operating expenses of less than $200,000) to 22 percent for medium-sized art museums (operating expenses between $200,000 and $1 million) to 31 percent for large art museums (operating expenses greater than $1 million).

The SOI data do not permit the same kind of analysis of earned-income share in relation to size for other museums (where there are too few entities at different points along the size distribution), historical societies (where earned income is much less important in general), or higher education (where the governmental role complicates and obscures other relationships). There is one last general point that can be made, however: except in unusual situations, where governmental funders provide significant support (such as the Minnesota Historical Society and the Field Museum of Natural History), most large organizations earn a considerable amount of their income. Excluding organizations that receive significant governmental funding, we can identify only five entities in our sample that have both total expenditures of $10 million or more and earned-income shares of less than 25 percent: the Cleveland Museum of Art, the Museum of Fine Arts in Houston, the Whitney Museum of American Art in New York, the Walker Art Center in Minneapolis, and the Detroit Institute of Arts.

The shares of total revenue provided by private contributions are, as indicated in the previous chapter, largely mirror images of the earned-income shares, at least for arts/culture organizations with small amounts of governmental support. Therefore, we will not provide separate scattergrams or any extended commentary on the relationship between this revenue source and organizational size. The one general point to emphasize is that very small organizations in these fields tend to be heavily dependent on private contributions. For example, for performing arts organizations with total expenditures under $5 million (with most having total expenditures in the range of $1 million to $1.5 million), the correlation between size and the private-contributions share of revenues is –0.33. A large proportion of those performing arts entities with budgets below $1.5 million count on contributions for at least 40 percent of their total revenues. Small art museums included in the American Association of Museums' 1989 survey show an even more pronounced pattern of the same kind: 69 percent of total revenues came from private sources (55 percent from contributions alone, and 14 percent from investment income).[4] The explanation is straightforward: it often takes a dedicated group of donors to launch an enterprise, and if the enterprise then flourishes, it will grow in size and attract other forms of support, including earned income.

The governmental share of total revenue varies with size in a quite distinctive way within the arts/culture fields. In the case of the orchestra field, where we have a relatively broad distribution of organizations by size, there is a decidedly nonlinear relationship, with the proportion of governmental support highest among medium-sized organizations (see the top panel of Figure 9.6). We suspect that the governmental share is highest for these mid-sized orchestras because eligibility for at least some kinds of government support requires (de facto) the attainment of a certain size, but the absolute size of governmental grants is also unlikely to exceed some maximum value. This combination of constraints at the bottom and at the top of the size distribution may well explain why the proportion of governmental support is highest for medium-sized arts organizations. Again, the ASOL study confirms our findings. Among ASOL members, the percentage of total revenue derived from governmental sources was 8.2 percent for orchestras with budgets below $1.8 million, 10.1 percent for orchestras with budgets of $1.8–5 million, 15.4 percent for orchestras with budgets of $5–8.5 million, but only 6.2 percent for orchestras with budgets of $8.5–38.7 million.[5]

Historical societies appear to be subject to the same forces as orchestras, but the paucity of observations from the SOI sample makes it difficult to describe with any precision the relationship between size and governmental support. We do know, however, that there are two clear outliers: the Ohio Historical Society and the Minnesota Historical Society, which are by far the largest historical societies, and which both have extraordinarily high governmental shares of revenue (84 percent and 72 percent, respectively, as contrasted with a median share of 6.4 percent for all historical societies). These two societies are instances in which nonprofit organizations are in effect agencies of the state, and the usual notions about an upper limit on governmental support do not apply. When these two outliers are removed from

Figure 9.6.   Governmental Share of Total Revenue by Size of Organization, Orchestras and Research/Doctorate Universities, 1987/1988.

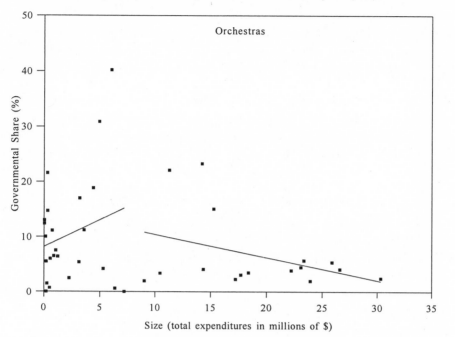

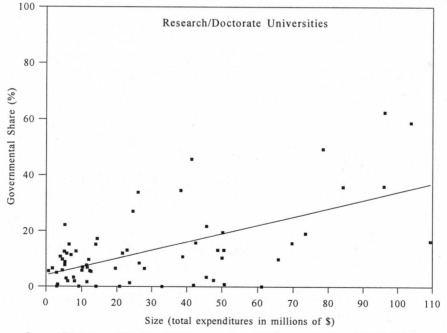

Source: Statistics of Income Division, Internal Revenue Service, 1987/1988.

the sample, the correlation between size and governmental share for historical societies resembles the plot for orchestras, with a mild positive relationship at lower levels of expenditure and a mild negative relationship at higher levels (the scattergram is not shown).

Research/Doctorate universities reflect another set of relationships altogether, in part because of the wider range of outputs which they produce (much research, as well as undergraduate and graduate training). These institutions do receive some governmental support for student aid and other purposes, but sponsored research funding is most important. To compete effectively for large amounts of sponsored research money, universities have to be consequential in size as well as in quality. Above some cutoff level, however, it is success in attracting sponsored research grants that leads to large size, not the other way around. Sponsored research also differs from most other types of governmental support in that funding is based on the appeal of particular projects and principal investigators; there is no overall budget for an individual institution.

These considerations explain why the governmental share of revenue increases rather steadily with size for the private Research/Doctorate universities (see the bottom panel of Figure 9.6). The correlation coefficient is +0.59, significant at the 95 percent level of confidence. It is also revealing that the two institutions in the northeast corner of the scattergram, M.I.T. and Johns Hopkins, have rather modest enrollments and are large in size mainly as a consequence of their success in attracting governmental grants and contracts.

Age and Revenue Profile

As already noted, the strength of the age-size nexus is such that it is difficult to determine the separate influence of age per se on revenue profile. Suffice it to say that with one exception, noted immediately below, the only statistically significant set of other-things-being-equal relationships is the one linking age to investment income.

The one exception is the statistically significant relationship between age and contributed income within the entire arts/culture sector (including performing arts, museums, and historical societies), even after we take account of the effects of size. The partial correlation coefficient is negative and significant at the 95 percent confidence level, although it is hardly robust (−0.17). The explanation, we believe, is the same as the one used above to explain why contributed income is most important (relative to other revenue sources) for small organizations: in many instances, private donors have to believe in an organization and be prepared to support it financially in order for it to be launched; then, after a successful launch, other sources of revenue may be obtained.

The puzzle is why a similar, inverse relationship is not found when we examine only those organizations in the performing arts part of the arts/culture sector (once again holding size constant). In the case of the performing arts, considered separately, the partial correlation coefficient even has the wrong sign—that is, it is positive, rather than negative—but it fails to pass any normal test of statistical significance.

Investment income is the one revenue source that one would surely expect to be correlated with age. The rationale is straightforward: the older an organization is, the more time it has had to build up an endowment or some other form of financial capital which can yield income. Time may be especially helpful to such organizations as colleges and universities, which rely heavily on donations from successive generations of alumni to build their endowments. Older institutions are also helped by the greater willingness of most individuals and foundations to give endowment support to entities which have demonstrated some staying power. We would expect age to be correlated with investment income for one other reason: the steady reinvestment of some part of the total return earned on an endowment will itself lead to higher investment income in the future, even if no new gifts are received.

The SOI data are generally consistent with these expectations. Even when size is held constant, age and the investment-income share are positively correlated, and some of the partial correlation coefficients are significant at the 95 percent level of confidence, especially in the higher education sector.

Another approach is to look at investment income as a percentage of all private support (defined as the sum of private contributions plus investment income; relating investment income to all private support rather than to total revenue is really a crude way of holding the earned-income and governmental shares constant). When we examine the crude association between the average ages of entire fields and the relative importance of investment income vis-à-vis all private support, we find a quite consistent relationship. The investment share of total private support is the highest (mostly in the range of 35 to 40 percent) in the higher education and historical society sectors, which have median ages of 98 to 133. It is much lower (in the range of 5 to 16 percent) in the performing arts fields, which have median ages between 22 and 57. The museum fields represent a middle case. They have investment shares of between 23 and 28 percent and median ages between 54 and 70.

The within-field patterns for some of the older sectors are summarized in Table 9.2. The pattern within higher education is very clear, especially within those sectors which contain the most highly endowed institutions. It is striking—an odd coincidence, more than anything else—that the investment income shares of total private support are almost identical in the Research/Doctorate universities and the Liberal Arts I colleges. (Investment income is a higher percentage of total revenues within the colleges because

Table 9.2. Average Investment-Income Share of Total Revenue and of Private Support, by Field and Age, 1987/1988.

		Average Investment Income as a Share						
		Of Total Revenue (%)			*Of Private Support (%)*			
Field	*Sample Size*	*Young*	*Medium-Aged*	*Old*	*Young*	*Medium-Aged*	*Old*	
Research/Doctorate universities	66	5.3	7.8	10.1	34.4	36.0	44.4	
Liberal Arts I colleges	123	11.0	10.9	15.4	34.4	37.4	44.3	
Historical societies	34	30.3	27.9	41.4	39.4	41.5	48.8	
Art museums	63	22.5	24.9	16.8	25.6	31.7	24.4	

Source: Statistics of Income Division, Internal Revenue Service, 1987/1988.

Note: "Private support" is the sum of contributed income and investment income. "Young," "medium-aged," and "old" are defined as the top quartile, the middle half, and the bottom quartile of the age distribution, respectively.

they have less sponsored research funding.) Investment income and age are also clearly correlated within the group of historical societies for which we have SOI data.

The mystery is why there is absolutely no consistent pattern among the art museums (see the bottom line of Table 9.2). This finding is a surprise, since one would have expected the same factors mentioned above in connection with higher education to operate here as well. The group of old art museums (those in the top quartile of the age distribution) earn less investment income, vis-à-vis current private contributions, than do the medium-aged museums. Others will have to explain what dynamic is responsible for this pattern.

To understand many phenomena of this kind, it is necessary to examine the histories of individual institutions over time. Neither the SOI sample nor the BMF database allows such comparisons, and that is why we compiled longitudinal data for thirty-two individual arts/culture organizations. The lessons learned from this study of trends at the level of the individual institution are reported in the next chapter.

Notes

1. See Whetten (1987) for a review of the literature on the application of the life-cycle analogy to the study of organizations.
2. The characteristics of the SOI sample proved to be a further source of difficulty. Because the sampling design of the SOI database is heavily weighted toward organizations with large assets, we were precluded from investigating relationships among age, size, and revenue profiles across as large a number of cases at the small end of the size distribution as would have been desirable. There simply are not enough observations in certain cells.
3. Authors' tabulations of data from the American Symphony Orchestra League (Wolf Organization, Inc., 1992).
4. Calculated from special tabulations provided by the Association of American Museums.
5. Authors' tabulations of data from the American Symphony Orchestra League (Wolf Organization, Inc., 1992).

TEN

Trends in Expenditures and Revenue Profiles

Having examined the interconnections among fields of activity, size, revenue profiles, and age at a single point in time—and having found that there are in fact systematic relationships among these variables—we pose the next obvious question: Have key relationships shifted over time, or do they appear to be more or less immutable?

It is important to know, for instance, if the nonprofit institutions included in this part of our analysis have come to depend more heavily on earned income. At issue is the extent to which, as some have postulated, nonprofits in America have become more commercialized.[1] A related question is whether particular sources of revenue have been especially strong "engines of growth" for certain types of nonprofits. Is it true that rapid growth in size has been possible only for those nonprofits which have exploited opportunities to increase earned income? Conversely, has contributed income (from private or governmental sources) become more or less critical to the finances of various types of entities? And does the answer to this question depend on the age as well as the type of the entity?

In this chapter, we are also interested in the overall rate of increase in expenditures per se and in the relationships among rate of growth in outlays, field of activity, and revenue profile. Have expenditures risen more rapidly than the general price level? Did rates of growth in real expenditures increase or decrease in the 1980s, as contrasted with the 1970s?

The Arts/Culture Institutional Database

Given the evident importance of these questions, one would think that at least some regularly published data on trends would be readily available. Regrettably, that is not the case.[2] As has already been explained, the Business Master File (BMF) of the IRS is constantly updated, and each version contains financial data for only one point in time. Old versions are destroyed in the process of updating the master file. While the Statistics of Income (SOI) surveys provide some panel data, going back to 1982 and now extending to 1989, this source did not meet our needs. It does not begin early enough to capture anything that might be considered a trend (at the minimum, it is important to be able to compare the 1970s and the 1980s, and this cannot be done with the SOI data). Further complicating such a comparison is the fact that the Form 990s themselves, which are the source of the raw data, were modified so substantially prior to the 1980s that no comparable figures are available from the Form 990s before then. Another problem with the SOI data is that the sample of institutions of interest to us is very small, particularly prior to 1987. For students of the nonprofit sector, and especially for those interested in questions of public policy, the development and maintenance of at least a minimal set of time-series data should be a top priority.

Faced with these realities, we concluded that we had no choice but to build our own time-series database. We started by selecting institutions in certain fields of special interest to us (culture and the arts, including museums and historical societies) that appeared in several of the SOI samples, in the hope that we could use the SOI data that were already available.[3] Subsequently, however, we decided that it would be better to go back to primary sources and obtain audited financial statements at five-year intervals (1972, 1977, 1982, 1987, and 1992) directly from individual organizations. Only in that way could we be confident about the consistency of the data over time.

We ended up working with 32 organizations. The full list of participants is given in Appendix G, Table G.10-1, along with descriptive measures of size and age (total expenditures in 1992, and year established). Thanks to the cooperation of these organizations, we were able to obtain complete sets of financial statements for five years, with only three exceptions (no records were available for the San Francisco Opera in 1972 and 1977 or for the Pittsburgh Symphony in 1972). We then culled data from these 157 separate sets of audited financial statements. Labor-intensive and laborious as this process was, it enabled us to assemble a consistent set of time-series data spanning two decades.

Our set of 32 organizations includes 3 operas, 5 orchestras, 4 ballets, 5 theaters, 7 art museums, 3 science museums, and 5 historical societies. We would characterize this population as falling somewhere between a large set of case studies and a small sample. It is obviously not a true sample in that, among other things, it is weighted heavily in favor of the larger and longer-established entities (note the high levels of expenditures and the "old" years of establishment in Appendix G, Table G.10-1). By definition, newer organizations could not be included (no data would have existed for the 1970s). We also thought it would be best to focus on reasonably well-known entities so that we could interpret their financial records in a tolerably knowledgeable way. The findings presented below should be read with these caveats in mind and should not be construed as describing trends applicable to younger or smaller entities. The results are best thought of as describing trends for the more prominent institutions in the chosen fields. It is reassuring, however, to find that the revenue profiles of these 32 organizations match astonishingly well with the corresponding data from the SOI sample.[4]

For other information about the institutions included in this analysis, and about the assumptions we used in translating the data contained in their financial reports into our accounting categories, see Appendix F. Because these data are unique and are likely to be of independent interest to others (in part as benchmarks for future studies), we reproduced the main statistics for individual institutions and particular years in Appendix G.

Trends in Total Expenditures

General Patterns

Between 1972 and 1992, the average annual rate of increase in total expenditures for the 32 nonprofit institutions we examined was 10.6 percent.[5] When we deflate these increases by a measure of changes in the overall price level (using the government's implicit price deflator for gross domestic product, or GDP), we obtain an average annual rate of increase of 4.5 percent in real dollars. This average rate of increase is surprisingly high—amazingly high, even. It is nearly twice the average annual growth in real GDP over the same period, which was 2.5 percent.

When we group average annual growth rates for individual organizations by broad field, nominal rates of increase range from an average of 9.3 percent per year for historical societies to 14.6 percent per year for ballet companies. The corresponding real growth rates range from 3.3 percent per year for historical societies to 8.3 percent per year for ballet (see Figure 10.1).* In general, we find that historical societies and museums grew less rapidly over the entire twenty-year period than did performing arts organizations.

It is even more important to note that high growth rates characterize

---

* There is no right answer to the question of whether it is better to compare nominal growth rates or real growth rates. We do want to take account of economy wide trends in prices, but we also know that different inflation factors are appropriate to different fields of activity. (The rapid increases in energy costs in the late 1970s and early 1980s, for example, had much more of an impact on manufacturing industries than on most service providers.) We are unable, however, to distinguish between, on the one hand, increases in outlays which, in an inflationary environment, are used to provide the same bundle of outputs as before and, on the other hand, increases in outlays which are used to provide more output. Lacking field-specific inflation factors, we will focus the rest of this discussion on the real growth rates obtained by use of the general price deflator, but we emphasize that individual organizations must pay their bills in current dollars, of course, and there is no assurance that their sources of revenue will keep pace with the price level.

Figure 10.1. Average Annual Growth Rate of Real and Nominal Expenditures by Field, 1972–1992.

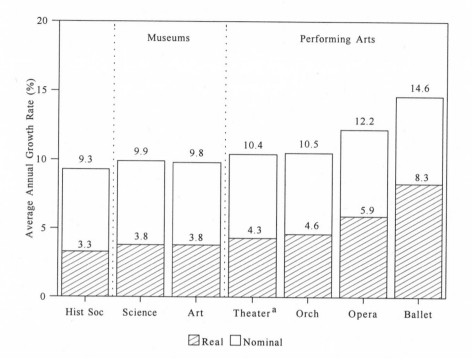

^a Excludes New York Shakespeare Festival.
Source: Arts/culture institutional database. See also Appendix G, Table G.10-2.

most individual organizations within all the fields (see Appendix G, Table G.10-2). Out of the 32 nonprofits in our group, only 2 had negative real growth over this twenty-year period: the New York Shakespeare Festival, and the Brooklyn Institute of Arts and Sciences. (It may be more than a coincidence that both are New York City institutions and may have been affected severely by the fiscal crisis of the 1970s.) Only 5 organizations (including the pair with negative rates) had real growth rates that were below the overall rate of increase in the real GDP.

What accounts for these high rates of increase in expenditures? Anecdotal evidence suggests that the explanation is not a ready abundance of cash and a general absence of financial pressures. For example, the New-York Historical Society, which experienced such serious financial problems that it had to close at least temporarily and is still struggling to put a new financial plan into effect, shows roughly the same average annual increase in real expenditures as the entire group of nonprofits (4.7 percent per year).

One key to understanding such apparently anomalous behavior is to consider trends in the use of restricted funds by many nonprofits. Increases in restricted funds often fail to improve the overall financial health of an organization. They can even worsen its financial condition if they fail to cover fully the incremental costs of new activities which are supposed to be paid for by the restricted revenues. Thus total revenues (and total expenditures) can rise fairly rapidly at the same time that the financial health of an organization is deteriorating. This simple but fundamental point is sometimes hard to grasp, especially if one is used to assuming that a dollar of revenue is a dollar of revenue, as is generally the case in the for-profit sector.

At the risk of oversimplifying an important and complex set of relationships, we would propose four possible explanations (by no means mutually exclusive) for the distinctly above-average rates of increase in expenditures by the prominent nonprofits we examined.

First, the labor-intensive nature of the activities carried out by these organizations, and the tendency for productivity in the nonprofit sector to rise less rapidly than productivity in the rest of the economy, has put inexorable upward pressure on costs, causing them to rise more rapidly than prices in general. This phenomenon is sometimes referred to as "Baumol's Disease" or "Bowen's Law."[6]

Second, the adherence by nonprofit institutions to the "nondistribution constraint" (which prohibits them from returning any "profits" to "owners") means that there is a strong tendency to spend whatever funds are acquired. There is a definite bias toward expanding services and other activities, and success in the nonprofit world is often defined in these terms.

Third, a host of field-specific factors were at work during the 1970s and 1980s, including the expansion of key governmental programs (especially the National Endowments for the Arts and Humanities). In the 1970s and the early 1980s, there were also great pressures on organizations in the arts/culture fields to expand outreach programs, which generated some new revenues but also pushed up expenditures, sometimes even more rapidly. This phenomenon is an example of the need to consider carefully the full effects of financing new programs with restricted funds.

Fourth, some (rather small) part of our set of organizations was founded in the 1950s or the 1960s and thus experienced the rapid growth characteristic of organizations in the "infant" or "adolescent" stage of the life cycle. As our colleague Rachel Bellow has observed, births of organizations in the performing arts in particular can occur after very short gestation periods, with rapid development occurring immediately thereafter. (See the discussion of the age-size relationship in the previous chapter.) But this phenomenon, however real, cannot explain much of the high growth seen in our data set, because most of the institutions were established much earlier. Many of the mature members of the group also experienced relatively rapid growth during the 1970s and the 1980s. If our sample had included a larger number of young organizations, the average annual growth rates might have been higher yet.

Whatever emphasis is put on one or another of these factors, or on still others, the central point remains: the data obtained from the financial reports convincingly document the tendency for increases in expenditures among these classes of nonprofits to outpace increases in both the general price level and real gross domestic product. The evidence on this point is unambiguous.

Differences by Subperiod

Measured in nominal dollars, average growth rates in total expenditures in all seven of our fields were higher between 1972 and 1982 than they were between 1982 and 1992. Given the differences between the two subperiods in the overall rate of inflation (8.1 percent per year versus 3.7 percent), this finding is hardly surprising. The picture is more complex, and more interesting, when we correct for differences in the rate of inflation between the subperiods and compare growth rates measured in real dollars. It is no longer easy to choose between the two subperiods: 16 organizations experienced faster growth in real terms during the 1972–1982 subperiod, and 15 experienced faster growth during the 1982–1992 subperiod (see Appendix G, Table G.10-2).

When we group organizations by field, however, there are systematic differences between the subperiods (see Figure 10.2). The historical societies and art museums grew more rapidly in real terms in the more recent subperiod, and rates of growth were the same in the two subperiods for science museums. In sharp contrast, every performing arts field except symphony orchestras exhibited significantly faster growth during the 1970s than during the 1980s. To state this finding another way, the performing arts fields grew considerably faster than the historical societies and museums during the first subperiod, but this advantage disappeared in the 1980s, when the two broad sets of fields grew at essentially the same rate.

Our interpretation is that most of the performing arts organizations we examined (except the symphony orchestras) grew at abnormally high rates during the 1970s, primarily as a result of field-specific factors. The growth of budgets at the National Endowment for the Arts, combined with the active grantmaking of the Ford Foundation, had a major impact on these entities, as well as on the overall size of the universe of performing arts groups (see Chapter Five). The relative youthfulness of some of the organizations (especially 2 of the 4 ballet companies) contributed to rapid average rates of growth. It is also our impression that the development of outreach activities, designed to broaden the appeal of productions and to attract new audiences, had stronger and earlier effects on many performing arts organizations than on museums.

Figure 10.2. Average Annual Growth Rate of Real Expenditures by Field, 1972–1982 and 1982–1992.

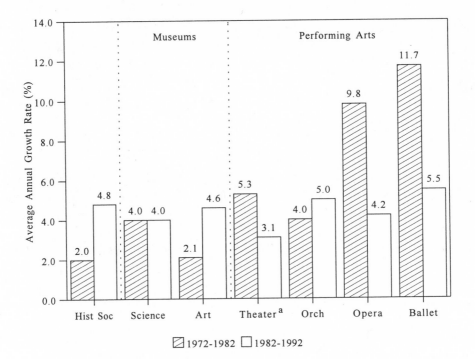

_a_ Excludes New York Shakespeare Festival.
Source: Arts/culture institutional database. See also Appendix G, Table G.10-2.

Engines of Growth

Has the extraordinarily rapid growth in expenditures for the nonprofit institutions we examined been driven by any single revenue source? Has there been a dominant "engine of growth"? When we began this analysis, we suspected that earned income had been disproportionately important. In the abstract, it seemed to us that earned income was potentially much more expandable than private contributions or investment income, especially over reasonably short periods. Thus our initial conjecture was that any organization that grew very rapidly must surely have had its growth fueled primarily by increases in earned income.

We were wrong. Examination of the data disproves this hypothesis, at least when stated in its extreme form. To test the hypothesis, we selected all high-growth cases, which we defined as instances in which organizations had at least doubled total expenditures over any of the three ten-year intervals covered by our analysis (1972–1982, 1977–1987, or 1982–1992). Nearly half the institutions in our set met this demanding criterion—a surprising finding in and of itself (see Appendix G, Table G.10-3). Yet in only two cases—the Boston Ballet and the New York Shakespeare Festival—did growth in earned income account for more than three-quarters of the overall growth in revenues. The Boston Ballet is the most dramatic example of consistent high growth fueled by rapidly rising earned income, and the components of its revenue growth are depicted in Figure 10.3.

The power of earned income to drive growth is seen even more vividly in Figure 10.4, which depicts the history of revenues at the New York Shakespeare Festival. Between 1972 and 1982, total revenue increased from just over $2 million to more than $61 million, and earned income accounted for nearly 95 percent of this exceptional growth, increasing from just about $750,000 to roughly $57 million. (This exceptional growth in earned income was due directly to the phenomenal box-office success of *A Chorus Line*, which was a property of the Festival.) Over the next ten years, total revenues declined to just over $8 million, and earned income fell even more rapidly.

Figure 10.3. Trends in Revenue Components, Boston Ballet, 1972–1992.

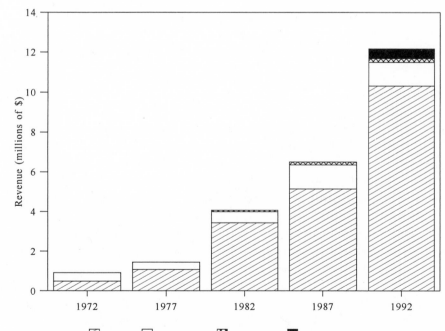

Source: Arts/culture institutional database. See also Appendix G, Table G.10-5.

Figure 10.4. Trends in Revenue Components, New York Shakespeare Festival, 1972–1992.

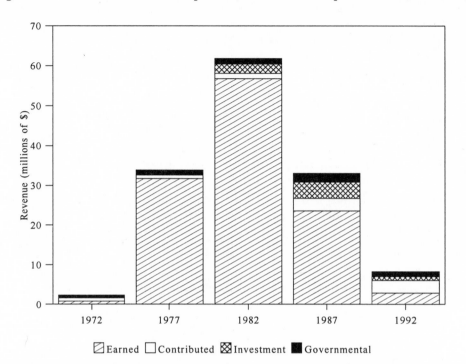

Source: Arts/culture institutional database. See also Appendix G, Table G.10-5.

Indeed, private contributions exceeded earned income in 1992. This roller-coaster pattern, reflecting dramatic shifts in earned income, is what we expected to find more often. But the experience of the New York Shakespeare Festival, while it illustrates how volatile earned income can be, is the only such case we found among our 32 organizations.

At the opposite end of the spectrum is an organization which grew very rapidly, and very steadily, without any significant contribution from earned income. The Virginia Historical Society had essentially the same overall rate of increase in total expenditures as did the Boston Ballet, and yet only 5 percent of its added revenue was earned income (see Figure 10.5). Between 1982 and 1992, increased private contributions accounted for over 80 percent of the increase in its revenues (see Appendix G, Table G.10-3). The New-York Historical Society also qualifies as a high-growth case in the 1980s, its financial woes notwithstanding. Here too the dominant engine of growth was private contributions, not earned income, which contributed only 9 percent of the overall increase in revenues. This story is more complex, however, and we shall return to it when we discuss trends in investment income.

Figure 10.5.   Trends in Revenue Components, Virginia Historical Society, 1972–1992.

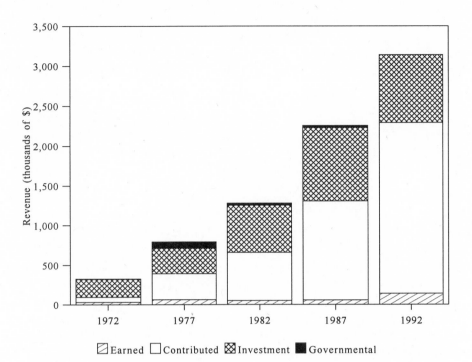

Source: Arts/culture institutional database. See also Appendix G, Table G.10-5.

None of the organizations described above is typical. In the overwhelming majority of high-growth cases, it was a combination of revenue
sources which permitted rapid overall increases in expenditures. In only one
other organization out of a total of 15 (Arena Stage between 1977 and 1987)
did any single revenue source contribute as much as two-thirds of the total
increase in expenditures (see Appendix G, Table G.10-3).

Having been compelled by this evidence to abandon the dominant "engine of growth" interpretation of rapid increases in total expenditures, we
asked a more neutral question: What role had each revenue source played in
financing the overall increases in expenditures which occurred between 1972
and 1992? The main finding (see Table 10.1) is that earned income played the
major role only for those fields of activity within which (for reasons discussed
in Chapter Eight) earned income is naturally more important than other revenue sources—principally, the performing arts organizations and science museums. For historical societies and art museums, which traditionally depend
more heavily on private contributions and investment income, those sources
tended to be more important than earned income in fueling growth.

Table 10.1 Components of Growth in Total Revenue by Field, 1972–1992.

	Average Share of Growth from:			
	Earned (%)	Contributed (%)	Investment (%)	Governmental (%)
Opera	50	41	5	3
Orchestra	61	15	17	7
Ballet	62	33	5	1
Theater	50	29	11	11
Art museums	25	35	24	17
Science museums	50	14	18	18
Historical societies	11	63	27	–1
Total	41	34	17	9

Source: Arts/culture institutional database.

The general lesson is "once an elephant, always an elephant"—that is, performing arts organizations differ from one another in many particulars, and they exhibit varying patterns of growth, but certain similarities remain, including strong dependence on earned income. Historical societies have their own particular characteristics; they too differ from one another in various respects, but all of them are likely to grow or not to grow according to their success in attracting sources of revenue other than earned income.

General Trends in Earned Income

The "once an elephant, always an elephant" proposition receives further support when we examine trends in earned-income shares among all the organizations and all the years for which we have data. There have been some shifts in the relative importance of different sources of revenue, but the overall pattern is one of stability (see Appendix G, Tables G.10-4 and G.10-5). Organizations that depended primarily on earned income in 1972 almost always continued to depend primarily on earned income in 1992. Similarly, institutions that depended mainly on private contributions twenty years ago have continued to depend mainly on private contributions.

A more interesting question is whether there has been any general tendency for earned income to increase as a share of total revenue—any trend which would hold for organizations of all types, including those that depend mainly on earned income and those that depend mainly on other sources of revenue. If there has indeed been increasing commercialization in the nonprofit sector, it ought to be reflected in a general increase in earned income as a percentage of total revenues. The answer our data provided to this question is a rather weak yes. There has been some tendency for earned income to increase, relative to other sources, but the pattern is hardly uniform or overwhelming.

At 18 of the 30 organizations for which we have complete information, earned income was higher as a percentage of total revenues in 1992 than in 1972. At the remaining 12 organizations, it was lower (see Table 10.2). The mixed nature of these results holds for almost all types of entities. The earned-income share rose for 4 art museums and fell for 3. It rose for 9 performing arts entities and fell for 6. We also see that the extent of the increase in the earned-income share was often quite modest. In only 8 cases did it rise by more than 10 percentage points over these twenty years.

Science and natural history museums are the one field in which every institution reported increases in the relative importance of earned income. The small size of this set (just 3 organizations) warns against making too much of this result, but we believe it reflects something real: an increased tendency for science museums in particular to rely on admissions receipts. It is significant, we think, that the earned-income share for the Franklin Institute (the purest science museum in the set) rose very sharply, from 50 percent in 1972 to 80 percent in 1992.

There is more to be learned by looking at what appear to be humps and troughs between 1972 and 1992 in the dependence on earned income by organizations within two broad fields: the performing arts (except symphony orchestras), and art museums. Among most performing arts organizations in our universe, the share of earned income rose noticeably between 1972 and 1982 (often from the low 50 percent range to the low to middle 60 percent range) but then declined by about the same amount between 1982 and 1992. The result is a hump-backed curve. (See the top panel of Figure 10.6, which includes standard deviations to illustrate the range of values.)

We interpret this pattern as reflecting a natural tendency to raise prices and increase box-office revenues in the 1970s, when there was an up-

Table 10.2. Trends in Earned-Income Share by Field, 1972–1992.

	Number of Organizations Whose Earned-Income Share:				
	Increased by x percentage points			Increased	Decreased
Field	x < 5	5 < x < 10	x > 10	(total)	(total)
Opera	0	1	0	1	1
Orchestra	0	1	2	3	1
Ballet	0	0	2	2	2
Theater	1	2	0	3	2
Art museums	1	2	1	4	3
Science museums	1	0	2	3	0
Historical societies	1	0	1	2	3
Total	4	6	8	18	12

Source: Arts/culture institutional database. See also Appendix G, Table G.10-4.
Note: The Pittsburgh Symphony and the San Francisco Opera are not included because of missing data.

Figure 10.6.   Average Earned-Income Share of Total Revenue, 1972–1992.

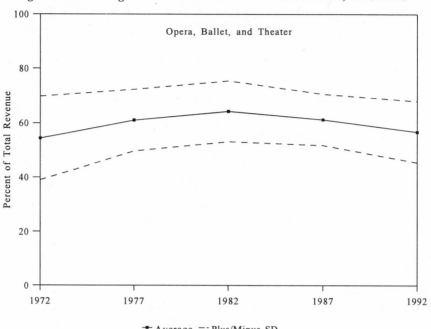

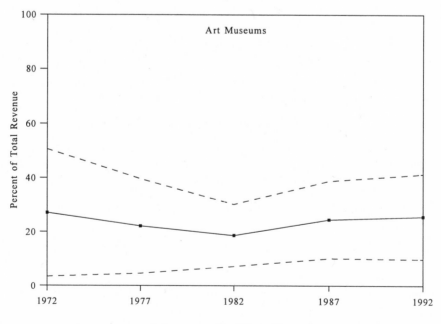

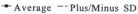

Source: Arts/culture institutional database. See also Appendix G, Table G.10-4.

surge in interest in the performing arts. Most performing arts organizations are box office–based, and we would expect them to have raised revenues from that source first, if they could, since it is more under their direct control than any other source. Then, in the 1980s, these organizations appeared to encounter resistance to higher ticket prices and to have no alternative but to seek increased support from other sources—in particular, to mount more aggressive fundraising campaigns.[7]

An opposite picture appears when we draw the same kind of figure for art museums (see the bottom panel of Figure 10.6). Here, we see first a rather significant decline in earned-income share during the first of the two decades under review (with the share typically falling from just under 30 percent to about 20 percent) and then a recovery to about the original level in 1992. This troughlike pattern implies that contributed income, the dominant source of support for most of these organizations, was rising more rapidly in the 1970s than in the 1980s, relative to other sources.

Our impression is that many art museums traditionally were reluctant to charge admission at all or even to ask aggressively for voluntary contributions. It would have been natural for these entities to seek first to raise contributions, their basic form of support, and only later, when further increases in contributed income became harder to realize, to focus on earned income. Another part of the explanation may have to do with the trend toward "blockbuster" exhibitions in the 1980s, which often provided opportunities to increase museum-shop sales. (The sharp jump in the earned-income share at the Metropolitan Museum of Art in 1987, for example, is closely related to peak-level profits from operations of museum shops and related activities.)

Trends in Private Versus Governmental Support

So far, we have focused on earned-income shares and have drawn no distinctions among other sources of income. An obvious next question is: How important has governmental support been, relative to private contributions and investment income? For the 32 organizations we studied, the general answer is that governments (local, state, and federal) together have provided roughly one-fifth to one-third of all nonearned income, with private patrons (past and present) contributing the balance (see Appendix G, Table G.10-6, for the detailed data). In the main, theaters, art museums, and science museums have received more governmental support than the other fields of activity, but the differences by field are not pronounced.

The data are so varied that generalizations are hazardous, but there is evidence of a gentle upward creep in the governmental share of nonearned income between 1972 and either 1982 or 1987 (depending on the organization in question). A clearer pattern exists over the most recent five-year period. With few exceptions, the governmental share was lower in 1992 than in

1987. A combination of the fiscal pressures felt by governments and the philosophical move toward privatization presumably explains this shift. In some states, drastic reductions in appropriations for state arts councils have had a major impact on the finances of those nonprofits that came to depend heavily on this source of support (Massachusetts and New Jersey are frequently cited as cases in point).

Trends in Investment Income Versus Contributed Income

We saw from the SOI data presented in Chapter Nine that the importance of investment income varies with the age of a nonprofit institution. These new data confirm that association. In the case of long-established organizations, such as symphony orchestras, museums, and historical societies, investment income is often in the range of 40 to 50 percent of all private support (current contributions plus investment income). Organizations in newer fields, such as ballet and theater, have smaller endowments and are more dependent on current gifts (see Appendix G, Table G.10-7, for the detailed data). The twenty-year time frame which we are using in this chapter does not allow us to identify the longer-term trends that are especially important in the case of efforts to build endowments. Shifts over five-year intervals, or even over twenty-year periods, are most likely to reflect the behavior of financial markets and the extent to which an organization has chosen to include high fractions of total returns in its current income—either by structuring its portfolio to favor investments providing a high current yield or by adopting a spending rule which allows the organization to treat significant amounts of capital gains as current income.

We will present here only one example, albeit a dramatic one, of the importance of policy decisions about investment income and the treatment of returns on endowment. The New-York Historical Society offers the object lesson, and it is instructive to compare two graphs for this organization, one in which investment income is defined to include only dividends and interest and one in which investment income is defined to include realized capital gains as well (see Figure 10.7).

Both panels of the figure show the substantial increase in contributed income obtained by the society between 1987 and 1992 (primarily as a result of vigorous fundraising efforts by Barbara Debs, who became interim director in August 1988 before being elected president in April 1989). Most of this new money was project money, however, with new expenditures offsetting new revenues, and it did not eliminate the chronic operating deficits from which the society had been suffering. The endowment continued to be consumed in order to finance these deficits, and one evident consequence (see the top panel of Figure 10.7) was a subsequent reduction in investment income, as traditionally defined. It was lower in absolute amount in 1992 than

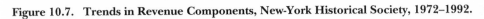

Figure 10.7. Trends in Revenue Components, New-York Historical Society, 1972–1992.

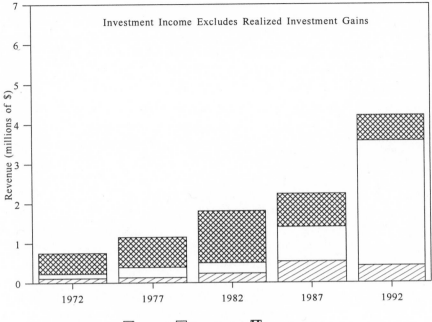

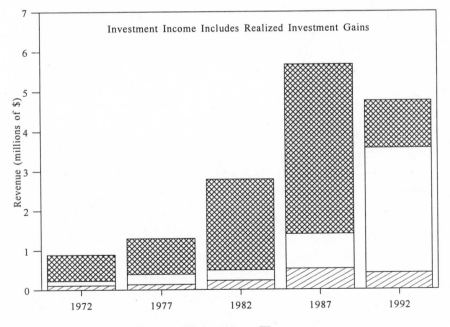

Source: Arts/culture institutional database. See also Appendix G, Table G.10-5.

it had been in 1977, primarily because of shrinkage in the corpus of the endowment.

During much of the 1980s, realized gains on investment assets, achieved because of the favorable equity markets of the time, were spent by the society. The magnitudes involved are shown in the bottom panel of the figure, which includes these realized gains with other investment income. The peak reached in 1987 is truly extraordinary. Spending realized gains, rather than reinvesting them, had the predictable effect of preventing the endowment from growing as much as it would have grown otherwise. The long-term consequences of such practices can be very serious, as the recent history of this important cultural institution reveals all too clearly.[8]

Two general conclusions emerge from this analysis of trends. First, the average annual rate of increase in expenditures for the organizations included in our data set has been distinctly and almost uniformly above the average for the economy as a whole. Second, there has been no single engine of growth fueling these rapid increases in expenditures.

The history of each organization is the product of the forces and the personalities peculiar to it, but trends in general revenue patterns have been undramatic. In most cases, earned income has grown somewhat, relative to other revenue sources, but there is certainly no evidence of any runaway trend toward commercialization, nor is there any evidence of other pronounced shifts in funding patterns. The answer to the most basic question posed at the start of this chapter is unequivocal: over the last twenty years, the relationship between field of activity and revenue profile has been highly stable if not immutable.

Notes

1. For discussions of commercial activity by nonprofit organizations, see Lifset (1988), DeVita and Salamon (1987), Bennett and DiLorenzo (1989), and Grønbjerg (1993). Weisbrod is also currently at work on this subject.

2. By far the most extensive time-series data to date have been compiled by Galaskiewicz and Bielefeld (1990). They surveyed a 20 percent stratified sample of 1,625 public charities headquartered in Minneapolis–St. Paul in 1979–1980, 1984–1985, and 1988–1989. Liebschutz (1992) also tracked six nonprofit agencies in Rochester, New York, during the 1980s, and Grønbjerg (1993, pp. 81–95) examined trends in funding patterns among six social service agencies and seven community development organizations in Chicago.

3. We did not include higher education, for two reasons. First, the financial statements of colleges and universities are so complex that they

would have required a different mode of analysis and interpretation. Second, almost all of these institutions depend so heavily on tuition (earned income) that marked shifts in revenue profiles are highly unlikely.

4. Precise comparisons between the SOI data discussed in Chapter Eight and the data in this chapter can be made by examining Appendix G, Tables G.8-1 and G.10-4. For example, in both sets of data, the earned-income share dominates in the performing arts. It is much less important for historical societies and art museums, and it again occupies an intermediate position in the case of science museums. The patterns for private and governmental support are also much the same as those reported in Chapter Eight. The only exception is art museums, where, for the purposes of this chapter, we happen to have chosen two entities (the Baltimore Museum of Art, and the Brooklyn Institute of Arts and Sciences) which receive more governmental support than is typical of museums.

5. This percentage is the unweighted mean of the average annual rates of increase for each of the 32 individual organizations. Giving each organization equal weight seemed to be the most appropriate way of summarizing our set of findings because we are interested in individual organizations, and we did not want the larger organizations to dominate the overall statistics. The average annual growth rate for each organization was calculated by means of regression analysis (as explained in Chapter Three). Growth rates for each organization are presented in Appendix G, Table G.10-2.

6. Baumol and Bowen (1966), Bowen (1968), Baumol, Blackman, and Wolff (1989, chapter 6), and Moynihan (1993).

7. It would obviously be desirable to divide increased earned income for performing arts organizations between revenue due to higher ticket prices and revenue due to increased attendance, but the available data do not permit us to achieve this split. We do not understand why the picture for symphony orchestras differs from that for the other performing arts fields. Perhaps the presence of significant fundraising capacity at an earlier time is part of the explanation. In any case, confronted with mounting financial problems, orchestras have begun to target new audiences in an effort to increase earned income (Stehle, 1993; Holland, 1993; Schwarz, 1993).

8. Our colleague Kevin Guthrie is preparing a case study (really a fairly extensive history) of the New-York Historical Society. His work will develop these themes at far greater length and will also show the lasting effects of other policy decisions, including those affecting acquisitions and the relationship of the society to the city and state governments.

CONCLUSION

<hr>

Key Findings and Directions for Further Research

Some books conclude with restatements of major theses and injunctions for action. This is not that kind of book. From the first, we conceived of it as a "framing study," intended to facilitate and encourage further work in a broad, important, neglected field: the study of the institutions which inhabit key parts of the nonprofit universe. Perhaps the best way to conclude is by summarizing what we believe we have learned from conducting this study and then suggesting some areas that deserve more attention.

We have learned, first, that doing empirical work in the nonprofit domain requires knowledge of databases, definitions, and conventions which are largely inaccessible to neophytes—an accurate description of our condition when we started this project. We would like to think, and do think, that access to the mysterious world of the IRS Business Master File can be eased by the road map we have provided in Chapter One. Such a road map, complete with definitions of major routes and warnings about cul de sacs and detours, would have helped us enormously. We hope that our tree diagram (Chapter One, Figure 1.1) will help others navigate this treacherous territory more expeditiously. (An enthusiastic reader of an early draft of the manuscript suggested that the tree diagram will come to be regarded by users of the Business Master File as equivalent in importance to fire and the wheel—a proposition which we would like to embrace, but do not!)

Broad Dimensions of the Nonprofit Sector

A related lesson is that it is all too easy to lose perspective and feel overwhelmed by the apparently huge dimensions of the nonprofit universe. In

fact, only about half of the roughly one million tax-exempt entities are charitable nonprofits—or, as they are often called, 501(c)(3)s. Of these charitable
nonprofits, only about one-quarter (roughly 125,000) are independent entities working actively in substantive fields and reporting annual revenues of
as much as $25,000. For most purposes, it is sufficient to focus on this much
smaller number of so-called positive filers. A probe we launched in New York
City causes us to doubt that more than a small fraction, perhaps 20 percent,
of the nonfilers even exist. In short, it is very easy to exaggerate the true number of actively functioning charitable nonprofits with tax-exempt rulings.

There are many descriptive questions that can be asked about this institutional population, including its distribution by field of activity and the
characteristic sizes and ages of entities in different fields. We found geographic patterns to be of particular interest. We were intrigued to discover
the degree to which both public charities (operating in fields ranging from
arts/culture and education to human services and recreation/leisure) and
grantmaking foundations remain much more heavily concentrated today in
regions such as New England than one would expect on the basis of population or wealth. Conversely, almost all types of nonprofits remain underrepresented in the South. The regularity of these patterns is quite remarkable, and
the long reach of historical forces, including religious influences, is evident.

Institutional Births

We were able to chart the year-to-year pattern of institutional formation in
major parts of the nonprofit sector over the last quarter-century by examining "ruling years"—the years in which entities were granted tax-exempt status. This method of analyzing trends in institutional births demonstrates
both the youthfulness of many public charities (over 80 percent of those active today received their rulings within the last two decades) and the extent
to which institutional birthrates have been influenced by such legislation as
the Tax Reform Act of 1969.

While our data confirm the dynamic character of the growth in the
number of new public charities over the last three decades (especially during the late 1960s and the first half of the 1970s), we also find that entry rates
have slowed markedly since 1985. The number of entrants into the universe
of grantmaking foundations, by contrast, is seen to have increased more
rapidly during the latter half of the 1970s and much of the 1980s than some
commentators had expected—although here, too, there is evidence of a recent slowdown in the entry rate. No one seems to know what explains the deceleration in rates of institutional formation among both public charities
and grantmaking foundations in the late 1980s and the early 1990s.

It is clear, however, that the dramatic growth in the number of new
public charities since 1965 has never been steady or uniform, either across
fields or over time. We were able to use National Taxonomy of Exempt Enti-

ties (NTEE) codes to classify organizations by primary field of activity and then determine which fields experienced the highest entry rates during the first of our two subperiods (1965–1975) and which during the second (1975–1988).

Broad patterns emerge, which may be related to the major social, economic and political transformations of the last twenty-five years. Entry rates in six fields (arts/culture, education, health, employment, human services, and animal services) were much higher during the first subperiod than during the second, and so we labeled this group *old enthusiasms*. The rapid rates of institutional formation characteristic of these fields in the first subperiod can be linked in most cases to the Great Society initiatives of the 1960s. We labeled two other fields (science/technology and community improvement) *new enthusiasms* because they had precisely the opposite characteristic: their entry rates were much higher in the more recent subperiod than in the first subperiod. Three other fields (conservation/environment, international affairs, and recreation/leisure) are noteworthy for the steady growth in number of new entrants during both subperiods, while one field, youth development, exhibited very little growth.

Aggregative trends in broad areas of the nonprofit world can be highly suggestive, but they need to be supplemented by studies of more precisely defined sectors. We looked in somewhat greater detail at just three such sectors. Of all the major nonprofit sectors, higher education is, along with religion, the oldest and most institutionalized. Its history is particularly illuminating because it demonstrates so vividly the tendency for distinct types of entities (Liberal Arts I colleges, Research/Doctorate universities, Two-Year colleges) to be formed in waves. The development of a new template leads to rapid increases in the number of new institutions of a certain type. That particular institutional niche is then filled. Another new template is created, leading to the establishment of institutions of another type, and so on.

The evolution of the much younger civil rights sector illustrates a different and much more recent phenomenon—namely, a tendency in society toward greater institutional specialization (that is, a tendency for new organizations to be established for the purpose of addressing the needs of more narrowly defined subsets of the population). For example, we find rapid proliferation in the number of institutions concerned with the rights of immigrant groups from specific countries in Eastern Europe and in Southeast Asia, as well as groups focused on gay and lesbian rights. By contrast, there has been much less growth in recent years in the number of new, broadly based "legal services" groups, perhaps because that niche was largely filled by the mid-1970s.

The third specific sector which we examined in detail, the performing arts, reveals still other forces at work. The leveraged effects of powerful external funders, especially the National Endowment for the Arts and the Ford Foundation, can be seen clearly in spurts of institutional formation. Large differences in start-up costs among fields (much larger for operas than for dance troupes) are reflected in the amount of expansion that occurred within existing institutions, relative to the number of new institutional births. Intense competition for audiences across fields, as well as within them, also appears to have affected entry rates in theater and dance.

Institutional Deaths

Institutional births are very important because they are sources of creativity within fields, as well as major determinants of the overall size of a sector. It is just as important, however, to study institutional deaths, although such analyses are rarely undertaken. One of the more original contributions of this study is an initial attempt to analyze exit rates during the 1980s within specific arts/culture fields. In general, the results are consistent with theoretical expectations. Younger entities are more likely to fail than older entities, a reflection of what has been called "the liability of newness." Exits are least common in such fields as museums, in which the costs of exiting are unusually high because of the problems of disposing of substantial assets. Many of the market-driven incentives and mechanisms which cause mergers, buyouts, and liquidations in the for-profit sphere are absent in the nonprofit world. Much more thought needs to be given to the question of whether some nonprofits live too long, and whether new mechanisms are needed to assist in the orderly dissolution of entities that have served their purposes.

Field of Activity and Size

In the third part of our study, which focuses on size, age, revenue profiles, and other characteristics of institutions operating in specific fields, we learned a great deal about the advantages (and limitations) of the information available from IRS Form 990 and from the surveys conducted by the Statistics of Income Division of the IRS. We hope the appendixes, tables, and figures summarizing this information will be useful to others who wish to pursue in more detail questions which we could only touch upon lightly.

One important if obvious finding is that field of activity (or type) determines most key institutional characteristics. The typical size of an entity varies systematically by field of activity, and the basic reason is that fixed costs differ so markedly. At one extreme are the research universities, with their laboratories, libraries, hospitals, and complex infrastructures. At the other extreme we find local historical societies and innovative dance troupes. The median level of gross receipts for the research universities in our sample was over $200 million, as contrasted with medians of about $80,000 for historical societies and $100,000 for dance. The running costs of small entities (which we approximate by calculating the expenditures of the organization at the 25th percentile of the size distribution for institutions of a given type) also vary substantially between performing arts organizations and museums, as well as among the sectors of higher education.

One interesting discovery was that in almost every field there are a few very large institutions which have taken advantage of special opportunities. We were surprised to learn that the budgets of the largest organizations were as much as eight to fifteen times larger than the budgets of similar organizations at the 95th percentile of the relevant size distribution. In short, field of activity determines, with some rough precision, minimal levels of expenditures, but there has been room at the top for extraordinary growth.

Revenue Profiles

There are also predictable differences in revenue profiles among types of nonprofits. In particular, earned income plays a much more dominant role in some fields than in others. The explanation has to do primarily with the nature of the output—with differences across fields in how easy it is to charge for services provided. In turn, the ability to charge directly for services or products depends heavily on whether the service or good provided confers significant private benefits on the recipient, who could readily be excluded from receiving the benefits. In the case of higher education, for example, tuition is the dominant revenue source for private institutions because students and their families believe that they will earn a good return on the investment they make in schooling, and so they are willing to pay in order to enroll. Historical societies, by contrast, offer such services as preservation of manuscripts, services which have spillover benefits and more of a public-good character; consequently, historical societies tend to receive relatively little earned income. In this respect, most museums are more like historical societies than like colleges, although some of them, especially science museums and large art museums, have come to depend quite heavily on earned income.

The performing arts are a most interesting middle case, which we examined in some detail. In general, about half of the revenue of a typical performing arts entity comes from ticket sales and other forms of earned income. Since audiences presumably benefit directly from attending performances, the key question is why the earned-income share in the performing arts is not higher than it is. The existence of voluntary price discrimination is part of the answer, as are considerations of equity, the educational values associated with performances of literary works, cost structures in the arts, and traditional assumptions about the roles of both private and public patrons.

Charitable nonprofits that depend heavily on a particular external revenue source may run the risks of sudden withdrawal of funding and threats to their independence (if a dominant donor seeks to intervene inappropriately). For both of these reasons, diversification of funding sources is important, and we constructed a measure of diversification which distin-

guishes organizations dependent on a primary source of revenue from organizations with hybrid revenue profiles. This crude effort at classification
suggests that performing arts organizations have the most diversified set of
revenue profiles among the limited number of nonprofit fields which we investigated. We know, however, that no formulaic measure can fully capture
the complicated recipient-funder relationships.

Institutional Age

Age is another institutional characteristic that varies systematically across our
sectors. The "ruling year" variable allowed us to quantify differences in average age, as well as to identify the number of quite young and rather old institutions in each of our sectors. Perhaps fittingly, museums of natural history
have the largest share of arts/culture entities over twenty-five years of age
(nearly 60 percent). At the other extreme, only 2 percent of dance companies are this old.

There are also predictable differences in life cycles, which are associated, we believe, with differences in the nature of the characteristic assets
held by the various types of organizations. Performing arts groups, dependent primarily on performers and other "living assets," often grow rapidly
and then reach maturity while still quite young. Museums, which collect objects, generally experience slower but steadier growth; almost all old museums are quite large. We also found that there is at least a weak positive
correlation between age and earned income, whereas private contributions
tend to be most important when organizations are young and are just beginning to establish their reputations.

Trends in Expenditures and Revenue Profiles

We had hoped to be able to determine, fairly definitively, whether the kinds
of financial patterns and profiles described above have shifted noticeably
over time. Unfortunately, however, there are no published time-series data
that permit answers to such questions. This is obviously a major deficiency.
In seeking to build a new database, we learned again how very difficult it is
to work with the disparate financial statements produced by nonprofit organizations—a subject in itself. Problems of data collection and interpretation
notwithstanding, we were able to assemble data for 32 generally large and
well-established organizations spanning two decades. Two noteworthy findings resulted from this final part of our study and deserve mention.

First, total expenditures increased much more rapidly between 1972
and 1992 than we had suspected before we looked at these data. Overall, total
expenditures for our 32 organizations increased at an average rate of 10.6
percent per year (or 4.5 percent per year, after correction for inflation). The
real gross domestic product for the economy at large rose only 2.5 percent

per year over this same interval. This surprisingly rapid escalation of expenditures is not a sign of financial health but rather reflects, we believe, a combination of forces related to the nature of nonprofit organizations as economic entities, the growth of restricted funding, and factors peculiar to some of the specific fields which we studied.

Second, contrary to our expectations and to what others have suggested, we did not find evidence of any persistent tendency for earned income to increase, relative to other funding sources. At most, there has been a mild upward drift in the earned-income share. Revenue profiles appear to be much more stable over time than we had expected them to be. In general, organizations which depended heavily on private contributions in 1972 continued to depend on private contributions to roughly the same extent in 1992. This "once an elephant, always an elephant" attribute characterized institutions in all sectors, including both faster-growing and slower-growing institutions.

Our information on the histories of these thirty-two organizations is superficial, of course, and can serve only to suggest the broadest kinds of patterns and trends. Some of the most important questions concerning the management of large nonprofit institutions, such as the place of endowment in their financial plans and the use of spending rules to balance the needs of the future against the claims of the present, can be explored only by looking much more intensively at the experiences of particular organizations. There is a great need for case studies, and we hope that this book will serve to provide at least a partial framework for further research of this kind.

We also hope that this study will encourage further investigation of the many questions that can be examined most productively by analyzing the institutional dynamics and behavior patterns characteristic of fields and sectors. For example, there is much more to be learned about the pricing strategies employed by different sets of institutions—how they are influenced by the successes and failures of fundraising campaigns, their implications for financial stability, and their effects on program content and on efforts to reach wider audiences. At a still more general level, the recoding of the NTEE data that is now under way will permit much more fine-grained analyses of trends in institutional births within subfields and geographic regions, and of the economic, social, and political factors which encourage or inhibit the creation of new entities of various kinds. Similarly, it will be possible to examine patterns of institutional demise in more sophisticated ways, and to pay more attention to small organizations. Further studies of trends in financial characteristics could be most revealing, but they will require new time-series data, which are badly needed.

No one can doubt that nonprofit institutions will continue to play a major role in American society. They serve crucial purposes, and they deserve to be understood better, especially by their own leaders, board members, and advocates. It can be argued that "to know thyself is the ultimate form of aggression,"[1] but we believe that greater self-knowledge will allow these vitally important institutions to function ever more effectively.

Note

1.　Levy (1981).

Appendixes

APPENDIX A

The
Business Master File (BMF)
Database

Chapter One describes the basic structure of the Exempt Organizations/Business Master File maintained by the IRS (which we refer to as the BMF) and defines its major classification systems. The intent of this appendix is to supplement the material in the text with a number of technical points which are important for those who wish to work with the BMF database. We do not discuss every data field available in the BMF but rather focus only on those fields that require further explanation.

How to Obtain Data from the BMF

Individuals who wish to extract data from the BMF may do so by contacting the IRS National Office in Washington, D.C., and requesting a document titled *Instructions for Requesting Information on Exempt Organizations*. This document describes the fees and the procedures that must be followed. It also briefly defines each available field, although it does not interpret the fields. Output is available either as a magnetic tape or as a computer printout.

Foundation Codes and Lapsed Public Charities

Foundation codes classify organizations as public charities or as private foundations. As shown in Table A.1, within the private foundation world, the foundation code differentiates grantmaking foundations (foundation code 4) from operating foundations (codes 2 and 3, both of which we include in our definition of operating foundations).

Organizations with any other foundation code are defined as public charities. We include all these organizations in our primary fields (see Ap-

Table A.1. Business Master File Foundation Codes.

Code	Description
2	Private operating foundation exempt from paying excise taxes on investment income
3	Private operating foundation
4	Private grantmaking (nonoperating) foundation
10	Church
11	School
12	Hospital or medical research organization
13	Organization which operates for benefit of college or university and is owned or operated by a governmental unit
14	Governmental unit
15	Organization which receives a substantial part of its support from a governmental unit or the general public
16	Organization that normally receives no more than one-third of its support from gross investment income and unrelated business income and, at the same time, more than one-third of its support from contributions, fees, and gross receipts related to exempt purposes
17	Organizations operated solely for the benefit of and in conjunction with organizations described in 10 through 16, above
18	Organizations organized and operated to test for public safety

Source: Internal Revenue Service.

pendix G, Table G.1-1), with the exception of organizations with foundation codes 13 and 17 (supporting organizations) and those with foundation code 10 (churches), which we exclude altogether for reasons explained in the text. Two sections of the tax code (foundation codes 15 and 16) provide for classification as a public charity based on the proportion of an organization's total revenue that is obtained through public support. The first section requires an organization to receive one-third of its total support from governmental units or from direct or indirect contributions from the general public (section 509(a)(1), section 170(b)(1)(a)(vi)). The second section also allows for related business income or fees for services to be counted as public support but requires that investment income and unrelated business income not exceed one-third of total income (section 509(a)(1)(2)).[1]

The vast majority of public charities qualify for tax-exempt status under one of these two public-support tests. In October 1991, 77 percent of all public charities were classified in one of these two categories, another 13 percent were classified as churches, and the remaining 10 percent were distributed among the other foundation codes. Of those organizations that qualified under the public-support tests, slightly more than half (53 percent) met the first test (foundation code 15). Many of the codes have very few organizations associated with them. For example, in 1991 there were only 55 organizations that tested for public safety (foundation code 18).

When the IRS grants tax-exempt status to a new public charity, it usually issues an "advance ruling" because the charity has not operated long

enough to qualify for a "definitive," or final, ruling. At the end of a proba-
tionary period, the organization must demonstrate that it actually has met
the conditions required by the tax code. If it has met the appropriate conditions, it is then granted a final ruling. If it has not (for example, by failing
to meet one of the public-support tests), it lapses into the status of a private
foundation. Note that the foundation code does not differentiate between
private foundations that are actually lapsed public charities and those that
are true grantmaking foundations. It is possible to make this distinction,
however, by comparing the foundation code with another field on the BMF,
known as the prior foundation code. In our analysis, if the prior foundation
code is anything other than code 4, the foundation is assumed to be a lapsed
public charity.

Affiliation Codes

Affiliation codes define the organizational family structure. Organizations
may be classified as parents (affiliation code 6), subordinates (affiliation code
9), or independents (affiliation code 3). In our analysis, we group the parents
(a total of 1,019 in October 1991) with independents. There are a few organizations with other affiliation codes (for example, codes 1, 2, 7, and 8). We
also group these organizations (a total of 2,314 entities) with independents.

Parents and subordinates are linked by means of a four-digit group exemption number (GEN), which is also available on the BMF. Parents may file
a single Form 990 as a group return for all of their subordinates, or the subordinates may file separately. In addition to the group return, each parent
must also file a separate Form 990 for itself. Private foundations are not permitted to use group rulings or to file group returns.

Gross Receipts

The BMF contains a field for each organization's total income, also referred
to as *gross receipts*. This field should be used with some caution, since it is defined by the IRS in a very specific way that does not correspond to the general usage of the term *income*. The Form 990 instructions define gross
receipts as "the total amount it [the organization] received from all sources
during its annual accounting period, *without subtracting any costs or expenses*"
(italics added).

Clearly, the failure to subtract offsetting costs may exaggerate an organization's total revenue. Specifically, the IRS does not allow the following
costs to be netted out of total revenue: rental expenses, cost of assets sold, direct fundraising costs, and cost of goods sold. For organizations with substantial endowments, especially those that actively manage them, the
consequences may be monumental. As an example, suppose an organization
buys securities for $100 million and later sells them for $105 million. Under

generally accepted accounting principles, this transaction would result in net income of $5 million. Under the IRS definition, however, gross receipts would increase by $105 million. This difference explains why the 1991 BMF records gross receipts of $838 million for the Metropolitan Museum of Art, when its true revenues are in the neighborhood of $170 million.

The IRS definition of gross receipts may also exaggerate true revenues for another reason: Form 990 does not distinguish between current and non-current revenue. For example, contributions to an endowment or a capital fundraising campaign are mixed in with funds generated by normal operations. Under the principles of fund accounting, revenues are generally segregated into various funds (an operating fund, an endowment fund, a building fund, and so forth), but on Form 990, all of an organization's separate funds are aggregated.

These distortions primarily affect large organizations—those with substantial endowments, significant flows of capital, active fundraising efforts, large "retail type" operations, and so on. For smaller organizations with simpler revenue structures, the amount of income recorded in the BMF is likely to be a fairly close approximation of reality.

Positive Filers, Zero Filers, and Nonfilers

As described in Chapter One, not all organizations are required to file Form 990 with the IRS. Those with annual gross receipts (as defined above) of normally less than $25,000 do not have to file. (*Normally* refers to the average of the prior three tax periods.) We refer to organizations that are required to file as *positive filers*. However, many organizations that fall below the $25,000 threshold send in a Form 990 even though they are not required to do so. When these very small organizations file and provide actual figures on Form 990, the IRS replaces their entries with zeros in the BMF; hence we call them *zero filers*. In our analysis, we combine zero filers and "never filers" into the category *nonfilers*, since none of these organizations is required to file. Of the 146,965 independent nonfilers reported in Chapter One, about 60 percent are zero filers.

It should be noted that although small organizations are not required to submit a Form 990 at all, they are requested by the IRS to file an initial 990 return, confirming that their receipts do not exceed $25,000. Some organizations ignore this request. If a small organization complies with the request for an initial filing and has less than $25,000 in revenues, the IRS then "turns off the filing switch"—that is, if the organization files the initial preaddressed return, it will not be mailed a Form 990 package in later years and need not file Form 990 again until either its gross receipts reach the $25,000 minimum or the organization is dissolved. Organizations which follow these instructions help the IRS update its records, eliminate follow-up inquiries by the IRS, and ensure the organization's listing in the Treasury Department's "Blue Book" (*The Cumulative List of Organizations*).[2]

Status Codes and Status Years

The status code is used to indicate whether an organization is active or inactive. Organizations with status codes of less than 20 are active; organizations with codes greater than or equal to 20 are inactive. The IRS does not normally provide data on organizations with inactive codes.

The inactive file used in most of our analysis includes only organizations with two inactive status codes: code 20 (organizations whose exempt status has formally been terminated), and code 21 (organizations that the IRS is unable to locate). In addition to codes 20 and 21, there are seven other inactive status codes (codes 22, 23, 24, 25, 26, 28, and 29). With the exception of code 28, these codes include very few organizations—a total of about 2,400 in 1991. Code 28, however, had about 47,000 entities assigned to it in 1991. This code includes all subordinate organizations that have been dropped from a group ruling, on the basis of information from either the parent or the subordinate. (Still other status codes apply to organizations that were denied tax-exempt status.)

Status year is the year when the organization was assigned its most recent status code. Thus, in the case of an inactive organization, it is the year when the organization became inactive. For an active organization, it is intended to be the self-reported date of formation, or legal inception, of the organization (in contrast with the ruling year, which is the date tax-exempt status was granted). IRS officials have warned us, however, that the status year is an unreliable indicator of the formation of an organization. One reason is that a large number of organizations failed to provide their dates of formation when the original Exempt Organizations Master File was established in the 1960s.

Activity Codes

Activity codes are intended to describe an organization's field of activity. Organizations with multiple purposes may have up to three different codes. However, activity codes are often unreliable. The primary problem is that the codes were originally self-assigned and are therefore subject to myriad varying interpretations. At best, the activity codes are useful as a supplemental piece of information to help describe a particular organization.

As mentioned, the IRS originally asked organizations to fill in their own activity codes on Form 990, but it later abandoned this practice because the results were so inconsistent. IRS field agents now code organizations when they apply for exempt status, and so the codes are presumably more accurate in recent years. Discussions are currently under way to have the IRS adopt the National Taxonomy of Exempt Organizations (NTEE) coding system. (See Chapter Two for a description of this classification system.)

Ruling Years

Ruling Year Versus Establishment Year

As noted in Chapter Three, we use the ruling year to date the birth of an organization. There are many qualifications that must be borne in mind in interpreting this variable. One question concerns its relationship to the establishment year, as defined by the organization.

In an effort to see how much difference there is between the ruling year and an organization's own definition of when it was formed, we studied information available for eighty-two members of Opera America.[3] One surprising discovery was that in 13 percent of the cases, the ruling year is earlier than the self-reported date of founding. The probable explanation is that the organization changed its name or structure but was allowed to retain its tax-exempt status without seeking a new ruling, presumably because it was still serving essentially the same purposes. In these situations, the ruling year would appear to be the more reliable indicator of institutional birth. In another 52 percent of the cases, the ruling year is either identical with the stated year of founding or lags one or two years behind it, as one might expect. In the remaining 35 percent of the cases, the ruling year is more than two years later than the stated year of founding. Most of the cases at this end of the distribution (all but 5 with lags of ten years or more) involve entities that received rulings prior to 1970. In these early years, the IRS was in the process of assembling its Business Master File, and great significance should not be attached to the precise dates of rulings recorded in the file. Trends in entrants over the more recent decades are of primary interest; from that perspective, the ruling-year variable seems reliable.

Ruling Years for Subordinate Organizations

For reasons given in Chapter One, the body of our analysis focuses on independent organizations, not on subordinates. In working with the ruling-year variable, it is particularly important to exclude subordinates, since they do not need separate tax-exempt rulings. As a result, ruling years for subordinates are neither very consequential nor very reliable.

A telling example is provided by Ducks Unlimited and its 4,122 associated subordinate organizations. All of these entities are registered in Illinois, the state of the parent, and all show the 1956 ruling year of the parent. The result is an artificial spike in the aggregate time-series data on ruling years. At least 3,735 of these subordinate organizations did not even appear in the BMF until sometime between 1987 and 1989, even though they all show 1956 as the ruling year. There is no way of knowing whether 1956, 1989, or some other intermediate point is the appropriate year of formation for any particular Ducks Unlimited subordinate. It is clear that the failure to distinguish between the establishment of new independent organizations and the founding of subordinate organizations can lead to significant confusion in the interpretation of entry trends among nonprofits.

Ruling Years in the Active and Inactive Files

In Chapter Three, where we are measuring all public-charity and private-foundation entrants, we use ruling years for organizations in both the active and the inactive portions of the BMF, since we want to measure the flow of all nonprofit organizations into the universe in a year. However, in Chapter Four, where we examine the number of entrants into individual fields, we are unable to include inactive organizations, since NTEE codes have not been applied to the inactive file.

Even when we are able to use organizations from the inactive file, a problem still remains. In January 1981, the Exempt Organizations Master File, which had been a separate file for nonprofits, was merged with the Business Master File. At that time, an administrative decision was made to delete from the BMF the records of previous entrants which had become inactive by 1980. Thus the total number of entrants for years prior to 1980 is understated because some of the early entrants became inactive prior to 1980. See Appendix C for a full discussion of related issues.

Ruling Years Prior to 1965

A final comment needs to be made on the period covered by our analysis. We do not show ruling years before 1965, even though that information is available. The reason is that pre-1965 ruling years are unreliable indicators of trends. In 1961, the IRS decided to build the database which became the Exempt Organizations Master File. It was designed to contain all the data that had accumulated over the years on tax-exempt organizations. Old files were examined, and questionnaires were distributed. The process of cleaning out the file and assembling these data led to a sudden spurt in the number of organizations with the ruling years 1962–64. Some of the apparent growth in the annual number of entrants between 1962 and 1964 was surely real, but much of it was simply a product of this process.

Notes

1. See Simpson (1990) for a thorough definition of the public-support tests.
2. Department of the Treasury (1992).
3. Perry (1991).

APPENDIX B

Searching for
Performing Arts Nonfilers
in Manhattan

I n our efforts to determine the size of the nonprofit sector, we were struck by the large number of very small 501(c)(3)s. Indeed, more than half of the almost 500,000 501(c)(3)s in the Business Master File (BMF) were not required to file tax returns, because they had less than $25,000 in annual gross receipts. We thought it was important to estimate how many of these small organizations actually existed, and what an organization with such a modest budget could accomplish. Therefore, during the fall of 1993, we employed Jackson Lee, a student at the City University of New York, to track down the 290 performing arts organizations in Manhattan that are included as independent organizations in the BMF database but were not required to file tax returns. We chose New York City because of its proximity, and we focused on performing arts organizations because of our knowledge of this sector, and because there is a healthy concentration of such organizations in New York City.

Selection of Organizations

Of the 290 independent nonfiler performing arts organizations with Manhattan zip codes in the BMF database in October 1991, there were 141 theater organizations, 97 dance troupes, 23 orchestras, 22 opera companies, and 7 ballet groups. Our list of nonfilers technically includes both strict nonfilers (111 organizations had never filed returns) and zero filers (179 organizations had filed returns at least once, but their responses were converted to zeroes because they had less than $25,000 in gross receipts).

Telephone Search

We began our search by consulting the white pages of the telephone book. Of the 290 organizations on our list, only 23 were listed in the phone book.[1] We were able to speak to someone at 16 of these organizations and determined that 13 of them were still in existence but that 3 had been defunct since before October 1991. We left multiple messages on answering machines at the remaining 7 organizations but never received responses.

Cross-Referencing with Art Directories

Once we had exhausted the use of the telephone directory, we contacted organizations in New York City that work on behalf of small performing arts organizations, as either support or advocacy organizations.[2] Three of these groups—A.R.T/New York, the Lower Manhattan Cultural Council, and the New York State Council on the Arts—sent us membership lists or funding reports, which we then cross-referenced with our list. Through this cross-referencing, we were able to locate 13 organizations that we had not found in the phone book. Many of these organizations were included in more than one directory.

Site Visits and Follow-ups

Next, Jackson Lee combed the city in an attempt to find the remaining 238 organizations for which we had street addresses. (For 13 organizations, we only had post office boxes.) Lee consulted building directories, doormen, and even neighbors in order to determine whether each organization existed. Any organization listed on a building directory, or whose existence was confirmed by a doorman or a neighbor, was counted as "found," even if Lee was unable to speak directly to a representative of the organization. If Lee was unable to speak with someone when he visited, or if he found an address but could not verify the organization's existence, he sent a follow-up letter explaining the nature of our study and requesting information. Lee also sent letters to the 13 organizations with post office boxes. Altogether, he mailed eighty-three letters. Despite these painstaking efforts, Lee was able to locate only 33 additional organizations, 4 of which had recently moved, but which presumably had been active in 1991, and 1 of which had been defunct for many years.

Implications for the Size of the Nonprofit Sector

All told, we were able to find 69 of the 290 organizations we attempted to locate. This total includes all 23 organizations listed in the phone book, even the 7 that never returned our calls; the 13 organizations listed in the art directories; and the 33 organizations that Lee found through his visits, or that responded to our mail inquiries. Since 4 of these 69 organizations had ceased functioning before 1991, we could confirm that only 65 of the 290 nonfilers, or 22 percent, were active in October 1991.

We found many fewer organizations than we had expected to find. Some of the organizations we were unable to locate may have changed addresses or gone out of business during the period between October 1991 (when we compiled our list from the BMF) and the fall of 1993 (when Lee conducted his search), but anecdotal evidence from doormen and neighbors suggests that most of the organizations probably did not exist at the listed locations in 1991, either. The IRS is unable to clean its files systematically, which explains why many organizations remain in the active files long after they have become inactive.

We initially thought that the zero filers on our list might be easier to locate than the nonfilers because the zero filers had at least filed returns. However, although we were able to find a larger share of zero filers than nonfilers, we could not locate many of either group. Altogether, we found 17 percent of the 111 nonfilers in our sample and 28 percent of the 179 zero filers. Our inability to locate a sizable fraction of either group suggests that it is appropriate to combine the nonfilers and the zero filers into one "nonfiler" category.

Extrapolating our results to the larger nonprofit universe is difficult because of the focused nature of our sample, in terms of both geography and type of institution. We know, for example, that there is a greater concentration of nonprofit organizations in New York City than in most other areas of the country, and that performing arts organizations are able to exist and to be formed on a much more modest scale than other types of nonprofits.[3] Nevertheless, the fact that we could locate only 22 percent of the performing arts nonfilers in Manhattan still suggests that most of the organizations that the IRS classifies as nonfilers or zero filers are probably inactive organizations.

Activity of "Found" Nonfilers

We were able to get detailed information on 26 of the 69 organizations we found. Three of the organizations are no longer active—in at least two cases, for personal reasons. For example, the Courante Dance Foundation, an organization which used to stage eighteenth-century French dances, has been dormant since the founder had a child.

Of the remaining 23 organizations, 18 regularly stage productions. The number of annual performances ranges from one to almost fifty. Those organizations that stage many performances typically offer multiple performances of the same production. The Blue Heron Theater, for example, undertakes two fifteen-performance productions each year.

Nearly all the organizations use professional performers, but most have volunteer staffs, operate out of someone's apartment, and rent performance and rehearsal space as needed. The professional performers also often volunteer their services, receiving only travel money and, in some cases, modest honoraria. A few organizations, including Stage-Left, Inc., use amateur performers.

Most of the organizations have very focused missions. For example, the Any Place Theater, formed in 1980 by a group of performers who fervently believed in outreach, stages productions "any place"—in homeless shelters, nursing homes, prisons, and battered-women's shelters. The New York Deaf Theater was established in 1979 for a very different but equally specific purpose: to provide artistic, administrative, and technical support for the production of sign-language plays and performances.

Five organizations from which we received information did not produce performances. Playformers is a small support group of professional writers. Dramatree offers a full schedule of acting and speech classes. The Masterworks Laboratory Theater is primarily a training laboratory. Ballet Who is an advocacy organization. The Amato Opera Circle, Inc., is a membership organization of Amato Opera patrons, established to support and promote the opera company.

Although all the organizations have small budgets, many have been in existence for a long time. Three of the organizations—the Masterworks Laboratory Theater, the Cosmopolitan Symphony Orchestra, and the New York Pro Arte Chamber Orchestra—are more than twenty-five years old. Many of the other organizations are more than ten years old. Given their long histories as small organizations, it is likely that these organizations will remain small.

Conclusions

Some (about 20 percent) of the performing arts nonfilers in Manhattan do exist and undertake projects on a small scale, but most of the nonfilers in this set no longer exist. This finding has major implications for size estimates of the nonprofit sector because over half of the almost 500,000 501(c)(3)s in the BMF are nonfilers. Our conclusions also underline the importance of empirical research. Clearly, there is no substitute for field research in understanding how certain types of numbers are to be interpreted.

Notes

1. Grønbjerg (1989) had an equally difficult time locating telephone numbers for nonprofit organizations in Chicago for the Urban Institute's Nonprofit Sector Project. She reasoned, "In contrast to businesses, which need to advertise their services and products and which can thus

be found through such sources as the Yellow Pages of the telephone directory, many nonprofit activities involve only a handful of individuals who meet on an intermittent basis to engage in recreational or special interest activities. Examples include choirs, garden clubs, book clubs, community organizations and self-help groups. Because the members of such groups may have little interest in attracting other like-minded persons, they may not advertise their activities (except in specialized media), and they may not have separate phone listings. Hence, telephone directories are likely to be incomplete" (p. 66).

2. Grønbjerg (1989) found that "the best source of information on nonprofit arts and cultural groups is the lists of grant applicants at arts and humanities councils" (p. 75).

3. For a study of how the New York nonprofit sector compares to the nonprofit sectors in fifteen other communities across the United States, see Grossman (1986).

APPENDIX C

Measuring
Institutional Populations

The purpose of this appendix is to describe the simulation model we used to test how various assumptions about exit rates affect the measurement of trends in institutional populations. As discussed in Chapter Three, the need for these simulations arose because of our inability to measure the number of organizational deaths accurately.

Using the data available from the inactive file for the period 1981–1991, we constructed high and low estimates of exit rates and then compared the number of entrants under each scenario with counts based on surviving entrants alone. The results show that even with a high estimate of exit rates, the observed patterns of changes in entrants are not materially altered. In particular, the analysis in Chapter Four of the difference in rates of increase between the two subperiods (early and late) is not affected by changing assumptions about exit rates.

Our simulation model borrows the concept of "age pyramids" from the field of demography. For each year between 1965 and 1988, we constructed a table containing the number of organizations in each age cohort. The size of each age cohort is equal to the number of organizations that were one year younger the preceding year, less the number of organizations in that cohort which exited during the year. This approach allows us to specify age-specific exit rates and thus model how the population changes from year to year. Our model differs slightly from conventional age pyramids in that we construct them backwards. In other words, we start with the most recent age pyramid and then, on the basis of a set of age-specific exit rates, we work back to 1965, reconstructing the number of actual entrants in each year. We can then compare these results with the ones we observe by studying surviving entrants alone.

Assumptions About Exit Rates

Each scenario requires two assumptions about exit rates, both of which vary from field to field. The first is a set of age-specific exit rates, one for each age between one and twenty-three. We assume that these rates do not change over time; in other words, the probability of exiting for an organization five years old was the same in 1988 as it was in 1965. Applying these exit rates to the age structure of the population in any particular year results in a total number of exits for that year, which can then be divided by the total number of organizations in existence that year to calculate a crude annual exit rate. When we refer to a particular scenario as based on a 2 percent exit rate (for example), we mean that it is based on a set of age-specific exit rates that result in an average crude exit rate of 2 percent over the 1965–1988 period.[1]

On the basis of our analysis of the inactive file, we selected two estimates of crude exit rates, a high one and a low one, which, we believe, encompass the range of exit rates across fields. As discussed in Chapter Six, the estimated exit rates for all public charities between 1984 and 1992 averaged 2.3 percent per year (see Table 6.1). In our analysis of individual fields (Table 6.2), annual exit rates ranged from 3.2 percent (job training) to 0.8 percent (historical societies). A study by Bielefeld of nonprofit exit rates between 1980 and 1988 in Minneapolis–Saint Paul found roughly similar rates.[2] In three fields with reasonable sample sizes (health/welfare, cultural, and recreational), the implied annual exit rates were 2.2 percent, 2.6 percent, and 4.4 percent, respectively. The average for all ten fields included in Bielefeld's study was 2.8 percent per year. On the basis of these results, we selected a crude exit rate of 4 percent as our high estimate and a crude exit rate of 1 percent as our low estimate.

The second assumption required by our model pertains to the structure of the age-specific exit rates. Our assumption, based in part on our analysis of exits in Chapter Six, is that exit rates decline with age. In other words, there is a "liability of newness": a young organization has a higher probability of exiting than an old organization. The question is how quickly the rate declines. Do organizations that are fifteen years old exit at one-half the rate of organizations ten years younger? Or is three-quarters of that rate a better estimate?

Having no theoretical propositions to guide us in answering this question, we turned again to the limited empirical evidence that is available. Among the eight fields in the inactive file that we coded, we found that the exit rate declined, on the average, 4 percent for each year of age. (With this assumption, the exit rate would be one-third lower for an organization ten years older.) If anything, we suspect that this rate of decline is on the low side, since some of the fields (for example, higher education) had exit rates that declined by as much as 8 percent per year. Only one field, dance, did not show a declining exit rate (dance actually increased by about 1.5 percent per year).

The empirical data also suggest that exit rates are relatively low for very young organizations (roughly, those under five years of age). This finding presumably reflects the fact that an organization's founders are not likely to "throw in the towel" until they have exhausted all means of survival. In addition, there is a lag between the time an organization ceases operations and the date that fact is recorded by the IRS. To simplify the analysis, we assume (somewhat arbitrarily) that organizations have the highest probability of dying when they are five years old.

After trying a wide range of values for the rate at which exit rates decline with age, we found this variable to have a much smaller overall effect than the crude death rate. Large changes in rate of decline are swamped by relatively small changes in the exit rate. In the end, we simply assumed in all scenarios that the exit rate declined at a constant rate of 4 percent per year as organizations aged. Under the high estimate of the crude exit rate (4 percent), age-specific mortality rates ranged from about 6.2 percent per year (for organizations five years old) to about 3.0 percent (for organizations twenty-three years old). The range under the low estimate was roughly 1.6 percent to 0.8 percent.

Simulation Results

The results of our analysis are shown in Table C.1. For each of the twelve fields examined in Chapter Four, we repeated our analysis of entrants, using the high and low estimates of crude exit rates. The results from Table 4.1 (which effectively assumes a zero percent exit rate) are included for comparison. We also prepared one pair of figures for the arts/culture field to illustrate the results (Figure C.1).

Under the low estimate of exit rates, the pattern of entrants is virtually identical, as can be seen in the top panel of the figure. Under the high estimate, the gap between the two lines widens, and yet the general pattern is still recognizable. As shown in Table C.1, the average annual increase in entrants is consistently lower under both the high and the low estimates—by about 1 percentage point and 4 percentage points, respectively. In both cases, however, the effect is greater in our second period, 1975–1988. For the group of fields we have labeled *old enthusiasms*, this bias has the effect of accentuating the difference between the two periods, since the number of entrants increases relatively faster in the first period. The difference between the two periods is dampened for the *new enthusiasms*, yet it still remains positive.

In addition to testing our assumptions about exit rates for each of the twelve fields, we also looked at all public charities. Here, we can add another element to the analysis, since we have partial information about exits in the inactive file (recall that the information is partial because the file does not contain data on organizations that became inactive prior to 1981). In Figure C.2 there are three lines. The lowest line, representing surviving entrants

Table C.1. Simulated Average Annual Rates of Increase in Entrants,
Using Low and High Estimates of Exit Rates[a] by Primary Field and Subperiod, 1965–1988.

Primary Field	Low Estimate (Exit Rate = 1%) Average Annual Increase in Entrants (%)				High Estimate (Exit Rate = 4%) Average Annual Increase in Entrants (%)				Surviving Only (Same as Table 4.1) Average Annual Increase in Entrants (%)			
	1965–88	1965–75	1975–88	Differ-ence	1965–88	1965–75	1975–88	Differ-ence	1965–88	1965–75	1975–88	Differ-ence
Old enthusiasms												
Arts/culture (A)[b]	6.3	10.2	2.7	−7.5	2.7	7.3	−1.3	−8.6	7.6	11.2	4.1	−7.1
Education (B)	4.6	8.5	3.3	−5.2	1.0	5.6	−0.8	−6.4	5.8	9.5	4.7	−4.8
Health (E,F,G,H)	5.4	10.9	2.6	−8.3	1.8	7.9	−1.5	−9.3	6.7	11.9	4.0	−7.9
Employment (J)	1.4	8.4	−1.1	−9.4	−2.0	5.5	−4.8	−10.3	2.6	9.3	0.3	−9.0
Human services (P)	6.5	13.3	2.4	−10.9	2.9	10.2	−1.6	−11.8	7.8	14.3	3.8	−10.5
Animal services (D)	5.9	12.4	4.4	−8.0	2.3	9.4	0.4	−9.1	7.2	13.5	5.9	−7.6
New enthusiasms												
Community improvement (S)	3.8	2.2	5.9	3.6	0.2	−0.5	1.7	2.2	5.0	3.2	7.3	4.1
Science/technology (U)	5.0	1.1	6.2	5.1	1.3	−1.6	2.0	3.6	6.2	2.1	7.6	5.5
Continuing enthusiasms												
International affairs (Q)	11.0	8.6	13.0	4.3	7.2	5.7	8.5	2.8	12.4	9.7	14.5	4.8
Conservation/environment (C)	6.1	9.1	5.9	−3.2	2.5	6.2	1.8	−4.4	7.4	10.1	7.4	−2.7
Recreation/leisure (N)	8.2	13.2	6.2	−7.0	4.5	10.2	2.1	−8.1	9.5	14.2	7.7	−6.5
Other												
Youth development (O)	−0.6	1.4	−0.7	−2.2	−4.1	−1.3	−4.7	−3.3	0.6	2.4	0.7	−1.7
All public charities	6.7	10.6	4.4	−6.1	3.1	7.6	0.4	−7.2	8.0	11.6	5.9	−5.7

Source: Business Master File, October 1991, active, independent only.

[a] "Exit rate" is the average crude exit rate between 1965 and 1988.

[b] Letters following each field refer to NTEE primary codes.

Figure C.1. Simulated Trends in Entrants by Ruling Year, Arts/Culture, 1965–1988.

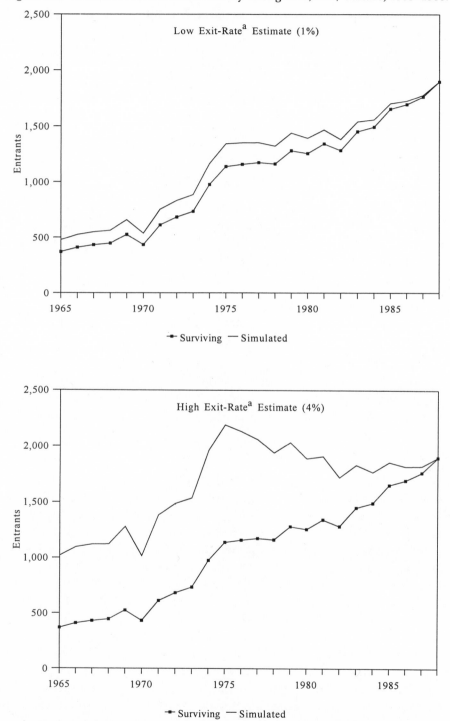

Source: Business Master File, October 1991, active, independent only.
[a]"Exit rate" is the average crude exit rate between 1965 and 1988.

Figure C.2. Simulated Trends in Entrants by Ruling Year, All Public Charities, 1965–1990.

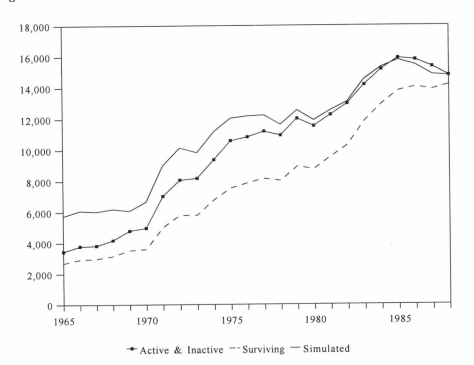

Source: Business Master File, October 1991, active and inactive, independent only.
Note: The "simulated" line assumes an average crude exit rate of 2.6 percent.

only, corresponds to data available for the individual fields (in other words, active organizations only). The middle line includes both active and inactive organizations, using the data that are available in the inactive file. The assumptions underlying the third line were chosen so that the pattern of entrants between 1981 and 1990 would match the combined active-inactive line as closely as possible. The resulting crude exit rate is 2.6 percent, along with age-specific exit rates that decline at 1.4 percent per year. As expected, prior to 1981 the two lines diverge, since the upper line now includes the estimated number of organizations that exited before 1981. The degree of divergence is, however, smaller than we had expected it to be.

We conducted one final "reality check" to test the assumptions underlying our simulation. IRS annual reports provide the total number of tax exemptions that are granted each year, which should correspond roughly to the total number of entrants in that year. That total is not directly comparable to our calculations, however, because it includes all tax-exempt organizations, not just independent public charities. Nevertheless, if we assume that the proportion of total exemptions granted to independent public charities is relatively constant, we can obtain a general sense of whether our simulated figures are believable. In 1990 and 1991, the average share of total exemptions that went to public charities was about 40 percent (roughly 15,000 out of a total of 38,000). In 1965, the total number of exemptions granted was 11,929. Using a 40 percent ratio, we calculate that about 4,772 public charities would have received tax-exempt rulings. Under our simulation, the number of entrants in 1965 was 5,744, which is about 20 percent greater—implying that, if anything, our assumptions about exit rates are on the high side.

Notes

1. One difficulty is how to treat organizations with ruling years prior to 1965. As explained in Appendix A, we do not consider the ruling year to be a reliable measure of institutional birth for these organizations. As a result, we have no knowledge of the age structure of the institutional population for years prior to 1965. It is reasonable to assume, however, that the exit rate for this cohort of organizations was higher in 1965 (when the population was young) than it was in 1988. As a rough approximation, our simulation model divides the period 1965–1988 into three subperiods and assigns a separate crude exit rate for the pre-1965 cohort to each period. From 1965 to 1972, the rate used is the average of the set of age-specific exit rates chosen for each simulation. From 1973 to 1980, the rate is half the rate of the first period. From 1981 to 1988, the rate is half the rate of the second period. Because the base population in 1965 is relatively small, changing these assumptions has only a minor effect on the results. Organizations whose ruling years were unknown were excluded from the analysis.
2. Bielefeld (1993).

APPENDIX D

The Higher Education, Civil Rights, and Performing Arts Databases

In Chapter Five, we examined patterns of institutional formation in three specific sectors: higher education, civil rights, and performing arts. The purpose of this appendix is to describe how we constructed the databases for each sector. The actual data are summarized in Appendix G, Tables G.5-1 (higher education), G.5-2 (civil rights), and G.5-3 (performing arts).

Higher Education

The data in the higher education section of Chapter Five and Part Three were taken from the *1992 Higher Education Directory*.[1] We used the *Directory*, rather than the Business Master File (BMF) or Statistics of Income (SOI) sample, to define our higher education universe, for three reasons:

1. We were primarily interested in accredited, degree-granting institutions. But, as explained in Chapter Four, the BMF education field at the primary field level, as defined by the National Taxonomy of Exempt Entities (NTEE), contains a large number of ancillary organizations, as well as primary and secondary schools. At present, the NTEE coding system is not reliable enough beyond the primary field level to identify accurately those institutions that are bona fide colleges and universities. Furthermore, the NTEE does not differentiate between accredited and nonaccredited institutions.

2. We wanted to include public as well as private nonprofit institutions because the private-public duality is more pronounced in higher education than in any other area of activity encompassed within this study. While it

would be desirable, in principle, to study interactions between private and public providers of every kind of charitable product, it is difficult to do so in practice because public providers fall outside the BMF. Higher education, however, offers an unusually good opportunity to examine private-public overlaps because of the existence of such all-inclusive data sources as the *Directory*.

3. The *Directory* provides more reliable dates of establishment for higher education institutions than the BMF does. The venerable age of many colleges and universities means that their ruling years are unreliable. Recall that ruling years are often not precise in the case of organizations established prior to 1965, and certainly are inaccurate for organizations founded prior to 1913. Lumping all pre-1965 institutions of higher education together would obscure the picture we are trying to present.

Our definitions for the sectors of higher education are based on the Carnegie Classification of institutions of higher education.[2] Research/Doctorate combines four Carnegie classifications: Research I (for example, Stanford University), Research II (Temple University), Doctorate-Granting I (the College of William and Mary), and Doctorate-Granting II (Pepperdine University). The distinctions among these four Carnegie groupings are related to the level of priority given to research, the number of doctorates granted, and the number of academic disciplines.

Our definitions of Comprehensive I institutions (Hawaii Pacific College), Liberal Arts I colleges (Amherst College), and Two-Year colleges (Mercer County Community College) are the same as the ones used in the Carnegie system. Comprehensive I colleges and universities offer graduate education through the master's degree, and more than half of their baccalaureate degrees are awarded in two or more occupational or professional disciplines. Liberal Arts I colleges are highly selective undergraduate institutions that award more than half of their baccalaureate degrees in the arts and sciences. Two-Year colleges generally award associate degrees.

Other Four-Year comprises two categories: Comprehensive II universities (the University of Tampa) and Liberal Arts II colleges (Oklahoma Baptist University). These institutions are similar to Comprehensive I and Liberal Arts I, but they are smaller and less selective. The Carnegie system also has separate categories for professional schools and other specialized institutions. In Figure 5.4, we group the professional and specialized schools into two categories: *religious* (theological seminaries, Bible colleges, and other institutions offering degrees in religion) and *professional* (all other specialized institutions, such as medical, law, and business schools).

Our analysis of higher education included only institutions that still existed in 1992. We did not account for the number or the dates of establishment of those institutions that closed prior to 1992. (We were able to test the effect of this omission on overall trends, and it appears to have made very little difference; see Chapter Five.) We also classified institutions on the basis of what they were in 1992. Many, perhaps even most, of them would have been classified differently when they were founded. Many Liberal Arts I colleges, for example, were founded as academies or secondary schools, and many Research/Doctorate universities were originally liberal arts colleges.

Civil Rights

The data source for our civil rights database is the BMF, since no other comprehensive directory of civil rights organizations exists. We included only independent, active organizations because the inactive portion of the BMF is not coded by field, and the ruling-year variable is not reliable for subordinates.

Our starting point was the *R* section of the NTEE taxonomy, which is designated for organizations whose primary purpose is related to civil rights, social action, or advocacy. In addition to removing all obvious coding errors, we eliminated the following groups of organizations:

- Organizations coded R30 (intergroup/race relations) and R40 (voter education/registration), because these organizations did not seem to be directly involved in the promotion of civil rights. Examples of R30 and R40 organizations are the Center for Peaceful Relations, the Committee for Better Racial Assurance, and the California Voter Foundation. R40 included a large number of Leagues of Women Voters.
- Entities that appeared to be primarily "social action" community groups—in some cases, concerned about a particular issue (for example, Arizonans Concerned About Smoking) and, in other cases, concerned about issues in a particular geographic area (Concerned Citizens of Morrison County, Minnesota).
- Entities that promote general democratic or American values, such as Democracy in Action and the Freedoms Foundation at Valley Forge. Most of these organizations were coded R15, R20, or R60.

Although the R section is designated for civil rights groups, we found enough overlap with other NTEE codes to warrant the inclusion of organizations from other sections of the taxonomy. Specifically, we included organizations with the following three codes:

- Women's centers (P83): The assigning of organizations to this category, or to women's rights (R24), appeared to be arbitrary. For example, the Women's Alliance is coded P83, but the Black Women's Alliance is coded R24.
- Ethnic/immigrant centers (P84): As in the case of women's centers, it was difficult to distinguish among ethnic/immigrant centers (coded P84) and two similar codes in the R section of the taxonomy: immigrants' rights (R21) and minority rights (R22). To avoid inconsistencies, we added most of the P84 organizations to our civil rights universe.

- Legal services (I80): Because the activities of these organizations are typically devoted to helping minorities, immigrants, the poor, and the generally disadvantaged, it seemed appropriate to include this category in our database.

Thus our civil rights database includes most of the organizations coded with primary field R (except for the R30s and R40s), as well as many entities coded P83, P84, or I80. Overall, nearly 80 percent of the entities in the BMF with these codes were included, leaving us with a total universe of 3,032 organizations. We then divided this universe into the five categories referred to in Chapter Five (and shown in Appendix G, Table G.5-2), as follows:

- Legal services: In most cases, we could not identify the legal organizations with a specific population group, and so we left legal services as a discrete category.
- Minority/immigrant rights: We grouped ethnic/immigrant centers and services (P84), immigrants' rights (R21), and minority rights (R22) together because organizations in all three classifications provided services or otherwise worked on behalf of well-defined groups.
- Women's centers/rights: We included both women's centers (P83) and women's rights groups (R24) in this category because their activities were in many cases indistinguishable.
- Abortion-related groups: We combined reproductive rights (R61) and right-to-life (R62) organizations to form this category.
- Other civil rights: Any organization coded in the R20s and R60s that was not included in another category, or was not eliminated for one of the reasons described above, was included in this final category.

Because of the overlap between civil rights and other portions of the NTEE taxonomy (as well as our doubts about the reliability of NTEE coding beyond the primary level), we were concerned that we might have missed another large pocket of civil rights organizations, coded in some other (unknown) section of the NTEE. To test this proposition, we obtained a list of organizations from the *Hispanic Americans Information Directory*,[3] and then attempted to locate a small subset of them in the BMF. This cross-referencing convinced us that there is no other pocket for civil rights entities in the NTEE taxonomy.

Performing Arts

There is a wide variety of arts organizations included in the NTEE. In Chapter Five, however, we limited our analysis to producing entities in five performing arts fields: theater (A65), opera (A64), dance (A62), ballet (A63), and orchestra (A69).

Our data source for the performing arts was the BMF, and we excluded subordinates and confined ourselves to independent organizations. The subordinate-to-parent ratios for the performing arts fields that we have selected are lower than 1 percent, compared to 32 percent for all public charities, reflecting the fact that franchise-like structures do not suit the unique missions of performing arts organizations. Because we used the BMF, our universe also excluded other "nonindependent" organizations, such as symphonies that are part of universities, and for-profit organizations (for example, Broadway theaters).

In the performing arts sector, unlike other sectors, we were able to include both active and inactive organizations. In order to include inactive organizations, we carefully reviewed the inactive portion of the BMF and coded all those entities which fell into our performing arts fields. The inclusion of inactive organizations enabled us to track interest in these fields more accurately. It is important to remember, however, that all the organizations that became inactive before 1981 were removed from the BMF by the IRS, and so our universe is still incomplete.

Here again, we were sensitive to the possibility of misclassifications within the NTEE. We removed obvious coding errors but could not systematically identify all errors, because there are no formal accreditation processes for performing arts organizations which would make it possible to define fields with the precision possible within higher education.

We did eliminate all entities whose titles included the words *guild*, *council*, *league*, *friends*, and *women's association*, since such organizations usually function in ancillary roles (raising money, recruiting volunteers, and so on) and are unlikely to produce works themselves.

In addition, we removed all opera "houses" (because "house" venues are no longer used exclusively for the production of operas), all supporting organizations, and, where we could identify them, service and presenting organizations. Finally, to avoid double counting, in cases in which one performing arts organization was represented by two or more corporate entities, we counted only the entity with the largest gross receipts.

To ensure that our analysis included at least the largest and most established organizations in each field, we also cross-referenced the NTEE classifications with listings of organizations participating in the major service organizations—Theatre Communications Group (TCG), Dance/USA, Opera America, and the American Symphony Orchestra League (ASOL). The primary roles of the service organizations are to disseminate information, encourage collegial exchange, and monitor growth among their constituents. The service groups tend to recognize organizations that are national in stature and therefore larger, more stable financially, and more sophisticated artistically than the majority of institutions that comprise an entire field. For example, there are over 4,000 institutions classified as theaters in the BMF taxonomy, but only 208 of them, or 19 percent, are members of TCG.

Through this cross-referencing, we were able to identify service-member organizations not classified under the primary NTEE headings. Of TCG's 208 members, 29 percent were classified outside the A65 (theater) field; 19 percent of Opera America's 101 American member companies were not coded A64 (opera); 29 percent of Dance/USA's 107 members were not coded either A62 (dance) or A63 (ballet); and 41 percent of ASOL's 795 members were not classified A69 (symphony).

Some of these omissions were coding errors. For example, the Music-Theater Group, in New York, and the American Music Theater Festival, in Philadelphia, two members of Opera America, were presumably not coded A64 (opera) because their titles do not include the word *opera*.

Other apparent omissions were not coding errors but instances in which the organization was part of another nonprofit institution. For example, Seattle Group Theater, which is part of the University of Washington, does not (and should not) exist as an independent theater in the BMF. We believe that such affiliations explain why so few of ASOL's members were in the BMF, relative to the other performing arts groups. Many of the orchestras listed separately by ASOL are actually youth or chamber orchestras that are affiliated with another institution and therefore do not have independent tax-exempt status.

Notes

1. M. Rodenhouse (1992). We obtained the electronic version of *The 1992 Higher Education Directory* from John Minter Associates, Boulder, Colorado.
2. See Carnegie Foundation Technical Report (1987) and Bowen and Sosa (1989, pp. 191–192) for further discussion of the Carnegie Classification. In 1994, the classification was updated and revised.
3. Furtaw (1993).

APPENDIX E

The
Statistics of Income (SOI)
Database

I n Chapters Eight and Nine, we made use of data collected by the Statistics of Income (SOI) Division of the Internal Revenue Service. These data are based on Form 990, which nonchurch nonprofits with annual revenues greater than $25,000 are required to file annually with the IRS.

Form 990 (reproduced at the end of this appendix, in Exhibit E.1) requires organizations to provide detailed financial information, similar in many respects to the type of information included on an organization's audited financial statements (breakdowns of revenues, expenses, assets, liabilities, and so on). Although Form 990 is also the source of data for the exempt portion of the Business Master File (BMF), the IRS does not have the resources to enter all the information reported on Form 990 into the BMF. Instead, it enters a few summary figures, such as gross receipts (see Appendix A) and total assets. For this reason, the BMF is not sufficiently detailed to answer the types of questions we pose in Chapters Eight and Nine.

To allow more systematic analysis of the data reported on Form 990, since 1982 the SOI Division has conducted a series of annual studies based on a sample of all the public charities that are required to file Form 990. For every organization included in the sample, all the financial information reported on the Form 990 is entered into a database. Thus, in contrast with the BMF, which has limited information on every tax-exempt organization, the SOI database has detailed information on relatively few organizations.

Considerable care is taken to ensure that the data are entered correctly. (Note that this is not the case with the BMF, where the IRS is not able to verify the accuracy of the data.) The SOI studies have the further advantage of providing the only time-series data currently available on the finances of nonprofit organizations. At the time our research was conducted, data tapes were available for 1982 through 1988, with the exception of 1984, when the study fell victim to budget cuts.[1] The data tapes may be purchased for a nominal fee from Independent Sector, in Washington, D.C.

SOI Sample Design

It is important to understand how the SOI sample is constructed. First, as mentioned above, all churches, and organizations with gross receipts of $25,000 or less, are excluded, since they are not required to file Form 990. Excluding the small organizations has the effect of biasing the sample toward larger organizations. We believe this bias is of minimal consequence, however, since our research suggests that most of the nonfilers (other than churches) no longer exist (see Appendix B).

A more serious analytic problem is introduced by the method used to select the sample. The SOI sample is composed of two elements: (1) *all* public charities with assets greater than $10 million, and (2) a random sample, stratified by asset size, of all the other public charities (positive filers) in the BMF.[2] This sample design ensures that the IRS, with its limited budget for policing tax-exempt organizations, can monitor all the largest entities. It also means, however, that the number of small organizations (with assets less than $10 million) included in the sample is a function of the size of the budget allocated to the study. In other words, whatever money is left after data for the large organizations have been collected determines the size of the remaining sample.

In 1982, for example, the first year of the study, the SOI sample contained only 484 organizations with assets less than $10 million, compared to 4,390 with assets of $10 million or more. In recent years, the sample size has increased. In 1988, the total was 12,746 organizations, with over half above the $10 million threshold.

Since some of the specific fields of interest to us have many small organizations (especially when measured in terms of total assets), relatively few of them appear in the SOI sample. Thus our ballet category contains only 8 organizations, and we omitted dance entirely because so few dance troupes were included. Higher education, however, is very well represented, with a total sample of 665 (which is why we were able to use the SOI data on higher education in Chapter Seven).

Criteria for Selecting Organizations

As a first cut, we used the National Taxonomy of Exempt Entities (NTEE) codes to select organizations in seven fields from the 1987 and 1988 data files: opera, orchestra, ballet, theater, art museums, science museums, and "other museums." Institutions of higher education were selected by matching institutions with the *1992 Higher Education Directory*, thereby avoiding the problem of NTEE coding errors. The institutions were divided into the four categories used in Chapter Five and defined in Appendix D.

To ensure that we did not mistakenly include organizations that do not belong to a particular group (since the NTEE codes are not reliable beyond the primary field level), we included only those organizations recognized by their respective fields—either through membership in a service organization or through listing in a field-specific publication.[3] The following specific criteria were used: To be included in our sample, ballet companies had to be members of Dance/USA, opera companies members of Opera America, orchestras members of the American Symphony Orchestra League, and theaters members of the Theater Communications Group. Museums had to be listed in *The Official Museum Directory*, published annually by the American Association of Museums. Historical societies had to be listed in the *Directory of Historical Organizations in the United States and Canada*, published by the American Association for State and Local History and edited by Wheeler, and they had to be described as historical societies in the directory. (The directory includes many other types of historical organizations, such as historic preservation agencies, historic sites or parks, and historic museums.) A few unusually complex organizations, such as the Smithsonian, were excluded. Moreover, organizations that include many diverse functions, only one of which is in a field of interest to us, were dropped.

By using this approach to select organizations, we lost the randomness of the original SOI sampling procedure. As a result, we cannot conduct formal tests of statistical significance on our findings, nor can we make statistically based claims about the entire universe of nonprofit organizations in these fields. Nevertheless, we believe that the organizations we have selected are broadly representative of their fields, and that our conclusions have relevance beyond the particular organizations we are studying.

We divided museums into three categories, based on the descriptions given in *The Official Museum Directory*: art, science, and "other." Science museums fall into two general categories: natural history, and science/technology. The residual category of "other museums" is defined as museums that are not purely art or science museums, and it includes (among others) general museums, history museums, anthropology museums, cultural museums, and art/history museums. Highly specialized museums are not included.

Definition of Revenue Sources

In order to create a revenue profile for each organization, we grouped the various types of revenue reported on Form 990 into four categories, as described below. We then converted the dollar value for each revenue source into a percentage by dividing it by the organization's total revenue (defined below). Note that when we calculated average revenue shares, we took the average of the percentage values for all individual organizations, rather than first aggregating the revenues (by source) for all organizations and then calculating percentages. Our method has the advantage of weighting each organization equally, rather than allowing one or two very large organizations to swamp the results. The line numbers referred to below are the line numbers on Form 990 (see Exhibit E.1).

Earned income is the sum of "program service revenue" (line 2), and "gross profit (loss)" (line 10c). In addition, we included in earned income half of the amount reported as "membership dues and assessments" on line 3. Our reason for including half the dues figures is that, depending on the type of organization and the amount of the dues, membership dues may be considered earned (when, for example, a member receives benefits, such as access to facilities), contributed (when a member is strongly committed to the organization and wants to support it financially, without regard to personal benefit), or a combination of the two. Since we had no way of defining precisely how much of the dues should be assigned to each category, we arbitrarily divided membership dues equally between earned and contributed income.

Contributed income includes the other half of membership dues, plus "direct and indirect public support" (lines 1a and 1b), and "net income [from special fundraising events and activities]" (line 9c).

Investment income is the sum of "interest on savings and temporary cash investments" (line 4), "dividends and interest from securities" (line 5), "net rental income (loss)" (line 6c), and "other investment income (loss)" (line 7). Rental income is included with investment income because the instructions for Form 990 make it clear that this line refers to investment property. Rental income related to the organization's tax-exempt function (for example, providing low-rent housing) is reported on line 2, "program service revenue." For reasons described below, we did not include net realized gains from the sale of investments (included in line 8c).

Governmental support is simply the amount reported on line 1c, "government grants." Note that this line does not distinguish between federal and state or local support. In addition to government grants, some organizations receive tax revenues or governmental appropriations. Since there is no specific line on Form 990 to record this amount, some organizations report it on line 11 ("other revenue"). When we could independently verify it, we added the appropriate amount from "other revenue" to "government grants." Clearly, however, there are important differences between these revenue sources.

In the text, we also often refer to *private support*, which is simply the sum of contributed income and investment income. For many purposes, it makes sense to view investment income as the result of income contributed by private donors in earlier periods.

Definition of Total Revenue on Form 990

We defined *total revenue* somewhat differently than the way it is defined on line 12 of Form 990. First, we subtracted "other revenue" (line 11) from the total, since it is impossible to know what is included in this category. In a few cases, organizations reported large amounts of revenue as "other," possibly because of unusual circumstances in a particular year. We removed all organizations with "other revenue" over one-third of total revenue, since this would clearly distort their revenue profiles. On the average, "other revenue" for the remaining organizations was less than 4 percent.

We also subtracted any "gain (loss) [from the sale of assets other than inventory]" (line 8c). For most organizations, this amount primarily represents realized gains or losses from the sale of investments. We believe that including these gains distorts total revenues because they are typically paper gains that are largely a function of how actively an investment portfolio is managed. Frequent buying and selling of securities may result in large realized gains, but they are not a source of operating revenue for the organization—unless, of course, the organization is selling off assets to finance an operating deficit. Even so, it would not be appropriate to include these gains as investment income. Some organizations also use a spending rule in managing their endowments, in which case part of the endowment's total return (including realized gains) is spent as investment income. The data on Form 990 do not allow us to take such policies into account.

There is one other difficulty with the way total revenue is defined on Form 990. We are interested in measuring *operating* revenue—those funds used to finance the normal, ongoing operations of the organization. But, as defined on Form 990, total revenue is not equivalent to operating revenue. Unlike most standard financial statements for nonprofits—which, at least in one way or another, separate current revenues from capital additions—Form 990 lumps all revenues together. Every dollar that crosses the threshold is counted, no matter what its source or designated purpose. Since many nonprofit organizations receive, at least on occasion, large capital contributions or bequests, to include these amounts with regular annual contributions could significantly distort their annual revenue profiles.

We used two techniques to minimize this problem. Before describing these techniques, however, we want to emphasize that it is impossible to remove all noncurrent revenue from data reported on Form 990. Even our amended results overstate, to some (unknown) degree, the amount of contributed income. We took the following steps to minimize the effect of capital contributions:

- When possible, we averaged revenue amounts across two years, 1987 and 1988. For a few organizations, data were not available in 1988. In these cases, 1987 amounts were used. (In some cases, data in the 1987 SOI database are actually from 1986, because 1986 returns were occasionally substituted for 1987 returns when organizations that were sampled for 1987 had not yet filed a return by the time the data were entered.)

- We checked each organization's contribution figure. Organizations that qualify for tax-exempt status under either of the two public-support tests must answer a question on Schedule A of Form 990 about gifts, grants, and contributions received over the prior four years (line 15). (Colleges and universities do not have to answer this question, because they qualify as educational institutions.) Dividing this amount by four provides a rough approximation of the average level of contributions received by an organization. We compared this figure to the actual contributions reported in 1987. If an organization had an unusually large contribution figure in a given year, we used the four-year average as the amount of contributed income. "Unusually large" is defined as follows: total contributions for the current year must be more than 50 percent higher than the average of the prior four years, *and* the organization must have a surplus (as defined on line 18 of Form 990) of more than 50 percent of total expenditures. The second condition helps ensure that we identify only truly noncurrent contributions. The 50 percent cutoff points are arbitrary but, we believe, quite conservative: only the most obvious spikes in the data are adjusted.

In summary, we defined total revenue as the amount reported on line 12 of Form 990, less "other revenue" (line 11), and less "realized gains (losses)" (line 8c). In addition, we excluded large noncurrent contributions if they could be identified on the basis of the information reported on Schedule A of Form 990.

Notes

1. An SOI study was also conducted in 1975, but our efforts to locate these data were fruitless.
2. The SOI Division used the sampling methodology described in the text in all years except 1986. In that year, the number of small organizations sampled was increased substantially, but since the total sample size remained the same (for budgetary reasons), about half of the organizations above the $10 million threshold were dropped.
3. Sarnoff (1991), Perry (1991), American Symphony Orchestra League (1993), Samuels (1992), American Association of Museums (1990), and Wheeler (1990).

Exhibit E.1. IRS Form 990.

Form **990**	**Return of Organization Exempt From Income Tax**	OMB No. 1545-0047

Form **990**

Department of the Treasury
Internal Revenue Service

Return of Organization Exempt From Income Tax
Under section 501(c) (except black lung benefit trust or private foundation)
of the Internal Revenue Code or section 4947(a)(1) trust
Note: You may be required to use a copy of this return to satisfy state reporting requirements. See instruction D.

OMB No. 1545-0047

19**87**

For the calendar year 1987, or fiscal year beginning _____ , 1987, and ending _____ , 19 ____

Use IRS label. Otherwise, please print or type.	Name of organization	**A** Employer identification number (see instruction L)
	Address (number and street)	**B** State registration number (see instruction D)
	City or town, state, and ZIP code	**C** Section 4947(a)(1) trusts filing this form in lieu of Form 1041, check here ▶ ☐ (see instruction C10)

D Check type of organization—Exempt under section ▶ ☐ 501(c) ( ) (insert number), OR ▶ ☐ section 4947(a)(1) trust
E Accounting method: ☐ Cash ☐ Accrual ☐ Other (specify) ▶
| Check here if application for exemption is pending . . ▶ ☐ |

F Is this a group return (see instruction J) filed for affiliates? . . . . . ☐ Yes ☐ No
If "Yes," enter the number of affiliates for which this return is filed _____
Is this a separate return filed by a group affiliate? . . . . ☐ Yes ☐ No

G If "Yes" to either, give four-digit group exemption number (GEN) ▶

H ☐ Check here if your gross receipts are normally not more than $25,000 (see instruction B11). You do not have to file a completed return with IRS but should file a return without financial data if you were mailed a Form 990 Package (see instruction A). Some states may require a completed return.

I ☐ Check here if gross receipts are normally more than $25,000 and line 12 is $25,000 or less. Complete Parts I (except lines 13-15), III, IV, VI, and VII and only the indicated items in Parts II and V (see instruction I). If line 12 is more than $25,000, complete the entire return.

501(c)(3) organizations and 4947(a)(1) trusts must also complete and attach Schedule A (Form 990). (See instructions.)

Part I	Statement of Support, Revenue, and Expenses and Changes in Fund Balances	(A) Total	(B) Unrestricted/ Expendable	(C) Restricted/ Nonexpendable
			These columns are optional— see instructions	

	Support and Revenue				
1	Contributions, gifts, grants, and similar amounts received:				
a	Direct public support				
b	Indirect public support				
c	Government grants				
d	Total (add lines 1a through 1c) (attach schedule—see instructions). .				
2	Program service revenue (from Part IV, line f).				
3	Membership dues and assessments				
4	Interest on savings and temporary cash investments.				
5	Dividends and interest from securities				
6a	Gross rents				
b	Minus: rental expenses				
c	Net rental income (loss).				
7	Other investment income (Describe ▶)				
8a	Gross amount from sale of assets other than inventory . (Securities / Other)				
b	Minus: cost or other basis and sales expenses . .				
c	Gain (loss) (attach schedule) . .				
9	Special fundraising events and activities (**attach schedule**—see instructions):				
a	Gross revenue (not including $_____ of contributions reported on line 1a).				
b	Minus: direct expenses				
c	Net income (line 9a minus line 9b) . . .				
10a	Gross sales minus returns and allowances . . .				
b	Minus: cost of goods sold (attach schedule) . .				
c	Gross profit (loss)				
11	Other revenue (from Part IV, line g).				
12	Total revenue (add lines 1d, 2, 3, 4, 5, 6c, 7, 8c, 9c, 10c, and 11) . .				

	Expenses				
13	Program services (from line 44, column (B)) (see instructions) . .				
14	Management and general (from line 44, column (C)) (see instructions)				
15	Fundraising (from line 44, column (D)) (see instructions)				
16	Payments to affiliates (attach schedule—see instructions) . . .				
17	Total expenses (add lines 16 and 44, column (A))				

	Fund Balances				
18	Excess (deficit) for the year (subtract line 17 from line 12) . . .				
19	Fund balances or net worth at beginning of year (from line 74, column (A)) .				
20	Other changes in fund balances or net worth (attach explanation) .				
21	Fund balances or net worth at end of year (add lines 18, 19, and 20) .				

For Paperwork Reduction Act Notice, see page 1 of the instructions.   Form **990** (1987)

Form 990 (1987)   Page **2**

Part II	**Statement of Functional Expenses**	All organizations must complete column (A). Columns (B), (C), and (D) are required for most sections 501(c)(3) and (c)(4) organizations and 4947(a)(1) trusts but optional for others. (See instructions.)		
	Do not include amounts reported on lines 6b, 8b, 9b, 10b, or 16 of Part I.	**(A)** Total	**(B)** Program services	**(C)** Management and general	**(D)** Fundraising
22	Grants and allocations (attach schedule)				
23	Specific assistance to individuals				
24	Benefits paid to or for members.				
25	Compensation of officers, directors, etc.. . . .				
26	Other salaries and wages				
27	Pension plan contributions				
28	Other employee benefits				
29	Payroll taxes				
30	Professional fundraising fees				
31	Accounting fees.				
32	Legal fees				
33	Supplies				
34	Telephone				
35	Postage and shipping				
36	Occupancy				
37	Equipment rental and maintenance				
38	Printing and publications				
39	Travel.				
40	Conferences, conventions, and meetings . . .				
41	Interest				
42	Depreciation, depletion, etc. (attach schedule) . .				
43	Other expenses (itemize): **a** _____				
b	_____				
c	_____				
d	_____				
e	_____				
f	_____				
44	Total functional expenses (add lines 22 through 43) Organizations completing columns B-D, carry these totals to lines 13-15.				

Part III	**Statement of Program Services Rendered**

List each program service title on lines a through d; for each, identify the service output(s) or product(s), and report the quantity provided. Enter the total expenses attributable to each program service and the amount of grants and allocations included in that total. (See instructions for Part III.) | Expenses (Optional for some organizations—see instructions) |

a _____

_____

_____

_____ (Grants and allocations $)

b _____

_____

_____

_____ (Grants and allocations $)

c _____

_____

_____

_____ (Grants and allocations $)

d _____

_____

_____

_____ (Grants and allocations $)

e Other program service activities (attach schedule) . . . . . .   (Grants and allocations $)

f Total (add lines a through e) (should equal line 44, column (B)) . . . .

Exhibit E.1. IRS Form 990, Cont'd.

Form 990 (1987)   Page **3**

Part IV Program Service Revenue and Other Revenue (State nature.)	Program service revenue	Other revenue
a Fees from government agencies		
b		
c		
d		
e		
f Total program service revenue (enter here and on line 2)		
g Total other revenue (enter here and on line 11)		

Part V Balance Sheets   If line 12 or Column (B) of line 59 is more than $25,000, complete the entire balance sheet. If line 12, Part I, and Column (B) of line 59 are $25,000 or less, you may complete only lines 59, 66, 74, and 75. See instructions.

		(A) Beginning of year	End of year		
Note: Columns (C) and (D) are optional. *Columns (A) and (B) must be completed to the extent applicable. Where required, attached schedules should be for end-of-year amounts only.*			**(B)** Total	**(C)** Unrestricted/ Expendable	**(D)** Restricted/ Nonexpendable
	Assets				
45	Cash—noninterest-bearing				
46	Savings and temporary cash investments				
47	Accounts receivable ▶ _____ minus allowance for doubtful accounts ▶_____ .				
48	Pledges receivable ▶ _____ minus allowance for doubtful accounts ▶_____ .				
49	Grants receivable				
50	Receivables due from officers, directors, trustees, and key employees (attach schedule)				
51	Other notes and loans receivable ▶ _____ minus allowance for doubtful accounts ▶_____ .				
52	Inventories for sale or use				
53	Prepaid expenses and deferred charges				
54	Investments—securities (attach schedule)				
55	Investments—land, buildings and equipment: basis ▶ _____ minus accumulated depreciation ▶_____ (attach schedule) .				
56	Investments—other (attach schedule)				
57	Land, buildings and equipment: basis ▶ _____ minus accumulated depreciation ▶_____ (attach schedule) .				
58	Other assets ▶ _____ .				
59	Total assets (add lines 45 through 58)				
	Liabilities				
60	Accounts payable and accrued expenses				
61	Grants payable				
62	Support and revenue designated for future periods (attach schedule) .				
63	Loans from officers, directors, trustees, and key employees (attach schedule)				
64	Mortgages and other notes payable (attach schedule) . . .				
65	Other liabilities ▶_____				
66	Total liabilities (add lines 60 through 65)				
	Fund Balances or Net Worth				
	Organizations that use fund accounting, check here ▶ ☐ and complete lines 67 through 70 and lines 74 and 75.				
67a	Current unrestricted fund				
b	Current restricted fund				
68	Land, buildings and equipment fund				
69	Endowment fund				
70	Other funds (Describe ▶ _____) .				
	Organizations that do not use fund accounting, check here ▶ ☐ and complete lines 71 through 75.				
71	Capital stock or trust principal				
72	Paid-in or capital surplus				
73	Retained earnings or accumulated income				
74	Total fund balances or net worth (see instructions)				
75	Total liabilities and fund balances/net worth (see instructions) . .				

Form 990 (1987)   Page **4**

Part VI   List of Officers, Directors, and Trustees (List each one whether compensated or not. See instructions.)

(A) Name and address	(B) Title and average hours per week devoted to position	(C) Compensation (if any)	(D) Contributions to employee benefit plans	(E) Expense account and other allowances
--				
--				
--				
--				
--				

Part VII   Other Information

		Yes	No

76 Has the organization engaged in any activities not previously reported to the Internal Revenue Service? . . . . .
If "Yes," attach a detailed description of the activities.

77 Have any changes been made in the organizing or governing documents, but not reported to IRS? . . . .
If "Yes," attach a conformed copy of the changes.

78 *If the organization had income from business activities, such as those reported on lines 2, 9, and 10 (among others), but NOT reported on Form 990-T, attach a statement explaining your reason for not reporting the income on Form 990-T.*

   a Did the organization have unrelated business gross income of $1,000 or more during the year covered by this return?

   b If "Yes," have you filed a tax return on Form 990-T, Exempt Organization Business Income Tax Return, for this year?

79 Was there a liquidation, dissolution, termination, or substantial contraction during the year? (See instructions.) . . .
If "Yes," attach a statement as described in the instructions.

80 Is the organization related (other than by association with a statewide or nationwide organization) through common membership, governing bodies, trustees, officers, etc., to any other exempt or nonexempt organization? (See instructions.) .
If "Yes," enter the name of the organization ▶ --
--- and check whether it is ☐ exempt **OR** ☐ nonexempt.

81 a Enter amount of political expenditures, direct or indirect, as described in the instructions . . ▶

   b Did you file Form 1120-POL, U.S. Income Tax Return for Certain Political Organizations, for this year? . . . . .

82 Did your organization receive donated services or the use of materials, equipment, or facilities at no charge or at substantially less than fair rental value? . . . .
If "Yes," you may indicate the value of these items here. Do not include this amount as support
in Part I or as an expense in Part II. See instructions for reporting in Part III . . . . . . ▶

83 *Section 501(c)(5) or (6) organizations.*—Did the organization spend any amounts in attempts to influence public opinion about legislative matters or referendums? (See instructions and Regulations section 1.162-20(c).) . . . . .
If "Yes," enter the total amount spent for this purpose . . . .

84 *Section 501(c)(7) organizations.*—Enter: **a** Initiation fees and capital contributions included on line 12 .

   b Gross receipts, included in line 12, for public use of club facilities (See instructions.) . . . . . .

   c Does the club's governing instrument or any written policy statement provide for discrimination against any person because of race, color, or religion? (See instructions.) . . . .

85 *Section 501(c)(12) organizations.*—Enter amount of:

   a Gross income received from members or shareholders . . . .

   b Gross income received from other sources (do not net amounts due or paid to other sources against amounts due or received from them) . . . .

86 *Public interest law firms.*—Attach information described in the instructions.

87 List the states with which a copy of this return is filed ▶ --

88 During this tax year did you maintain any part of your accounting/tax records on a computerized system? . . . .

89 The books are in care of ▶ ------------------------------- Telephone no. ▶ -------------------
Located at ▶

90 *Section 4947(a)(1) trusts filing Form 990 in lieu of Form 1041.*—Enter the amount of tax-exempt interest received or accrued during the tax year. . . . . ▶

Please Sign Here

Under penalties of perjury, I declare that I have examined this return, including accompanying schedules and statements, and to the best of my knowledge and belief, it is true, correct, and complete. Declaration of preparer (other than officer) is based on all information of which preparer has any knowledge.

▶ Signature of officer	Date	▶ Title	

Paid Preparer's Use Only

Preparer's signature ▶	Date	Check if self-employed ▶ ☐
Firm's name (or yours, if self-employed) and address ▶	ZIP code	

★U.S.GPO 1987-0-183-070

Exhibit E.1.   IRS Form 990, Cont'd.

SCHEDULE A (Form 990) Department of the Treasury Internal Revenue Service	**Organization Exempt Under 501(c)(3)** (Except Private Foundation), 501(e), 501(f), 501(k), or Section 4947(a)(1) Trust Supplementary Information ▶ Attach to Form 990.	OMB No. 1545-0047 **1987**

Name	Employer identification number

Part I   Compensation of Five Highest Paid Employees
Other Than Officers, Directors, and Trustees (See specific instructions.)

Name and address of employees paid more than $30,000	Title and average hours per week devoted to position	Compensation	Contributions to employee benefit plans	Expense account and other allowances
-------------------------------				

Total number of other employees paid over $30,000 . . . . ▶

Part II   Compensation of Five Highest Paid Persons for Professional Services
(See specific instructions.)

Name and address of persons paid more than $30,000	Type of service	Compensation
---		

Total number of others receiving over $30,000 for professional services . . . . ▶

Part III   Statements About Activities

		Yes (1)	No (2)
1	During the year, have you attempted to influence national, state, or local legislation, including any attempt to influence public opinion on a legislative matter or referendum? **1**		
	If "Yes," enter the total expenses paid or incurred in connection with the legislative activities $ _____		
	Complete Part VI of this form for organizations that made an election under section 501(h) on Form 5768 or other statement. For other organizations checking "Yes," attach a statement giving a detailed description of the legislative activities and a classified schedule of the expenses paid or incurred.		
2	During the year, have you, either directly or indirectly, engaged in any of the following acts with a trustee, director, principal officer or creator of your organization, or any organization or corporation with which such person is affiliated as an officer, director, trustee, majority owner, or principal beneficiary:		
a	Sale, exchange, or leasing of property? **2a**		
b	Lending of money or other extension of credit? **2b**		
c	Furnishing of goods, services, or facilities? **2c**		
d	Payment of compensation (or payment or reimbursement of expenses if more than $1,000)? **2d**		
e	Transfer of any part of your income or assets? **2e**		
	If the answer to any question is "Yes," attach a detailed statement explaining the transactions.		
3	Do you make grants for scholarships, fellowships, student loans, etc.? **3**		
4	Attach a statement explaining how you determine that individuals or organizations receiving disbursements from you in furtherance of your charitable programs qualify to receive payments. (See specific instructions.)		

For Paperwork Reduction Act Notice, see page 1 of the separate instructions to this form.   Schedule A (Form 990) 1987

Schedule A (Form 990) 1987   Page **2**

Part IV	**Reason for Non-Private Foundation Status (See instructions for definitions.)**

The organization is not a private foundation because it is (check applicable box; please check only **ONE** box):

5 ☐ 1 A church, convention of churches, or association of churches. Section 170(b)(1)(A)(i).

6 ☐ 2 A school. Section 170(b)(1)(A)(ii). (Also complete Part V, page 3.)

7 ☐ 3 A hospital or a cooperative hospital service organization. Section 170(b)(1)(A)(iii).

8 ☐ 4 A Federal, state or local government or governmental unit. Section 170(b)(1)(A)(v).

9 ☐ 5 A medical research organization operated in conjunction with a hospital. Section 170(b)(1)(A)(iii). **Enter name, city, and state of hospital ▶** ....

10 ☐ 6 An organization operated for the benefit of a college or university owned or operated by a governmental unit. Section 170(b)(1)(A)(iv). (Also complete Support Schedule.)

11 ☐ 7 An organization that normally receives a substantial part of its support from a governmental unit or from the general public. Section 170(b)(1)(A)(vi). (Also complete Support Schedule.)

12 ☐ 8 An organization that normally receives: (a) no more than 1/3 of its support from gross investment income and unrelated business taxable income (less section 511 tax) from businesses acquired by the organization after June 30, 1975, and (b) more than 1/3 of its support from contributions, membership fees, and gross receipts from activities related to its charitable, etc., functions—subject to certain exceptions. See section 509(a)(2). (Also complete Support Schedule.)

13 ☐ 9 An organization that is not controlled by any disqualified persons (other than foundation managers) and supports organizations described in (1) boxes 5 through 12 above or (2) section 501(c)(4), (5), or (6) if they meet the test of section 509(a)(2). See section 509(a)(3).

Provide the following information about the supported organizations. (See instructions for Part IV, box 13.)

(a) Name of supported organizations	**(b)** Box number from above

14 ☐ 0 An organization organized and operated to test for public safety. Section 509(a)(4). (See specific instructions.)

Support Schedule (Complete only if you checked box 10, 11, or 12 above.) Use cash method of accounting.

Calendar year (or fiscal year beginning in) ▶	**(a)** 1986	**(b)** 1985	**(c)** 1984	**(d)** 1983	**(e)** Total
15 Gifts, grants, and contributions received. (Do not include unusual grants. See line 28.)					
16 Membership fees received					
17 Gross receipts from admissions, merchandise sold or services performed, or furnishing of facilities in any activity that is not a business unrelated to the organization's charitable, etc., purpose					
18 Gross income from interest, dividends, amounts received from payments on securities loans (section 512(a)(5)), rents, royalties, and unrelated business taxable income (less section 511 taxes) from businesses acquired by the organization after June 30, 1975					
19 Net income from unrelated business activities not included in line 18 . .					
20 Tax revenues levied for your benefit and either paid to you or expended on your behalf . . .					
21 The value of services or facilities furnished to you by a governmental unit without charge. Do not include the value of services or facilities generally furnished to the public without charge					
22 Other income. Attach schedule. Do not include gain (or loss) from sale of capital assets .					
23 Total of lines 15 through 22 . . .					
24 Line 23 minus line 17					
25 Enter 1% of line 23					////////

26 Organizations described in box 10 or 11:
   a Enter 2% of amount in column (e), line 24. . . . .
   b Attach a list (not open to public inspection) showing the name of and amount contributed by each person (other than a governmental unit or publicly supported organization) whose total gifts for 1983 through 1986 exceeded the amount shown in 26a. Enter the sum of all excess amounts here _____

(Continued on page 3)

Exhibit E.1.   IRS Form 990, Cont'd.

Part IV   Support Schedule (continued)(Complete only if you checked box 10, 11, or 12 on page 2.)

27   Organizations described in box 12, page 2:
  a Attach a list for amounts shown on lines 15, 16, and 17, showing the name of, and total amounts received in each year from, each "disqualified person," and enter the sum of such amounts for each year:

     (1986)............................(1985)...........................(1984)............................(1983)............................

  b Attach a list showing, for 1983 through 1986, the name and amount included in line 17 for each person (other than "disqualified persons") from whom the organization received more, during that year, than the larger of: the amount on line 25 for the year or $5,000. Include organizations described in boxes 5 through 11 as well as individuals. Enter the sum of these excess amounts for each year:
     (1986)   (1985)   (1984)   (1983)

28   For an organization described in box 10, 11, or 12, page 2, that received any unusual grants during 1983 through 1986, attach a list (not open to public inspection) for each year showing the name of the contributor, the date and amount of the grant, and a brief description of the nature of the grant. Do not include these grants in line 15 above. (See specific instructions.)

Part V   Private School Questionnaire
          To Be Completed ONLY by Schools That Checked Box 6 in Part IV

		Yes (1)	No (2)
29	Do you have a racially nondiscriminatory policy toward students by statement in your charter, bylaws, other governing instrument, or in a resolution of your governing body? **29**		
30	Do you include a statement of your racially nondiscriminatory policy toward students in all your brochures, catalogues, and other written communications with the public dealing with student admissions, programs, and scholarships? **30**		
31	Have you publicized your racially nondiscriminatory policy by newspaper or broadcast media during the period of solicitation for students or during the registration period if you have no solicitation program, in a way that makes the policy known to all parts of the general community you serve? **31**		
	If "Yes," please describe; if "No," please explain. (If you need more space, attach a separate statement.)		
32	Do you maintain the following:		
a	Records indicating the racial composition of the student body, faculty, and administrative staff? **32a**		
b	Records documenting that scholarships and other financial assistance are awarded on a racially nondiscriminatory basis? **32b**		
c	Copies of all catalogues, brochures, announcements, and other written communications to the public dealing with student admissions, programs, and scholarships? **32c**		
d	Copies of all material used by you or on your behalf to solicit contributions? **32d**		
	If you answered "No" to any of the above, please explain. (If you need more space, attach a separate statement.)		
33	Do you discriminate by race in any way with respect to:		
a	Students' rights or privileges? **33a**		
b	Admissions policies? **33b**		
c	Employment of faculty or administrative staff? **33c**		
d	Scholarships or other financial assistance? (See instructions.) **33d**		
e	Educational policies? **33e**		
f	Use of facilities? **33f**		
g	Athletic programs? **33g**		
h	Other extracurricular activities? **33h**		
	If you answered "Yes" to any of the above, please explain. (If you need more space, attach a separate statement.)		
34a	Do you receive any financial aid or assistance from a governmental agency? **34a**		
b	Has your right to such aid ever been revoked or suspended? **34b**		
	If you answered "Yes" to either 34a or b, please explain using an attached separate statement.		
35	Do you certify that you have complied with the applicable requirements of sections 4.01 through 4.05 of Rev. Proc. 75-50, 1975-2 C.B. 587, covering racial nondiscrimination? If "No," attach an explanation. (See instructions for Part V.) . **35**		

Schedule A (Form 990) 1987

Part VI Lobbying Expenditures by Public Charities (see instructions)
(To be completed ONLY by an eligible organization that filed Form 5768)

Check here ▶ **a** ☐ If the organization belongs to an affiliated group. (see instructions)
Check here ▶ **b** ☐ If you checked **a** and "limited control" provisions apply. (see instructions)

Limits on Lobbying Expenses	(a) Affiliated group totals	(b) To be completed for ALL electing organizations
36 Total (grassroots) lobbying expenses to influence public opinion		
37 Total lobbying expenses to influence a legislative body		
38 Total lobbying expenses (add lines 36 and 37)		
39 Other exempt purpose expenses (see Part VI instructions)		
40 Total exempt purpose expenses (add lines 38 and 39) (see instructions).		

41 Lobbying nontaxable amount. Enter the smaller of $1,000,000 or the amount determined under the following table—

If the amount on line 40 is—	**The lobbying nontaxable amount is—**
Not over $500,000	20% of the amount on line 40 . . . .
Over $500,000 but not over $1,000,000 . . .	$100,000 plus 15% of the excess over $500,000 . .
Over $1,000,000 but not over $1,500,000 . . .	$175,000 plus 10% of the excess over $1,000,000 . . .
Over $1,500,000	$225,000 plus 5% of the excess over $1,500,000 . .

42 Grassroots nontaxable amount (enter 25% of line 41) . . . .

(Complete lines 43 and 44. File Form 4720 if either line 36 exceeds line 42 or line 38 exceeds line 41.)

43 Excess of line 36 over line 42 . . . .

44 Excess of line 38 over line 41 . . . .

4-Year Averaging Period Under Section 501(h)
(Some organizations that made a section 501(h) election do not have to complete all of the five columns below. See the instructions for lines 45-50 for details.)

Lobbying Expenses During 4-Year Averaging Period

Calendar year (or fiscal year beginning in) ▶	(a) 1987	(b) 1986	(c) 1985	(d) 1984	(e) Total
45 Lobbying nontaxable amount (see instructions)					
46 Lobbying ceiling amount (150% of line 45(e))					
47 Total lobbying expenses (see instructions)					
48 Grassroots nontaxable amount (see instructions)					
49 Grassroots ceiling amount (150% of line 48(e))					
50 Grassroots lobbying expenses (see instructions)					

★U.S.GPO:1987-0-183-072

APPENDIX F

The Arts/Culture
Institutional Database

As described at the beginning of Chapter Ten, the arts/culture institutional database is constructed from data we collected ourselves, directly from individual organizations. This appendix describes how we collected and assembled the data.

Availability of Time-Series Data

We attempted to locate other sources of time-series data, but these attempts were all unsuccessful. Our first thought was to use the SOI data described in Appendix E as a starting point. Although these data extend back only to 1982, we believed it might be possible to supplement them by obtaining copies of Form 990 from earlier years. However, we were informed by the IRS that it destroys Form 990s after six years. In any case, we learned that Form 990 had a significantly different format before the 1980s, making it difficult to compare early returns with more recent data.

Since many state or local governments also require tax-exempt organizations to file returns (either copies of Form 990 or audited financial statements), we tried to obtain time-series data through state or city agencies. In New York City, we contacted the Department of Community Affairs (DCA) and the New York State Council for the Arts (NYSCA). We discovered that DCA keeps copies of audited statements, but only as far back as the late 1970s. NYSCA, which collects Form 990s and audited statements, referred us to the New York State Archives, where we learned that the files submitted by NYSCA are inconsistent, and that archive files prior to the early 1970s have been destroyed. We also contacted the attorney general's office in Connecticut but discovered that all returns are thrown out after seven years. (We believe that many other states also discard old returns.)

We relate this history only to underscore the point that it is virtually impossible to find consistent time-series data that extend farther back than the late 1970s or the early 1980s. In the end, we concluded that the only alternative was to assemble the data ourselves, by contacting individual organizations and asking them to send us copies of their audited financial statements.

To make the task manageable, we asked each organization to send statements for five years: 1972, 1977, 1982, 1987, and 1992. (Since most organizations' fiscal years do not correspond to calendar years, we requested statements for the fiscal year closest to each calendar year. In some cases, organizations were not able to supply statements for the precise year we wanted, and so we asked them to substitute a neighboring year.) Although it clearly would have been preferable to have data for every year (because any one of the years selected might be an unusual one for a particular organization), collecting and entering twenty years of data for each organization was beyond the scope of this project.[1]

Criteria for Selecting Organizations

Because we initially planned to use SOI data, we began with the list of arts/culture institutions we had selected from the SOI database. When we decided to collect audited financial statements instead, we first examined the files of The Andrew W. Mellon Foundation because organizations that receive grants from the foundation are required to submit copies of their financial statements. Out of this process emerged a list of five to ten institutions in each of the seven arts/culture fields: opera, orchestra, ballet, theater, art museums, science museums, and historical societies.

We then contacted each organization and requested additional statements for the years we were missing. A number of organizations were dropped from our original list, either because they were not able to supply statements or because they did not respond to our request. In one case (the Ohio Historical Society), reports from early years were not comparable with more recent reports. In the end, we obtained 157 sets of audited financial statements from thirty-two organizations, as shown in Appendix G, Table G.10-1. (Three sets of statements are missing: 1972 and 1977 from the San Francisco Opera, and 1972 from the Pittsburgh Symphony.)

It is important to note that the approach we used to construct our time-series data means that our sample contains mostly large and (as even a cursory inspection of the list reveals) well-known organizations in each field. At the very least, all the organizations in our data set have not only existed but have also compiled audited financial statements since 1972.

Interpreting Financial Statements

Once we obtained the statements, the task of interpreting them consistently presented another challenge. There are two related problems: first, comparing statements from year to year within an individual organization; and, second, comparing statements across organizations. These problems are exacerbated by the intricacies of fund accounting, a system of accounting in which separate funds are used to account for various restrictions placed on certain types of revenue.

Over the course of twenty years, most organizations experience significant changes in their accounting procedures and reporting formats, often corresponding to changes in key personnel. New standards are also established from time to time by the accounting profession (such as the publication of a new "statement of position" by the Financial Accounting Standards Board, in 1978). Changes may occur in the accounting method used (cash, accrual, or modified accrual), the method of valuing physical assets and investments (historical cost, market value, or lower-of-cost-or-market), the procedures used to record investment income (and whether or not a spending rule is used), the use of depreciation (and the method of depreciation used), the number of separate funds, the means of recording transfers between funds, the definitions of revenue and expense categories (and at what level to aggregate them), the conventions used to net certain costs against revenues, the method of recording capital additions and grants received for future periods, and so on.

In addition, organizations may merge with other institutions or spin off separate entities. For example, an organization may have a research division that later becomes a separate entity, or several similar organizations may decide to merge their endowment funds into one large fund, so that they can take advantage of economies of scale, a decision which may be reversed five years later.

It is also possible for an organization to be entirely consistent in its reporting standards but the standards may be so idiosyncratic that comparison with the records of other organizations is difficult. The Massachusetts Historical Society is a case in point. Its audited financial statements are very thorough and consistent from year to year, but they are also so unlike the statements of any other organization that they are almost incomprehensible to an outsider.

Definitions of Categories

These difficulties notwithstanding, we examined each set of audited financial statements and attempted to translate the raw data into a consistent set of categories that could be compared across time periods and organizations.

Each category is described below, along with any important assumptions and conventions that were used in interpreting the data.

Earned income is any revenue received in exchange for providing a good or a service. Examples of earned income include admission fees (typical for museums and historical societies), ticket sales (usually the largest item for performing arts organizations), tuition (for organizations with schools or training programs), sales of any type (including receipts for programs, recordings, and books), and net revenue from museum shops, cafeterias, and concession stands (the latter are often lumped together in a category called *auxiliary activities*). Rental income was included if it was clear from the context that the income was not from properties held as investments (in which case it was included with investment income).

Note that we define income from auxiliary activities and rental income as net income—that is, we subtract the cost of operating the activity from its gross revenues. Organizations follow different conventions for reporting this type of revenue: some report net revenue in the revenue portion of their financial statements; others report gross revenues and then show corresponding expenses under the expense section of their reports. For organizations with large amounts of auxiliary income, the choice of which format to use can make an enormous difference. In 1992, for example, the Metropolitan Museum of Art reported total revenues of $172 million. Included in this figure are gross revenues of $93 million from the museum's auxiliary activities. Netting out the $94 million of corresponding expenses (in this case, the auxiliary activities operated at a loss) reduces total revenues to $78 million.

Also included in earned income is half of membership dues, consistent with the definition of earned income we used in the SOI database (see Appendix E). Our reasoning here is the same. Members who pay dues generally receive some direct benefit, such as special announcements of coming events, and preferred access to them. But, in almost all situations, some component of dues also represents a contribution to the organization, over and above the value that generally would be assigned to the direct benefits received. Thus we arbitrarily assigned half of membership dues to earned income and half to private contributions. Membership dues were occasionally not reported as a separate category (for example, they were often included with admissions). In those cases, we included 100 percent of dues with earned income. We adopted this approach for the Philadelphia Museum of Art, the American Museum of Natural History, and the New-York Historical Society.

One other type of revenue that falls into the gray area is the revenue that museums and historical societies receive for deaccessioning objects in their collections. Here, we made judgments on a case-by-case basis. If a museum appeared to have a fairly regular stream of income from this source, we included it with earned income. If a particular deaccession seemed to be out of the ordinary—a large, one-time event—we considered it "noncurrent revenue" (discussed below).

Contributed income includes all private contributions, donations, gifts, bequests, and grants used for operating purposes. Grants from private foundations and corporations are also included, as are proceeds from special fundraising events. In an ideal world, it would be useful to distinguish between contributions from individuals and contributions from corporations and foundations. However, report formats are too inconsistent for this approach to be feasible. (Many organizations lump all private support into a single category in their financial statements.)

When possible, we netted out fundraising expenses or the cost of special fundraisers. Again, different reporting conventions in this area make consistency difficult to achieve. As explained in the discussion of earned income, half of membership dues was also counted as private contributions.

Where possible, we excluded all noncurrent revenues from contributed income.[2] By *noncurrent revenues* we mean contributions to an endowment, a building program, or any capital fundraising campaign. In addition, the income from any one-time, unusual event, which clearly was not part of current operations, was assigned to this category. Examples include the sale of fixed assets or unusual sales of art objects.

Investment income includes all interest and dividends reported in the financial statement. It does not, however, include realized or unrealized gains from the sale of investments. We excluded these amounts for the same reasons we left them out in the SOI database: they are usually paper gains, largely a function of how actively an investment portfolio is managed, rather than a reflection of normal operating revenue.

Our definition of investment income appears straightforward, but it was not always easy to apply. The main difficulty is the many different ways organizations report investment income. For example, some report all interest and dividends earned by an endowment fund and then transfer portions of it to other funds. Others report all interest and dividends in the operating fund, regardless of the fund in which they were earned. Financial statements of organizations that use a spending rule to guide their spending of endowment earnings are particularly difficult to interpret consistently. Organizations that use a spending rule often report simply the amount of investment income spent, without specifying whether that amount includes some portion of realized gains or whether it is actually less than total dividends and interest earned. In light of these complexities, we tried to apply as simple a rule as possible, which was to enter total dividends and interest earned, regardless of the fund in which it was earned and regardless of whether the organization used a spending rule.

Governmental support is any revenue received from federal, state, or local sources. We were unable to distinguish between federal support—usually grants from the National Endowment for the Arts (NEA)—and state or local support (such as appropriations from state or city governments, or grants from state arts councils), although it clearly would have been preferable to do so.

The major difficulty we encountered with this category is that some organizations do not report governmental support as a separate category in their financial statements. For example, organizations sometimes report total revenue received in the form of grants, but this sum might include both foundation and governmental grants. In some cases, we knew from other sources that the organizations had received regular NEA grants, yet we could not identify any governmental support on their financial statements (the Boston Ballet, for example). Occasionally, we were able to deduce information about governmental grants from the notes to the financial statements or from the text of annual reports. Any organization that we thought had received governmental support, but where governmental support could not be identified, was assigned the code *na* (data not available) in the database.

Total revenue is the sum of the four revenue categories just defined. Total revenue thus does not directly correspond to total revenue reported in the financial statements, for two reasons. First, as explained above, total revenue excludes realized and unrealized gains on investments, as well as revenues from auxiliary activities that have not been netted against expenses. Second, it does not include "other revenue"—any revenue reported on a financial statement that we could not identify.

Total expenditures are defined as total operating expenses. The figure we use for this category may also differ slightly from the amounts reported on financial statements, since we deducted any expenses that were netted against revenues. In some cases, we also subtracted expenses for large, one-time purchases (for example, the purchase of an unusually valuable work of art).

Notes

1. Collecting annual data is practical (indeed, essential) in conducting detailed case studies of individual organizations. Our colleagues at The Andrew W. Mellon Foundation, Jed Bergman and Kevin Guthrie, are currently studying several nonprofit institutions using this approach. Grønbjerg (1993) found that there was considerable year-to-year "turbulence" in her data for social service organizations in Chicago.

2. We could often identify the nature of the revenue by the fund in which it was recorded (for example, operating fund versus endowment fund). However, the following organizations did not make any distinction between current and noncurrent revenues in their financial statements:

Massachusetts Historical Society (all five years), Virginia Historical Society (all five years), Baltimore Museum of Art (1982 and 1987), Toledo Museum of Art (1972), and Lyric Opera of Chicago (1977). In other cases, some noncurrent revenues could be deduced, but we could not be certain that we had identified all noncurrent revenues.

APPENDIX G

Additional Tables

Table G.1-1. Components of the Charitable Nonprofit Universe, 1991.

Primary Field	Independent Organizations			Subordinate Organizations[a]			Total
	Positive Filers	Nonfilers	Total	Positive Filers	Nonfilers	Total	Total
Private foundations							
Grantmaking	32,759	3,592	36,351	0	0	0	36,351
Operating	1,624	256	1,880	1	0	1	1,881
Lapsed public charities	4,960	3,941	8,901	3	1	4	8,905
Total private foundations	39,343	7,789	47,132	4	1	5	47,137
Public charities							
Primary fields							
Arts/culture (A)	12,442	19,890	32,332	352	7,344	7,696	40,028
Education (B)	13,985	17,841	31,826	1,508	24,129	25,637	57,463
Conservation/environment (C)	1,618	2,791	4,409	23	1,100	1,123	5,532
Animal services (D)	1,677	1,826	3,503	10	4,696	4,706	8,209
Health (E,F,G,H)	18,316	10,539	28,855	899	3,885	4,784	33,639
Public protection (I)	1,857	1,870	3,727	20	43	63	3,790
Employment (J)	1,960	1,076	3,036	53	322	375	3,411
Food/agriculture (K)	1,262	1,217	2,479	79	105	184	2,663
Housing (L)	5,129	1,891	7,020	277	259	536	7,556
Disaster relief (M)	1,209	1,754	2,963	16	1,611	1,627	4,590
Recreation/leisure (N)	5,762	7,820	13,582	844	4,674	5,518	19,100
Youth development (O)	2,514	1,832	4,346	1,229	9,315	10,544	14,890
Human services (P)	18,192	10,507	28,699	534	4,049	4,583	33,282
International/foreign (Q)	913	1,202	2,115	77	644	721	2,836

Civil rights (R)	641	842	1,483	66	356	422	1,905
Community improvement (S)	7,619	5,853	13,472	236	3,537	3,773	17,245
Philanthropy (T)	2,109	2,079	4,188	23	70	93	4,281
Science/technology (U)	1,007	1,114	2,121	118	1,908	2,026	4,147
Social science (V)	473	313	786	1	40	41	827
Public affairs (W)	1,011	1,347	2,358	79	4,242	4,321	6,679
Religion (X)	4,222	8,006	12,228	316	1,760	2,076	14,304
Mutual benefit (Y)	175	148	323	8	143	151	474
Unknown (Z)	18,128	45,207	63,335	557	8,027	8,584	71,919
Total primary fields	122,221	146,965	269,186	7,325	82,259	89,584	358,770
Supporting organizations	9,669	8,375	18,044	142	1,375	1,517	19,561
Total public charities[b]	131,890	155,340	287,230	7,467	83,634	91,101	378,331
All 501(c)(3)s (excluding churches)[b]	171,233	163,129	334,362	7,471	83,635	91,106	425,468

Source: Business Master File, October 1991, active only.

Note: Letters following each field refer to NTEE primary codes.

[a] The tax code does not permit private foundations to be subordinate organizations. The five subordinate private foundations shown here are classification errors in the BMF.

[b] 56,320 organizations with the foundation code *church* are excluded from this table. When they are included, the total number of public charities in October 1991 was 434,651, and the total number of 501(c)(3)s was 481,788.

**Table G.2-1.   Ratio of All Subordinates to
Independent Positive Filers by Primary Field, 1991.**

Primary Field	Number of Independent Positive Filers	Number of Subordinates	Ratio
Arts/culture (A)	12,442	7,696	0.62
Education (B)	13,985	25,637	1.83
Conservation/environment (C)	1,618	1,123	0.69
Animal services (D)	1,677	4,706	2.81
Health (E,F,G,H)	18,316	4,784	0.26
Public protection (I)	1,857	63	0.03
Employment (J)	1,960	375	0.19
Food/agriculture (K)	1,262	184	0.15
Housing (L)	5,129	536	0.1
Disaster relief (M)	1,209	1,627	1.35
Recreation/leisure (N)	5,762	5,518	0.96
Youth development (O)	2,514	10,544	4.19
Human services (P)	18,192	4,583	0.25
International affairs (Q)	913	721	0.79
Civil rights (R)	641	422	0.66
Community improvement (S)	7,619	3,773	0.5
Philanthropy (T)	2,109	93	0.04
Science/technology (U)	1,007	2,026	2.01
Social science (V)	473	41	0.09
Public affairs (W)	1,011	4,321	4.27
Religion (X)	4,222	2,076	0.49
Mutual benefit (Y)	175	151	0.86
Unknown (Z)	18,128	8,584	0.47
All public charities	122,221	89,584	0.73

Source: Business Master File, October 1991, active only.
Note: Letters following each field refer to NTEE primary codes.

Table G.2-2. Number of Large and Small Organizations, Twelve Primary Fields, 1991.

Primary Field	Number of Organizations with Receipts of $1 Million or More	Number of Organizations with Receipts of $25,000–$50,000
Arts/culture (A)	1,374	2,580
Education (B)	3,477	2,063
Conservation/environment (C)	201	296
Animal services (D)	203	292
Health (E,F,G,H)	7,110	1,659
Employment (J)	550	166
Recreation/leisure (N)	328	1,420
Youth development (O)	410	260
Human services (P)	3,618	1,801
International affairs (Q)	167	138
Community improvement (S)	1,572	1,097
Science/technology (U)	263	141
Total	19,273	11,913

Source: Business Master File, October 1991, active, independent, positive filers only.
Note: Letters following each field refer to NTEE primary codes.

Table G.2-3. Geographic Distribution of Grantmaking Foundations and Public Charities, Twelve Primary Fields, 1991.

	Percent of Total Population	Grantmaking Foundations			All Public Charities			Arts/Culture (A)			Education (B)		
		Number	%	I	Number	%	I	Number	%	I	Number	%	I
United States	100.0	32,759	100.0	1.00	122,220	100.0	1.00	12,442	100.0	1.00	13,985	100.0	1.00
Regions													
Northeast	20.4	11,232	34.3	1.68	30,839	25.2	1.24	3,512	28.2	1.38	4,039	28.9	1.42
New England	5.3	3,072	9.4	1.77	10,317	8.4	1.59	1,079	8.7	1.64	1,475	10.5	1.99
Middle Atlantic	15.1	8,160	24.9	1.65	20,522	16.8	1.11	2,433	19.6	1.30	2,564	18.3	1.21
Midwest	24.0	8,703	26.6	1.11	29,267	23.9	1.00	2,672	21.5	0.89	2,793	20.0	0.83
East North Central	16.9	6,206	18.9	1.12	19,343	15.8	0.94	1,793	14.4	0.85	1,843	13.2	0.78
West North Central	7.1	2,497	7.6	1.07	9,924	8.1	1.14	879	7.1	1.00	950	6.8	0.96
South	34.3	8,015	24.5	0.71	35,193	28.8	0.84	3,429	27.6	0.80	3,923	28.1	0.82
Atlantic	17.5	4,658	14.2	0.81	19,901	16.3	0.93	1,988	16.0	0.91	2,224	15.9	0.91
East South Central	6.1	1,011	3.1	0.51	5,472	4.5	0.73	475	3.8	0.63	624	4.5	0.73
West South Central	10.7	2,346	7.2	0.67	9,820	8.0	0.75	966	7.8	0.73	1,075	7.7	0.72
West	21.2	4,809	14.7	0.69	26,921	22.0	1.04	2,829	22.7	1.07	3,230	23.1	1.09
Mountain	5.5	1,143	3.5	0.63	6,452	5.3	0.96	662	5.3	0.97	699	5.0	0.91
Pacific	15.7	3,666	11.2	0.71	20,469	16.7	1.07	2,167	17.4	1.11	2,531	18.1	1.15
Five States													
Massachusetts	2.4	1,627	5.0	2.07	4,866	4.0	1.66	537	4.3	1.80	728	5.2	2.17
New Jersey	3.1	1,009	3.1	0.99	3,363	2.8	0.89	302	2.4	0.78	453	3.2	1.04
New York	7.2	5,445	16.6	2.31	10,893	8.9	1.24	1,521	12.2	1.70	1,295	9.3	1.29
Illinois	4.6	2,219	6.8	1.47	5,142	4.2	0.91	494	4.0	0.86	549	3.9	0.85
California	12.0	2,726	8.3	0.69	14,957	12.2	1.02	1,582	12.7	1.06	1,881	13.5	1.12

	Percent of Total Population	Conservation/ Environment (C)			Animal Services (D)			Health (E,F,G,H)			Employment (J)		
		Number	%	I	Number	%	I	Number	%	I	Number	%	I
United States	100.0	1,618	100.0	1.00	1,677	100.0	1.00	18,316	100.0	1.00	1,960	100.0	1.00
Regions													
Northeast	20.4	421	26.0	1.28	341	20.3	1.00	4,946	27.0	1.32	426	21.7	1.07
New England	5.3	199	12.3	2.32	105	6.3	1.18	1,609	8.8	1.66	138	7.0	1.33
Middle Atlantic	15.1	222	13.7	0.91	236	14.1	0.93	3,337	18.2	1.21	288	14.7	0.97
Midwest	24.0	308	19.0	0.79	395	23.6	0.98	4,599	25.1	1.05	551	28.1	1.17
East North Central	16.9	199	12.3	0.73	270	16.1	0.95	3,060	16.7	0.99	361	18.4	1.09
West North Central	7.1	109	6.7	0.95	125	7.5	1.05	1,539	8.4	1.18	190	9.7	1.37
South	34.3	474	29.3	0.85	539	32.1	0.94	5,132	28.0	0.82	542	27.7	0.81
Atlantic	17.5	314	19.4	1.11	316	18.8	1.08	2,892	15.8	0.90	313	16.0	0.91
East South Central	6.1	50	3.1	0.51	85	5.1	0.83	884	4.8	0.79	74	3.8	0.62
West South Central	10.7	110	6.8	0.64	138	8.2	0.77	1,356	7.4	0.69	155	7.9	0.74
West	21.2	415	25.6	1.21	402	24.0	1.13	3,639	19.9	0.94	441	22.5	1.06
Mountain	5.5	107	6.6	1.20	112	6.7	1.21	948	5.2	0.94	110	5.6	1.02
Pacific	15.7	308	19.0	1.21	290	17.3	1.10	2,691	14.7	0.94	331	16.9	1.08
Five States													
Massachusetts	2.4	82	5.1	2.11	42	2.5	1.04	738	4.0	1.68	71	3.6	1.51
New Jersey	3.1	36	2.2	0.72	42	2.5	0.81	640	3.5	1.13	45	2.3	0.74
New York	7.2	126	7.8	1.08	126	7.5	1.04	1,514	8.3	1.15	142	7.2	1.01
Illinois	4.6	54	3.3	0.73	64	3.8	0.83	821	4.5	0.97	102	5.2	1.13
California	12.0	214	13.2	1.10	201	12.0	1.00	1,926	10.5	0.88	227	11.6	0.97

Table G.2–3. Geographic Distribution of Grantmaking Foundations and Public Charities, Twelve Primary Fields, 1991, Cont'd.

	Percent of Total Population	Recreation/Leisure (N)			Youth Development (O)			Human Services (P)		
		Number	%	I	Number	%	I	Number	%	I
United States	100.0	5,762	100.0	1.00	2,514	100.0	1.00	18,192	100.0	1.00
Regions										
Northeast	20.4	1,170	20.3	1.00	553	22.0	1.08	4,302	23.6	1.16
New England	5.3	440	7.6	1.44	192	7.6	1.44	1,491	8.2	1.55
Middle Atlantic	15.1	730	12.7	0.84	361	14.4	0.95	2,811	15.5	1.02
Midwest	24.0	1,557	27.0	1.13	663	26.4	1.10	4,739	26.0	1.09
East North Central	16.9	1,020	17.7	1.05	484	19.3	1.14	3,049	16.8	0.99
West North Central	7.1	537	9.3	1.31	179	7.1	1.00	1,690	9.3	1.31
South	34.3	1,475	25.6	0.75	727	28.9	0.84	5,196	28.6	0.83
Atlantic	17.5	801	13.9	0.79	350	13.9	0.80	2,807	15.4	0.88
East South Central	6.1	196	3.4	0.56	135	5.4	0.88	851	4.7	0.77
West South Central	10.7	478	8.3	0.78	242	9.6	0.90	1,538	8.5	0.79
West	21.2	1,560	27.1	1.28	571	22.7	1.07	3,955	21.7	1.03
Mountain	5.5	362	6.3	1.14	139	5.5	1.01	1,005	5.5	1.00
Pacific	15.7	1,198	20.8	1.32	432	17.2	1.09	2,950	16.2	1.03
Five States										
Massachusetts	2.4	229	4.0	1.66	91	3.6	1.51	708	3.9	1.62
New Jersey	3.1	131	2.3	0.73	78	3.1	1.00	498	2.7	0.88
New York	7.2	340	5.9	0.82	187	7.4	1.03	1,425	7.8	1.09
Illinois	4.6	230	4.0	0.87	105	4.2	0.91	808	4.4	0.97
California	12.0	927	16.1	1.34	337	13.4	1.12	2,130	11.7	0.98

	Percent of Total Population	International Affairs (Q)			Community Improvement (S)			Science/Technology (U)		
		Number	%	I	Number	%	I	Number	%	I
United States	100.0	913	100.0	1.00	7,618	100.0	1.00	1,007	100.0	1.00
Regions										
Northeast	20.4	281	30.8	1.51	1,977	26.0	1.27	238	23.6	1.16
New England	5.3	88	9.6	1.82	606	8.0	1.50	83	8.2	1.56
Middle Atlantic	15.1	193	21.1	1.40	1,371	18.0	1.19	155	15.4	1.02
Midwest	24.0	140	15.3	0.64	2,107	27.7	1.15	181	18.0	0.75
East North Central	16.9	97	10.6	0.63	1,459	19.2	1.13	119	11.8	0.70
West North Central	7.1	43	4.7	0.66	648	8.5	1.20	62	6.2	0.87
South	34.3	259	28.4	0.83	2,327	30.5	0.89	295	29.3	0.85
Atlantic	17.5	201	22.0	1.26	1,214	15.9	0.91	217	21.5	1.23
East South Central	6.1	16	1.8	0.29	419	5.5	0.90	23	2.3	0.37
West South Central	10.7	42	4.6	0.43	694	9.1	0.85	55	5.5	0.51
West	21.2	233	25.5	1.20	1,207	15.8	0.75	293	29.1	1.37
Mountain	5.5	25	2.7	0.50	293	3.8	0.70	71	7.1	1.28
Pacific	15.7	208	22.8	1.45	914	12.0	0.76	222	22.0	1.40
Five States										
Massachusetts	2.4	53	5.8	2.42	251	3.3	1.37	45	4.5	1.86
New Jersey	3.1	17	1.9	0.60	196	2.6	0.83	23	2.3	0.74
New York	7.2	150	16.4	2.28	739	9.7	1.35	83	8.2	1.14
Illinois	4.6	28	3.1	0.67	338	4.4	0.96	45	4.5	0.97
California	12.0	162	17.7	1.48	639	8.4	0.70	175	17.4	1.45

Source: BMF, October 1991, active, independent, positive filers only. 1990 population figures from *Statistical Abstract of the United States* (1991).

Note: Letters following each field refer to NTEE primary codes. Population index (*I*) is the fraction of total organizations in a region divided by the fraction of the U.S. population in the region. We use U.S. Census definitions of regions.

**Table G.3-1. Entrants by Ruling Year,
Public Charities and Grantmaking Foundations, 1965–1990.**

Ruling Year	Public Charities	Grantmaking Foundations
1965	3,448	1,184
1966	3,786	1,119
1967	3,827	1,116
1968	4,178	1,394
1969	4,785	1,451
1970	4,959	875
1971	7,044	823
1972	8,076	807
1973	8,188	630
1974	9,392	635
1975	10,613	601
1976	10,845	647
1977	11,211	608
1978	10,955	691
1979	12,025	767
1980	11,549	805
1981	12,259	923
1982	12,973	1,036
1983	14,176	1,190
1984	15,171	1,297
1985	15,896	1,525
1986	15,792	1,708
1987	15,353	2,728
1988	14,778	2,068
1989	15,842	1,736
1990	15,671	1,549

Source: Business Master File, October 1991, active and inactive, independent only.

Table G.4-1. Entrants by Ruling Year, Twelve Primary Fields, 1965–1988.

Ruling Year	Old Enthusiasms						New Enthusiasms			Continuing Enthusiasms		Other
	Arts/ Culture	Education	Health	Employment	Human Services	Animal Services	Science/ Technology	Community Improvement	Conservation/ Environment	International Affairs	Recreation/ Leisure	Youth Development
1965	369	464	329	49	291	46	37	252	44	15	106	144
1966	409	449	358	51	304	37	41	330	57	18	124	88
1967	431	472	377	80	302	43	34	256	63	15	135	103
1968	446	486	386	81	335	48	33	205	61	16	138	104
1969	526	557	417	93	318	45	31	194	74	15	225	115
1970	433	600	414	101	404	48	30	224	81	17	183	119
1971	612	753	625	109	595	79	42	371	129	18	236	135
1972	683	874	769	117	660	87	42	363	118	27	273	127
1973	734	875	782	95	681	103	41	307	97	38	303	129
1974	976	948	771	132	908	112	38	318	113	29	361	124
1975	1,139	971	957	123	954	128	47	325	112	35	391	144
1976	1,159	1,046	962	115	993	96	67	343	121	46	431	130
1977	1,175	1,021	913	117	1,018	116	48	344	128	45	415	136
1978	1,163	893	922	116	977	87	59	347	143	46	387	114
1979	1,282	1,092	963	111	1,063	108	58	356	142	46	454	105
1980	1,257	983	917	102	1,028	102	62	405	165	49	433	94
1981	1,343	1,033	945	97	1,087	114	80	442	167	60	566	95
1982	1,284	1,148	1,054	116	1,042	138	69	502	182	84	586	126
1983	1,452	1,443	1,229	117	1,190	143	92	519	197	114	653	137
1984	1,493	1,540	1,324	133	1,281	163	104	579	236	113	773	130
1985	1,654	1,590	1,362	142	1,327	176	107	610	239	139	767	139
1986	1,695	1,627	1,406	134	1,298	177	97	608	237	122	825	160
1987	1,764	1,500	1,371	116	1,448	183	111	681	244	172	814	124
1988	1,898	1,500	1,370	97	1,664	217	132	828	288	208	960	125

Source: Business Master File, October 1991, active, independent only.

Table G.5-1. Entrants by Date of Establishment, Higher Education.

Year Established	Research/Doctorate		Comprehensive I		Liberal Arts I		Other Four-Year		Specialized/Religious		Specialized/Professional		Two-Year		Total	
	Public	Private	Public	Private	Public	Private	Public	Private	Public	Private	Public	Private	Public	Private	Public	Private
Pre-1780	2	7	1	0	0	4	0	1	0	0	0	0	0	0	3	12
1780–1784	0	0	1	0	0	3	0	1	0	1	0	0	0	1	1	6
1785–1789	3	1	0	1	0	1	1	0	0	0	0	0	0	1	4	4
1790–1794	2	0	0	0	0	2	0	1	0	2	0	0	0	0	2	5
1795–1799	1	0	0	0	0	2	0	0	0	0	0	0	0	0	1	2
1800–1804	2	0	0	0	0	1	0	1	0	0	1	0	1	0	4	2
1805–1809	1	0	0	0	0	0	0	1	0	1	1	0	0	0	2	2
1810–1814	0	0	0	0	0	2	0	2	0	4	0	0	0	0	0	8
1815–1819	3	1	1	0	0	3	0	2	0	2	0	1	0	0	4	9
1820–1824	1	2	1	1	0	4	1	1	0	1	1	3	0	1	4	13
1825–1829	0	2	0	1	0	4	1	4	0	5	1	1	0	0	2	17
1830–1834	2	2	1	4	0	9	0	9	0	4	1	1	0	0	4	29
1835–1839	2	3	7	0	1	8	3	9	0	2	0	1	0	0	13	23
1840–1844	2	2	2	2	0	5	0	13	0	3	0	2	0	2	4	29
1845–1849	3	2	3	1	0	12	0	15	0	2	1	1	0	3	7	36
1850–1854	4	5	4	10	0	7	1	20	0	5	0	3	1	3	10	53
1855–1859	6	1	8	6	0	10	0	16	0	6	1	2	1	1	16	42
1860–1864	6	4	2	3	0	7	1	9	0	5	1	7	0	0	10	35
1865–1869	14	3	18	4	0	11	2	26	0	5	1	4	1	6	36	59
1870–1874	8	7	13	4	0	4	5	21	0	4	2	3	0	2	28	45
1875–1879	4	3	7	7	0	3	1	19	0	4	3	7	0	2	15	45
1880–1884	4	2	7	3	0	2	3	30	0	4	4	5	3	9	21	55
1885–1889	13	5	14	10	0	8	6	31	0	6	2	14	3	9	38	83
1890–1894	11	7	15	6	0	3	10	36	0	5	1	10	2	6	39	73
1895–1899	5	3	14	3	0	1	5	21	0	4	0	8	3	6	27	46

Year															
1900–1904	3	2	9	6	0	1	3	13	7	1	12	4	7	20	48
1905–1909	2	2	22	7	0	1	7	22	5	2	15	13	5	46	57
1910–1914	8	1	12	5	0	2	2	13	6	2	12	24	4	48	43
1915–1919	3	1	5	5	0	1	2	15	7	1	20	18	3	29	52
1920–1924	1	0	8	5	0	2	1	18	13	1	7	27	3	38	48
1925–1929	2	2	17	5	0	4	4	13	10	1	10	51	4	75	48
1930–1934	1	0	6	4	0	0	0	9	10	1	11	19	6	27	40
1935–1939	0	2	5	2	0	2	0	10	12	0	6	19	6	24	40
1940–1944	0	1	4	3	0	1	0	6	15	4	4	11	1	19	31
1945–1949	2	1	10	8	1	2	1	20	30	3	5	64	10	81	76
1950–1954	1	1	2	3	0	0	1	15	17	2	5	16	5	22	46
1955–1959	3	1	14	3	0	2	4	22	18	4	10	66	15	91	71
1960–1964	6	2	17	5	0	2	3	15	16	12	16	180	12	218	68
1965–1969	3	0	25	4	1	2	3	14	14	4	17	303	8	339	59
1970–1974	2	0	6	4	0	0	6	14	14	11	31	97	9	122	72
1975–1979	0	0	2	0	0	0	2	2	12	0	25	31	6	35	45
1980–1984	0	0	0	1	0	0	0	1	4	0	16	5	4	5	26
1985–1989	0	0	0	0	0	0	0	0	0	0	15	3	2	3	17

Source: 1992 Higher Education Directory, surviving only. See also Appendix D.
Note: Year of establishment was not available for 51 institutions.

Table G.5-2. Entrants by Ruling Year, Civil Rights, 1965–1988.

Ruling Year	Legal Services	Women's Centers/ Rights	Abortion- Related	Minority/ Immigrant Rights	Other Civil Rights	Total	Minority/Immigrant Rights					All Asian				
							All Asian	All Hispanic	Other Specific	Other General	Total	Viet- namese	Chinese	Filipino	Other Asian	Total
1965	10	4	0	6	3	23	0	3	3	0	6	0	0	0	0	0
1966	17	4	0	5	4	30	1	0	2	2	5	0	0	0	1	1
1967	33	2	1	4	4	44	0	0	2	2	4	0	0	0	0	0
1968	25	4	0	5	3	37	1	2	1	1	5	0	1	0	0	1
1969	20	1	0	5	8	34	0	1	3	1	5	0	0	0	0	0
1970	16	4	1	11	4	36	3	4	4	0	11	0	0	1	2	3
1971	24	6	6	10	14	60	1	2	4	3	10	0	1	0	0	1
1972	18	11	5	20	8	62	3	11	5	1	20	0	1	1	1	3
1973	30	4	10	15	5	64	7	4	4	0	15	0	1	4	2	7
1974	30	13	10	15	11	79	6	3	3	3	15	1	1	1	3	6
1975	30	10	11	22	14	87	7	4	10	1	22	0	3	1	3	7
1976	32	26	5	25	9	97	5	6	10	4	25	2	1	0	2	5
1977	43	23	8	25	15	114	8	11	5	1	25	2	2	3	1	8
1978	40	19	9	22	19	109	10	4	5	3	22	1	1	3	5	10
1979	47	21	7	28	12	115	9	6	9	4	28	3	0	3	3	9
1980	31	29	15	23	26	124	7	3	10	3	23	2	1	0	4	7
1981	23	26	9	25	31	114	9	6	6	4	25	5	0	2	2	9
1982	34	17	4	36	21	112	18	7	5	6	36	5	2	4	7	18
1983	30	24	15	33	21	123	16	8	5	4	33	3	0	2	11	16
1984	32	24	14	41	32	143	19	11	7	4	41	2	1	6	10	19
1985	30	27	21	41	27	146	15	9	12	5	41	4	1	1	9	15
1986	18	33	18	40	32	141	14	12	6	8	40	2	1	2	9	14
1987	33	43	29	76	30	211	24	14	28	10	76	2	4	4	14	24
1988	28	51	17	98	40	234	18	24	38	18	98	1	2	3	12	18

Source: Business Master File, October 1991, active, independent only.

Table G.5-3. Entrants by Ruling Year, Performing Arts, 1965–1988.

Ruling Year	Theater	Orchestra	Dance	Ballet	Opera
1965	67	24	3	9	11
1966	47	25	7	9	14
1967	49	22	9	13	10
1968	47	25	7	9	10
1969	63	33	15	15	19
1970	57	22	9	14	8
1971	87	40	12	18	5
1972	96	22	38	18	10
1973	105	26	37	32	17
1974	161	38	55	33	17
1975	199	56	44	31	15
1976	210	43	58	30	23
1977	220	55	54	25	25
1978	187	51	71	27	31
1979	205	61	76	34	28
1980	220	49	76	36	28
1981	240	43	69	40	30
1982	192	51	66	27	25
1983	221	70	64	31	17
1984	238	51	58	24	20
1985	249	61	74	35	20
1986	241	54	75	27	23
1987	227	63	53	33	12
1988	232	32	66	26	13

Source: Business Master File, October 1991, active and inactive, independent only.

Table G.6-1. Age-Specific Exit Rate by Field and Five-Year Cohort.

| Ruling-Year Cohort | Number of Institutions | | | Age-Specific Exit Rate(%)[a] |
	Exited 1981–1991 +	Active in 1991 =	Base Population	
Theater				
No ruling year	14	47	61	
Pre-1966	52	384	436	11.9
1966–70	53	210	263	20.2
1971–75	184	464	648	28.4
1976–80	319	723	1,042	30.6
1981 and later	329	1,898	2,227	14.8
Total	951	3,726	4,677	
Opera				
No ruling year	0	4	4	
Pre-1966	16	70	86	18.6
1966–70	17	44	61	27.9
1971–75	16	48	64	25.0
1976–80	45	90	135	33.3
1981 and later	29	162	191	15.2
Total	123	418	541	
Dance				
No ruling year	4	16	20	
Pre-1966	5	9	14	35.7
1966–70	14	33	47	29.8
1971–75	65	121	186	34.9
1976–80	99	235	334	29.6
1981 and later	87	543	630	13.8
Total	274	957	1,231	
Ballet				
No ruling year	2	6	8	
Pre-1966	14	42	56	25.0
1966–70	14	46	60	23.3
1971–75	36	96	132	27.3
1976–80	56	96	152	36.8
1981 and later	53	235	288	18.4
Total	175	521	696	

Table G.6-1. **Age-Specific Exit Rate by Field and Five-Year Cohort, Cont'd.**

Ruling-Year Cohort	Number of Institutions			Age-Specific Exit Rate(%)[a]
	Exited 1981–1991	+ Active in 1991	= Base Population	
Museums				
No ruling year	0	44	44	
Pre-1966	24	402	426	5.6
1966–70	37	193	230	16.1
1971–75	50	272	322	15.5
1976–80	80	424	504	15.9
1981 and later	80	1,149	1,229	6.5
Total	271	2,484	2,755	
Historical societies				
No ruling year	3	58	61	
Pre-1966	54	893	947	5.7
1966–70	70	633	703	10.0
1971–75	109	1,079	1,188	9.2
1976–80	134	1,296	1,430	9.4
1981 and later	152	3,039	3,191	4.8
Total	522	6,998	7,520	
Higher education				
No ruling year	5	18	23	
Pre-1966	130	973	1,103	11.8
1966–70	57	116	173	32.9
1971–75	88	166	254	34.6
1976–80	74	140	214	34.6
1981 and later	54	203	257	21.0
Total	408	1,616	2,024	
Job training				
No ruling year	6	33	39	
Pre-1966	38	102	140	27.1
1966–70	113	260	373	30.3
1971–75	181	381	562	32.2
1976–80	198	365	563	35.2
1981 and later	150	760	910	16.5
Total	686	1,901	2,587	

Source: Business Master File, October 1991, active and inactive, independent only.
[a] "Age-specific exit rate" equals "exited 1981–1991" divided by "base population."

Table G.7-1. Size of Organizations by Field.

	Number of Organizations	Size ($)			
		25th Percentile	50th Percentile	75th Percentile	95th Percentile
Field					
Performing arts					
Opera	224	75,898	262,718	1,087,188	5,560,383
Orchestra	647	66,330	153,231	460,533	4,887,554
Ballet	244	54,210	132,493	397,442	4,063,313
Theater	1,545	54,545	111,667	311,619	1,601,926
Dance	289	52,052	100,336	179,564	611,528
Museums/historical societies					
Science museums	44	444,276	1,340,678	3,907,922	23,235,480
Art museums	266	174,865	717,038	2,669,008	19,618,386
Natural history museums	31	204,514	1,291,151	4,916,002	20,607,503
Other museums	835	71,597	179,236	476,893	3,671,418
Historical societies	835	44,623	82,195	199,436	1,204,106
Higher education					
Research/Doctorate	66	69,879,094	201,998,336	476,757,980	961,290,000
Comprehensive I	112	21,540,079	30,551,640	42,919,872	87,575,508
Liberal Arts I	123	15,642,411	23,251,990	35,973,292	57,120,165
Other Four-Year	364	7,361,297	9,828,455	14,830,480	22,816,038

Source: Arts/culture—Business Master File, October 1991, active, independent, positive filers only; higher education, Statistics of Income Division, Internal Revenue Service, 1987/1988.

Note: For arts/culture, size is measured by gross receipts; for higher education, size is measured by total expenditures.

Table G.8-1. Average Revenue Shares by Field, 1987/1988.

Field	Sample Size	Average Revenue Shares (%)						Total Revenue ($)	
		Earned		Private		Governmental			
		Mean	Median	Mean	Median	Mean	Median	Mean	Median
Performing arts									
Opera	9	45.7	46.4	47.0	44.4	7.3	6.3	12,026,000	9,014,000
Orchestra	40	42.8	40.9	48.3	48.6	8.9	5.5	9,075,000	5,303,000
Ballet	8	51.4	57.6	40.2	34.9	8.4	7.3	10,780,000	9,379,000
Theater	25	52.6	56.3	39.5	37.3	7.9	6.2	5,016,000	4,025,000
All performing arts	82	46.9	49.3	44.7	43.7	8.4	6.1	8,328,000	4,855,000
Museums/historical societies									
Art museums	63	15.8	12.6	75.8	79.1	8.4	4.9	9,762,000	4,185,000
Science museums	19	42.0	38.3	44.8	38.1	13.2	12.2	10,258,000	4,950,000
Other museums	35	22.9	20.2	63.6	66.0	13.5	7.2	2,328,000	1,369,000
All museums	117	22.2	17.2	67.1	73.9	10.7	5.1	7,618,000	2,806,000
Historical societies	34	14.8	8.4	70.3	79.5	14.9	6.4	2,210,000	844,000
Higher education									
Research/Doctorate	66	66.9	70.7	20.1	17.9	13.0	9.6	324,430,000	205,360,000
Comprehensive I	112	77.2	78.6	15.3	14.4	7.5	6.4	40,522,000	33,427,000
Liberal Arts I	123	65.5	68.7	30.5	27.3	4.0	3.4	30,952,000	26,831,000
Other Four-Year	364	67.6	68.8	23.5	22.7	8.9	6.9	12,718,000	10,508,000
All higher education	665	68.8	70.8	23.1	21.5	8.1	6.1	51,710,000	17,274,000

Source: Statistics of Income Division, Internal Revenue Service, 1987/1988.

Table G.8-2. Distribution of Earned-Income Share by Field, 1987/1988.

Field	Sample Size	Earned Income Share of Total Revenue (%)						
		Maximum	75th Percentile	Median	Mean	25th Percentile	Minimum
Performing arts							
Opera	9	65.4	51.7	46.4	51.4	37.5	32.2
Orchestra	40	75.0	51.7	40.9	42.8	31.7	8.5
Ballet	8	68.9	60.8	57.6	51.4	39.9	25.8
Theater	25	94.2	65.7	56.3	52.6	41.7	13.7
All performing arts	82	94.2	60.0	49.3	47.7	32.8	8.5
Museums/historical societies							
Art museums	63	49.0	20.3	12.6	15.8	7.8	-0.3
Science museums	19	68.6	61.9	38.3	42.0	25.8	12.2
Other museums	35	66.3	35.2	20.2	22.9	7.7	0.5
All museums	117	68.6	31.7	17.2	22.2	9.2	-0.3
Historical societies	34	69.0	19.5	8.4	14.8	4.3	-2.7
Higher education							
Research/Doctorate	66	93.6	81.0	70.7	66.9	56.0	23.8
Comprehensive I	112	94.9	84.4	78.6	77.2	72.3	42.6
Liberal Arts I	123	84.6	73.6	68.7	65.5	58.7	23.0
Other Four-Year	364	100.0	77.5	68.8	67.6	60.1	23.6
All higher education	665	100.0	78.4	70.8	68.8	61.4	23.0

Source: Statistics of Income Division, Internal Revenue Service, 1987/1988.

Table G.9-1. Age-Size Distribution by Ruling Year, Arts/Culture.

Field	1991–1980			1979–1970			1969–1960			1959–1950			1949–1940			Pre-1940			Total		
	S	M	L	S	M	L	S	M	L	S	M	L	S	M	L	S	M	L	S	M	L
Performing arts																					
Opera	28	34	7	21	47	12	3	19	21	4	7	10	0	3	4	0	1	1	56	111	55
Orchestra	80	69	20	38	103	9	22	90	29	19	42	47	2	14	35	0	4	18	161	322	158
Ballet	33	48	9	24	53	23	4	18	23	0	2	5	0	0	1	0	0	0	61	121	61
Theater	214	370	108	101	217	159	37	83	58	21	58	33	7	20	15	1	13	9	381	761	382
Dance	47	74	31	20	58	32	3	8	5	1	0	0	0	1	0	0	0	0	71	141	68
All performing arts	402	595	175	204	478	235	69	218	136	45	109	95	9	38	55	1	18	28	730	1,456	724
Museums/hist. societies																					
Science museums	9	6	0	0	9	1	2	2	0	0	4	3	0	1	4	0	0	3	11	22	11
Art museums	28	20	3	24	35	2	12	30	13	2	24	6	1	22	15	0	2	27	67	133	66
Natural hist. museums	2	3	0	2	1	0	3	3	1	1	6	0	0	1	3	0	2	3	8	16	7
Other museums	110	188	53	66	122	42	24	57	51	4	29	22	0	11	20	1	2	14	205	409	202
All museums	149	217	56	92	167	45	41	92	65	7	63	31	1	35	42	1	6	47	291	580	286
Historical societies	53	69	10	76	134	25	50	115	51	20	53	42	6	37	58	2	5	23	207	413	209

Source: Business Master File, October 1991, active, independent, positive filers only.

Note: Size is based on gross receipts, and age is based on ruling year. Small (S) is defined as organizations with gross receipts less than or equal to the 25th percentile. Medium (M) is gross receipts greater than the 25th percentile but less than or equal to the 75th percentile. Large (L) is gross receipts greater than the 75th percentile. Ruling year was not available for 38 performing arts organizations, 19 museums, and 6 historical societies.

Table G.9-2. Age-Size Distribution by Date of Establishment, Higher Education.

Field	1991–1945			1944–1914			1913–1890			1889–1860			1859–1636			Total		
	S	M	L	S	M	L	S	M	L	S	M	L	S	M	L	S	M	L
Research/Doctorate	4	1	0	1	2	0	4	7	1	6	8	6	2	15	9	17	33	16
Liberal Arts I	2	3	0	6	3	0	1	5	1	7	13	13	14	38	17	30	62	31
Comprehensive I	10	5	2	5	12	4	5	11	4	5	16	9	3	12	9	28	56	28
Other Four-Year	9	26	9	19	20	8	19	37	26	29	60	21	15	39	28	91	182	92
All higher education	25	35	11	31	37	12	29	60	32	47	97	49	34	104	63	166	333	167

Source: Statistics of Income Division, Internal Revenue Service, 1987/1988.

Note: Size is based on total expenses, and age is based on year of establishment. Small (*S*) is defined as organizations with total expenses less than or equal to the 25th percentile. Medium (*M*) is total expenses greater than the 25th percentile but less than or equal to the 75th percentile. Large (*L*) is total expenses greater than the 75th percentile.

**Table G.10-1. Basic Information on Organizations
Included in the Arts/Culture Institutional Database.**

	Total Expenditures 1992 ($)	Year Established
Opera		
Houston Grand Opera	15,797,578	1955
Lyric Opera of Chicago	20,654,937	1954
San Francisco Opera	33,864,908	1923
Average	23,439,141	1944
Orchestra		
Baltimore Symphony	16,623,000	1916
Boston Symphony	35,880,000	1881
Los Angeles Philharmonic	32,035,000	1919
Pittsburgh Symphony	22,400,000	1926
St. Louis Symphony	17,428,975	1879
Average	24,873,395	1904
Ballet		
Boston Ballet	12,148,027	1963
Houston Ballet	10,207,565	1969
New York City Ballet	28,731,000	1948
San Francisco Ballet	16,795,149	1933
Average	16,970,435	1953
Theater		
American Conservatory	10,323,062	1965
Arena Stage	9,508,944	1950
Center Stage	3,773,431	1963
Guthrie Theater	10,636,822	1963
New York Shakespeare Festival	10,466,625	1954
Average	8,941,777	1959
Art museums		
Art Institute of Chicago	79,474,626	1879
Baltimore Museum of Art	7,176,179	1914
Brooklyn Institute of Arts and Sciences	16,153,273	1823
Corcoran Gallery of Art	9,571,521	1869
Metropolitan Museum of Art	87,708,785	1870
Philadelphia Museum of Art	20,507,169	1876
Toledo Museum of Art	6,796,860	1901
Average	32,484,059	1876

**Table G.10-1. Basic Information on Organizations
Included in the Arts/Culture Institutional Database, Cont'd.**

	Total Expenditures 1992 ($)	Year Established
Science museums		
American Museum of Natural History	51,985,654	1893
Field Museum	23,929,150	1824
Franklin Institute	18,935,141	1869
Average	31,616,648	1862
Historical societies		
Maryland Historical Society	1,986,720	1844
Massachusetts Historical Society	1,628,713	1791
New-York Historical Society	7,117,164	1804
Rhode Island Historical Society	1,406,459	1822
Virginia Historical Society	2,610,967	1831
Average	2,950,005	1818

Source: Arts/culture institutional database.

Table G.10-2. Trends in Total Expenditures for Individual Arts/Culture Organizations, 1972–1992.

	Total Nominal Expenditures ($)					Average Annual Growth in Nominal Expenditures (%)			Average Annual Growth in Real Expenditures (%)		
	1972	1977	1982	1987	1992	1972–92	1972–82	1982–92	1972–92	1972–82	1982–92
Opera											
Houston Grand Opera	635,973	4,909,134	6,834,196	7,999,046	15,797,578	14.8	26.8	8.7	8.5	17.4	4.9
Lyric Opera of Chicago	3,568,378	6,250,020	9,752,772	16,224,338	20,654,937	9.5	10.3	8.8	3.3	2.2	4.7
San Francisco Opera	na	na	17,720,237	21,667,230	33,864,908	na	na	6.7	na	na	2.9
Average	2,102,176	5,579,577	11,435,735	15,296,871	23,439,141	12.2	18.6	8.1	5.9	9.8	4.2
Orchestra											
Baltimore Symphony	1,425,702	2,996,413	4,053,770	10,812,000	16,623,000	13.2	11.0	15.2	6.9	2.8	11.0
Boston Symphony	6,465,528	10,351,104	18,600,694	25,504,000	35,880,000	9.0	11.1	6.8	3.0	2.9	3.0
Los Angeles Philharmonic	4,798,755	7,393,129	16,059,686	24,567,690	32,035,000	10.5	12.8	7.1	4.4	4.5	3.3
Pittsburgh Symphony	na	5,467,430	11,345,466	16,293,463	22,400,000	9.6	15.7	7.0	4.3	6.7	3.2
St. Louis Symphony	2,620,165	4,141,867	7,732,813	13,046,978	17,428,975	10.4	11.4	8.5	4.3	3.2	4.6
Average	3,827,538	6,069,989	11,558,486	18,044,826	24,873,395	10.5	12.4	8.9	4.6	4.0	5.0
Ballet											
Boston Ballet	792,828	1,503,362	4,275,517	6,557,776	12,148,027	15.5	20.7	11.0	9.1	11.6	7.0
Houston Ballet	356,238	1,334,728	4,172,450	5,542,651	10,207,565	17.7	27.9	9.4	11.2	18.4	5.5
New York City Ballet	4,803,718	6,826,057	13,963,748	21,212,000	28,731,000	9.9	11.3	7.5	3.8	3.0	3.6
San Francisco Ballet	837,235	3,351,405	6,593,595	11,327,653	16,795,149	15.5	22.9	9.8	9.1	13.8	5.9
Average	1,697,505	3,253,888	7,251,328	11,160,020	16,970,435	14.6	20.7	9.4	8.3	11.7	5.5
Theater											
American Conservatory	1,757,231	4,383,366	5,623,579	6,665,541	10,323,062	8.2	12.3	6.3	2.2	4.0	2.5
Arena Stage	1,248,452	1,926,605	4,541,484	8,238,653	9,508,944	11.7	13.8	7.7	5.5	5.4	3.8
Center Stage	420,474	820,327	1,737,987	2,904,125	3,773,431	12.0	15.2	8.1	5.8	6.7	4.2
Guthrie Theater	1,753,685	2,744,866	6,246,483	8,084,923	10,636,822	9.6	13.6	5.5	3.5	5.2	1.7
New York Shakespeare Festival	3,254,136	31,255,596	56,556,370	32,812,886	10,466,625	4.9	33.0	-15.5	-0.9	23.2	-18.5
Average	1,686,796	8,226,152	14,941,181	11,741,226	8,941,777	9.3	17.6	2.4	3.2	8.9	-1.3
Average excluding New York Shakespeare Festival	1,294,961	2,468,791	4,537,383	6,473,311	8,560,565	10.4	13.8	6.9	4.3	5.3	3.1

Table G.10-2. Trends in Total Expenditures for Individual Arts/Culture Organizations, 1972–1992, Cont'd.

	Total Nominal Expenditures ($)					Average Annual Growth in Nominal Expenditures (%)			Average Annual Growth in Real Expenditures (%)		
	1972	1977	1982	1987	1992	1972–92	1972–82	1982–92	1972–92	1972–82	1982–92
Art museums											
Art Institute of Chicago	9,845,382	14,502,247	29,240,057	65,748,338	79,474,626	12.0	11.5	10.5	5.8	3.2	6.6
Baltimore Museum of Art	965,528	1,639,279	2,811,601	5,871,984	7,176,179	11.2	11.3	9.8	5.0	3.0	5.9
Brooklyn Institute of Arts and Sciences	5,474,125	6,531,563	6,321,719	12,564,443	16,153,273	5.8	1.4	9.8	-0.1	-6.1	5.9
Corcoran Gallery of Art	1,412,125	2,120,171	4,410,715	6,085,225	9,571,521	11.1	15.3	8.1	5.2	6.7	4.2
Metropolitan Museum of Art	14,156,075	18,400,449	38,974,709	69,660,217	87,708,785	10.3	10.9	8.4	4.2	2.6	4.6
Philadelphia Museum of Art	3,726,209	5,322,139	9,892,812	17,484,724	20,507,169	9.5	10.3	7.7	3.5	2.1	3.9
Toledo Museum of Art	1,431,728	2,040,055	4,189,739	6,371,373	6,796,860	8.9	11.3	5.0	2.9	3.1	1.2
Average	5,287,310	7,222,272	13,691,622	26,255,186	32,484,059	9.8	10.3	8.5	3.8	2.1	4.6
Science museums											
American Museum of Natural History	10,233,450	16,640,247	27,015,582	37,134,226	51,985,654	8.4	10.2	6.8	2.4	2.0	3.0
Field Museum	3,874,620	7,775,635	11,347,513	16,757,061	23,929,150	9.2	11.3	7.7	3.2	3.1	3.9
Franklin Institute	1,912,026	3,614,518	8,797,034	10,402,251	18,935,141	12.0	14.9	9.0	5.8	6.8	5.2
Average	5,340,032	9,343,467	15,720,043	21,431,179	31,616,648	9.9	12.2	7.9	3.8	4.0	4.0
Historical societies											
Maryland Historical Society	489,401	925,469	1,284,086	1,759,594	1,986,720	7.3	10.2	4.5	1.4	2.1	0.7
Massachusetts Historical Society	297,830	522,463	811,416	1,031,512	1,628,713	8.5	10.5	7.2	2.5	2.3	3.4
New-York Historical Society	1,200,350	1,570,585	2,361,515	5,879,717	7,117,164	10.7	7.8	11.7	4.7	-0.3	7.7
Rhode Island Historical Society	259,855	476,061	788,537	916,734	1,406,459	8.6	11.7	6.0	2.6	3.4	2.2
Virginia Historical Society	286,496	505,140	778,431	1,177,689	2,610,967	11.5	10.5	14.2	5.2	2.3	9.9
Average	506,786	799,944	1,204,797	2,153,049	2,950,005	9.3	10.2	8.7	3.3	2.0	4.8

Source: Arts/culture institutional database.

Note: Average annual growth rates for the Pittsburgh Symphony begin in 1977; *na* means "data not available."

Table G.10-3. Components of Growth in Total Revenue, High-Growth Organizations.

	Period	Total Change (%)	Share of Growth from (%)				
			Earned	Contributed	Investment	Governmental	Total
Houston Grand Opera	1972–82	398	39	51	4	6	100
Baltimore Symphony Orchestra	1982–92	185	46	20	16	19	100
Boston Ballet	1972–82	166	94	4	2	0	100
Houston Ballet	1972–82	442	54	43	3	0	100
San Francisco Ballet	1972–82	265	64	25	3	7	100
Arena Stage	1977–87	139	66	17	6	11	100
Center Stage	1977–87	98	62	6	13	19	100
New York Shakespeare Festival	1972–82	705	94	1	4	1	100
Art Institute of Chicago	1977–87	153	26	52	16	7	100
Baltimore Museum of Art	1977–87	100	8	44	8	40	100
Detroit Institute of Art	1972–82	253	17	16	6	61	100
Metropolitan Museum of Art	1977–87	98	37	25	19	19	100
Franklin Institute	1972–82	105	50	45	–2	7	100
New York Historical Society	1982–92	110	9	119	–28	0	100
Virginia Historical Society	1982–92	139	5	83	13	–1	100

Source: Arts/culture institutional database.

Note: "High-growth organizations" are those that at least doubled total real expenditures over a ten-year period.

Table G.10-4   Trends in Revenue Shares for

	Earned Income (%)				
	1972	*1977*	*1982*	*1987*	*1992*
Opera					
Houston Grand Opera	58.0	75.1	45.3	50.6	42.6
Lyric Opera of Chicago	49.5	44.4	55.6	53.5	57.9
San Francisco Opera	na	na	69.9	52.5	61.1
Average	53.7	59.7	57.0	52.2	53.9
Orchestra					
Baltimore Symphony	30.9	35.7	34.7	48.2	43.0
Boston Symphony	58.2	69.1	67.0	71.7	75.4
Los Angeles Philharmonic	63.6	76.2	73.1	74.6	72.2
Pittsburgh Symphony	na	44.6	60.7	69.5	56.4
St. Louis Symphony	58.4	33.7	33.1	44.9	47.9
Average	52.8	51.9	53.7	61.8	59.0
Ballet					
Boston Ballet	52.6	74.7	84.5	78.9	84.8
Houston Ballet	24.8	52.6	51.8	53.8	55.8
New York City Ballet	80.6	56.5	73.3	62.2	50.2
San Francisco Ballet	58.1	55.0	63.4	61.3	56.4
Average	54.0	59.7	68.2	64.1	61.8
Theater					
American Conservatory	53.1	72.8	70.7	77.0	62.4
Arena Stage	68.1	58.7	70.8	64.2	54.4
Center Stage	37.8	49.9	57.5	58.7	43.5
Guthrie Theater	61.8	70.9	64.7	61.1	55.3
NY Shakespeare Festival	33.0	93.7	91.9	71.4	34.2
Average	50.8	69.2	71.1	66.5	50.0
Average excluding NY Shakespeare Festival	55.2	63.1	65.9	65.3	53.9
Art museums					
Art Institute of Chicago	30.4	35.7	30.6	27.7	41.0
Baltimore Museum of Art	6.0	4.3	5.9	7.3	11.6
Brooklyn Inst. Arts & Sci.	14.4	5.8	12.4	14.7	11.2
Corcoran Gallery of Art	73.5	53.4	37.4	49.5	51.1
Metropolitan Museum of Art	13.1	23.1	19.2	33.3	18.3
Philadelphia Museum of Art	12.2	12.3	9.4	13.0	14.8
Toledo Museum of Art	39.5	20.2	15.7	26.0	31.1
Average	27.0	22.1	18.7	24.5	25.6
Science museums					
American Mus. Nat. Hist.	8.1	31.6	38.1	41.3	40.3
Field Museum	16.9	31.5	13.3	10.9	18.2
Franklin Institute	50.3	53.1	50.4	76.2	80.6
Average	25.1	38.7	33.9	42.8	46.4
Historical societies					
Maryland Hist. Society	6.6	11.6	15.3	28.8	25.5
Massachusetts Hist. Society	1.3	1.2	0.0	0.0	0.3
New-York Hist. Society	14.8	11.5	12.8	23.7	10.0
Rhode Island Hist. Society	7.7	10.7	18.3	16.8	8.0
Virginia Hist. Society	9.3	7.9	3.9	2.5	4.4
Average	7.9	8.6	10.1	14.4	9.6

Source: Arts/culture institutional database.
Note: na means "data not available," or unknown.

Individual Arts/Culture Organizations, 1972–1992.

Private Support (%)					Governmental Support (%)				
1972	1977	1982	1987	1992	1972	1977	1982	1987	1992
38.1	20.1	49.6	44.5	51.6	3.9	4.9	5.1	4.9	5.8
50.5	50.6	41.0	46.5	40.5	na	4.9	3.4	na	1.6
na	na	23.5	40.8	33.8	na	na	6.5	6.7	5.1
44.3	35.4	38.0	43.9	42.0	3.9	4.9	5.0	5.8	4.2
39.6	41.4	40.4	22.0	36.8	29.6	23.0	24.9	29.8	20.2
39.4	28.1	28.8	24.6	23.6	2.4	2.8	4.2	3.6	1.0
34.1	21.4	24.2	24.0	24.6	2.3	2.4	2.7	1.4	3.2
na	49.9	33.0	25.5	39.7	na	5.4	6.3	5.0	3.9
41.6	36.2	50.1	39.5	42.1	0.0	30.1	16.8	15.6	10.0
38.7	35.4	35.3	27.1	33.4	8.6	12.8	11.0	11.1	7.7
47.4	25.3	15.5	21.1	11.3	na	na	na	na	4.0
75.2	47.4	48.2	46.2	44.2	na	na	na	na	na
12.1	30.9	18.6	27.8	45.9	7.3	12.6	8.1	9.9	3.9
26.0	37.5	28.2	31.3	38.6	16.0	7.5	8.5	7.4	4.9
40.2	35.3	27.6	31.6	35.0	11.6	10.1	8.3	8.7	4.3
38.0	19.8	19.3	23.0	29.5	8.9	7.4	9.9	na	8.1
31.9	27.4	21.5	24.3	34.4	na	13.9	7.7	11.5	11.2
62.2	50.1	23.0	27.0	35.0	na	na	19.5	14.4	21.4
30.6	22.1	35.3	38.9	44.7	7.5	7.0	na	na	na
37.4	2.7	5.9	21.9	50.6	29.6	3.7	2.3	6.8	15.2
40.0	24.4	21.0	27.0	38.8	15.3	8.0	9.9	10.9	14.0
40.7	29.8	24.8	28.3	35.9	8.2	9.5	12.4	12.9	13.6
59.4	52.7	61.8	64.1	50.1	10.2	11.6	7.7	8.2	8.9
18.7	26.0	26.0	46.1	55.0	75.3	69.6	68.0	46.6	33.4
44.5	50.0	40.5	33.2	46.0	41.1	44.2	47.1	52.1	42.8
25.6	42.1	51.9	43.4	40.3	0.9	4.4	10.7	7.1	8.7
68.6	61.9	53.1	48.8	66.7	18.3	15.0	27.7	17.9	15.0
35.2	39.2	53.7	61.1	60.8	52.6	48.6	36.9	25.8	24.4
60.5	79.8	84.3	74.0	68.9	na	na	na	na	na
44.6	50.2	53.0	53.0	55.4	33.1	32.2	33.0	26.3	22.2
59.3	45.3	40.0	37.2	44.4	32.5	23.1	21.9	21.5	15.3
55.7	35.9	55.8	49.3	44.8	27.4	32.6	30.9	39.8	37.0
34.5	33.3	41.0	15.8	16.0	15.2	13.7	8.6	8.1	3.4
49.8	38.2	45.6	34.1	35.1	25.0	23.1	20.5	23.1	18.6
78.7	63.4	65.5	58.1	68.9	14.8	25.1	19.1	13.1	5.6
97.9	76.3	96.5	100.0	99.7	0.8	22.5	3.5	na	na
85.2	88.5	87.2	76.3	90.0	na	na	na	na	na
60.3	43.3	31.4	34.6	35.2	31.9	46.0	50.4	48.6	56.9
89.8	82.1	94.1	96.4	95.6	0.9	10.0	2.0	1.1	na
82.4	70.7	74.9	73.1	77.9	12.1	25.9	18.7	21.0	31.2

Table G.10-5. Trends in Revenue Components (in Thousands

| | 1972 | | | | 1977 | | | |
| | Earned | Private | | Govt. | Earned | Private | | Govt. |
		Contr.	Invest.			Contr.	Invest.	
Opera								
Houston Grand Opera	371	229	15	25	3,858	1,032	na	250
Lyric Opera of Chicago	1,772	1,810	na	na	2,700	3,041	38	300
San Francisco Opera	na	na	na	na	na	na	na	na
Average	1,071	1,019	15	25	3,279	2,036	38	275
Orchestra								
Baltimore Symphony	501	518	124	480	1,041	965	242	670
Boston Symphony	3,791	1,815	754	157	6,630	1,726	971	269
Los Angeles Philharmonic	2,852	1,083	448	104	5,333	995	503	170
Pittsburgh Symphony	na	na	na	na	2,745	976	2,096	335
St. Louis Symphony	1,519	925	158	0	1,407	1,191	317	1,255
Average	2,166	1,085	371	185	3,431	1,170	826	540
Ballet								
Boston Ballet	482	435	0	na	1,076	365	na	na
Houston Ballet	74	224	0	na	737	664	na	na
New York City Ballet	3,249	482	5	294	3,607	1,975	na	807
San Francisco Ballet	433	194	na	119	2,006	1,366	na	275
Average	1,059	334	2	207	1,857	1,093	na	541
Theater								
American Conservatory	1,020	725	5	170	3,042	757	72	310
Arena Stage	930	430	6	na	1,162	482	59	275
Center Stage	183	301	0	na	387	387	1	na
Guthrie Theater	1,221	596	8	149	2,099	582	71	208
NY Shakespeare Festival	753	821	32	675	31,722	906	na	1,243
Average	821	575	10	331	7,682	623	51	509
Average excluding NY Shakespeare Festival	838	513	5	160	1,672	552	51	264
Art museums								
Art Institute of Chicago	3,509	3,678	3,186	1,182	4,951	3,288	4,034	1,613
Baltimore Museum of Art	52	106	58	661	69	385	28	1,103
Brooklyn Inst. of Arts & Sci.	796	1,370	1,083	2,266	386	2,074	1,264	2,951
Corcoran Gallery	888	140	170	11	1,220	757	206	102
Metropolitan Mus. of Art	1,721	1,794	7,246	2,414	4,120	4,328	6,709	2,678
Philadelphia Mus. of Art	415	572	625	1,787	663	1,044	1,077	2,630
Toledo Museum of Art	580	127	760	na	505	338	1,651	na
Average	1,137	1,113	1,875	1,387	1,702	1,745	2,138	1,846
Science Museums								
American Mus. Nat. Hist.	619	2,286	2,231	2,477	4,631	3,878	2,745	3,380
Field Museum	641	649	1,463	1,041	2,714	1,473	1,625	2,810
Franklin Institute	999	399	286	301	1,891	988	197	486
Average	753	1,111	1,327	1,273	3,079	2,113	1,522	2,226
Historical societies								
Maryland Hist. Soc.	35	243	171	78	103	409	155	223
Massachusetts Hist. Soc.	5	87	265	3	9	160	441	177
New-York Hist. Soc.	111	117	520	na	132	259	757	na
Rhode Island Hist. Soc.	17	87	47	71	48	105	89	206
Virginia Hist. Soc.	30	63	229	3	62	331	319	79
Average	40	120	247	39	71	253	352	171

Source: Arts/culture institutional database.
Note: na means "data not available," or unknown.

of Dollars) for Individual Arts/Culture Organizations, 1972–1992.

	1982				1987				1992		
Earned	Private		Govt.	Earned	Private		Govt.	Earned	Private		Govt.
	Contr.	Invest			Contr.	Invest.			Contr.	Invest.	
3,107	3,131	265	350	4,070	3,398	186	395	6,171	6,398	1,082	844
5,707	3,818	383	347	9,012	7,024	823	na	12,628	7,729	1,090	351
11,639	3,307	610	1,087	11,701	8,131	950	1,491	17,997	9,044	916	1,499
6,818	3,419	420	594	8,261	6,184	653	943	12,266	7,724	1,029	898
1,290	939	563	927	5,429	1,686	788	3,349	6,589	3,273	2,365	3,093
12,790	3,330	2,171	802	17,586	3,665	2,376	890	26,558	4,056	4,265	366
11,947	2,857	1,099	437	18,350	4,923	988	336	24,655	7,515	881	1,105
6,514	334	3,200	676	9,026	221	3,087	655	10,347	380	6,901	719
2,504	2,754	1,035	1,274	4,990	2,813	1,575	1,734	7,386	4,435	2,052	1,544
7,009	2,043	1,614	823	11,076	2,662	1,763	1,393	15,107	3,932	3,293	1,365
3,436	560	69	na	5,137	1,217	153	na	10,314	1,182	187	483
2,218	1,953	112	na	2,966	2,350	202	na	5,624	3,260	1,191	na
9,151	2,319	na	1,018	13,194	5,152	742	2,108	16,716	14,091	1,188	1,297
3,927	1,574	171	524	5,839	2,691	289	706	9,087	5,846	370	795
4,683	1,601	118	771	6,784	2,853	347	1,407	10,435	6,095	734	858
3,815	980	64	535	5,251	1,522	45	na	5,768	2,730	na	745
3,237	765	217	352	5,469	1,595	473	979	5,268	2,640	685	1,084
1,061	240	186	360	1,736	510	288	425	1,607	814	480	792
3,886	1,530	589	na	4,557	2,360	537	na	5,415	3,161	1,210	na
56,788	1,313	2,316	1,404	23,613	3,162	4,067	2,236	2,826	3,228	954	1,252
13,757	965	674	663	8,125	1,830	1,082	1,213	4,177	2,515	832	968
3,000	878	264	416	4,253	1,497	336	702	4,514	2,336	792	874
9,129	9,232	9,218	2,298	18,167	29,918	12,105	5,350	30,710	23,894	13,668	6,631
167	649	85	1,917	528	2,862	448	3,347	1,092	4,094	1,088	3,150
797	1,895	709	3,029	1,957	3,375	1,031	6,925	1,722	5,315	1,741	6,555
1,621	1,707	539	463	2,721	2,111	278	391	4,321	2,899	506	733
7,829	9,263	12,426	11,306	24,353	18,286	17,394	13,108	15,644	30,377	26,615	12,795
938	2,744	2,617	3,682	2,133	6,356	3,642	4,226	2,787	5,972	5,474	4,592
739	976	2,976	na	1,347	453	3,381	na	1,830	249	3,810	na
3,031	3,781	4,081	3,782	7,315	9,052	5,468	5,558	8,301	10,400	7,557	5,743
10,201	4,329	6,380	5,871	15,724	6,123	8,028	8,171	18,102	10,285	9,695	6,881
1,363	1,995	3,732	3,174	1,613	1,753	5,582	5,917	3,360	2,117	6,130	6,820
4,370	3,429	124	749	7,931	1,065	577	840	12,523	1,744	737	533
5,311	3,251	3,412	3,264	8,423	2,981	4,729	4,976	11,328	4,715	5,521	4,745
200	411	443	249	516	493	549	236	472	667	608	104
0	255	770	38	0	732	882	na	7	838	1,345	na
231	266	1,311	na	531	874	831	na	422	3,150	636	na
133	113	116	367	155	154	165	449	109	246	234	777
50	609	596	25	56	1,250	925	25	138	2,154	846	na
123	331	647	170	252	701	670	237	230	1,411	734	440

Table G.10-6. Governmental Share of Nonearned Income for
Individual Arts/Culture Organizations, 1972–1992.

	Governmental Share of Nonearned Income (%)				
	1972	1977	1982	1987	1992
Opera					
Houston Grand Opera	9.3	19.5	9.3	9.9	10.1
Lyric Opera of Chicago	na	8.9	7.6	na	3.8
San Francisco Opera	na	na	21.7	14.1	13.1
Average	9.3	14.2	12.9	12.0	9.0
Orchestra					
Baltimore Symphony	42.8	35.7	38.2	57.5	35.4
Boston Symphony	5.8	9.1	12.7	12.8	4.2
Los Angeles Philharmonic	6.4	10.2	10.0	5.4	11.6
Pittsburgh Symphony	na	9.8	16.1	16.5	9.0
St. Louis Symphony	0.0	45.4	25.2	28.3	19.2
Average	13.7	22.0	20.4	24.1	15.9
Ballet					
Boston Ballet	na	na	na	na	26.1
Houston Ballet	na	na	na	na	na
New York City Ballet	37.7	29.0	30.5	26.3	7.8
San Francisco Ballet	38.1	16.7	23.1	19.2	11.3
Average	37.9	22.9	26.8	22.7	15.1
Theater					
American Conservatory	18.9	27.2	33.9	na	21.4
Arena Stage	na	33.7	26.4	32.1	24.6
Center Stage	na	na	45.9	34.7	38.0
Guthrie Theater	19.8	24.2	na	na	na
New York Shakespeare Festival	44.2	57.8	27.9	23.6	23.0
Average	27.6	35.7	33.5	30.2	26.8
Art museums					
Art Institute of Chicago	14.7	18.1	11.1	11.3	15.0
Baltimore Museum of Art	80.1	72.8	72.3	50.3	37.8
Brooklyn Inst. Arts and Sci.	48.0	46.9	53.8	61.1	48.2
Corcoran Gallery of Art	3.4	9.6	17.1	14.1	17.7
Metropolitan Museum of Art	21.1	19.5	34.3	26.9	18.3
Philadelphia Museum of Art	59.9	55.4	40.7	29.7	28.6
Toledo Museum of Art	na	na	na	na	na
Average	37.9	37.0	38.2	32.2	27.6
Science museums					
American Mus. Nat. Hist.	35.4	33.8	35.4	36.6	25.6
Field Museum	33.0	47.6	35.7	44.6	45.3
Franklin Institute	30.5	29.1	17.4	33.8	17.7
Average	33.0	36.8	29.5	38.4	29.5
Historical societies					
Maryland Historical Society	15.8	28.3	22.6	18.5	7.6
Massachusetts Historical Society	0.8	22.8	3.5	na	na
New-York Historical Society	na	na	na	na	na
Rhode Island Historical Society	34.6	51.5	61.6	58.4	61.8
Virginia Historical Society	1.0	10.9	2.0	1.1	na
Average	13.1	28.4	22.4	26.0	34.7

Source: Arts/culture institutional database.
Note: na means "data not available," or unknown.

Table G.10-7. Investment Income as a Share of Private Support
for Individual Arts/Culture Organizations, 1972–1992.

	Investment Income as a Share of Private Support (%)				
	1972	*1977*	*1982*	*1987*	*1992*
Opera					
Houston Grand Opera	6.2	na	7.8	5.2	14.5
Lyric Opera of Chicago	na	1.2	9.1	10.5	12.4
San Francisco Opera	na	na	15.6	10.5	9.2
Average	6.2	1.2	10.8	8.7	12.0
Orchestra					
Baltimore Symphony	19.3	20.1	37.5	31.9	41.9
Boston Symphony	29.4	36.0	39.5	39.3	51.3
Los Angeles Philharmonic	29.3	33.6	27.8	16.7	10.5
Pittsburgh Symphony	na	68.2	90.5	93.3	94.8
St. Louis Symphony	14.6	21.0	27.3	35.9	31.6
Average	23.1	35.8	44.5	43.4	46.0
Ballet					
Boston Ballet	0.0	na	11.0	11.2	13.6
Houston Ballet	0.0	na	5.4	7.9	26.8
New York City Ballet	1.1	na	na	12.6	7.8
San Francisco Ballet	na	na	9.8	9.7	6.0
Average	0.4	na	8.8	10.3	13.5
Theater					
American Conservatory	0.7	8.6	6.1	2.9	na
Arena Stage	1.4	10.9	22.1	22.9	20.6
Center Stage	0.0	0.2	43.7	36.1	37.1
Guthrie Theater	1.3	10.9	27.8	18.5	27.7
New York Shakespeare Festival	3.8	na	63.8	56.3	22.8
Average	1.4	7.7	32.7	27.3	27.1
Art museums					
Art Institute of Chicago	46.4	55.1	50.0	28.8	36.4
Baltimore Museum of Art	35.3	6.7	11.6	13.5	21.0
Brooklyn Inst. Arts and Sci.	44.2	37.9	27.2	23.4	24.7
Corcoran Gallery of Art	54.8	21.4	24.0	11.6	14.9
Metropolitan Museum of Art	80.2	60.8	57.3	48.7	46.7
Philadelphia Museum of Art	52.2	50.8	48.8	36.4	47.8
Toledo Museum of Art	85.7	83.0	75.3	88.2	93.9
Average	56.9	45.1	42.0	35.8	40.8
Science museums					
American Mus. Nat. Hist.	49.4	41.4	59.6	56.7	48.5
Field Museum	69.3	52.5	65.2	76.1	74.3
Franklin Institute	41.7	16.7	3.5	35.1	29.7
Average	53.5	36.9	42.7	56.0	50.9
Historical societies					
Maryland Historical Society	41.3	27.5	51.9	52.7	47.7
Massachusetts Historical Society	75.2	73.4	75.1	54.6	61.6
New-York Historical Society	81.6	74.5	83.1	48.7	16.8
Rhode Island Historical Society	35.4	46.1	50.6	51.8	48.8
Virginia Historical Society	78.4	49.1	49.5	42.5	28.2
Average	62.4	54.1	62.0	50.1	40.6

Source: Arts/culture institutional database.
Note: na means "data not available," or unknown.

REFERENCES

Aldrich, H. E. *Organizations and Environments.* Englewood Cliffs, N.J.: Prentice-Hall, 1979.

American Association of Museums. *The Official Museum Directory, 1990.* Wilmette, Ill.: National Register Publishing Company, 1989.

American Association of Museums. *Data Report from the 1989 National Museum Survey.* Washington, D.C.: American Association of Museums, 1992.

American Symphony Orchestra League. "1992–93 Orchestra and Business Directory." *Symphony,* 1993, *44* (1), 53–86.

Baumol, W. J., Blackman, S.A.B., and Wolff, E. N. *Productivity and American Leadership: The Long View.* Cambridge: Massachusetts Institute of Technology Press, 1989.

Baumol, W. J., and Bowen, W. G. *Performing Arts: The Economic Dilemma.* New York: Twentieth Century Fund, 1966.

Beeman, A. L. *Wilson College: A Case Study.* Report prepared for the Lilly Endowment. Indianapolis, Ind.: Lilly Endowment, 1979.

Ben-Ner, A. "Nonprofit Organizations: Why Do They Exist in Market Economies?" In S. Rose-Ackerman (ed.), *The Economics of Nonprofit Institutions: Studies in Structure and Policy.* New York: Oxford University Press, 1986.

Bennett, J. T., and DiLorenzo, T. J. *Unfair Competition: The Profits of Nonprofits.* New York: Hamilton Press, 1989.

Berelson, B. *Graduate Education in the United States.* New York: McGraw-Hill, 1960.

Bielefeld, W. "Funding Uncertainty and Nonprofit Strategies in the 1980s." *Nonprofit Management & Leadership,* 1992, *2* (4), 381–401.

Bielefeld, W. "Care Givers in a Time of Change: Factors Affecting Nonprofit Mortality." In Spring Research Forum Working Papers, *Transmitting the Tradition of a Caring Society to Future Generations.* Washington, D.C.: Independent Sector, 1993.

Boris, E. T. "Creation and Growth: A Survey of Private Foundations." In T. Odendahl (ed.), *America's Wealthy and the Future of Foundations.* New York: Foundation Center, 1987.

Bowen, W. G. *The Economics of the Major Private Universities.* Berkeley, Calif.: Carnegie Commission on the Future of Higher Education, 1968.

Bowen, W. G. *Inside the Boardroom: Governance by Directors and Trustees.* New York: Wiley, 1994.

Bowen, W. G., and Breneman, D. W. "Student Aid: Price Discount or Educational Investment?" *Brookings Review,* 1993, *11* (1), 28–31.

Bowen, W. G., and Sosa, J. A. *Prospects for Faculty in the Arts and Sciences.* Princeton, N.J.: Princeton University Press, 1989.

Burke, C. B. *American Collegiate Populations: A Test of the Traditional View.* New York: New York University Press, 1982.

Carnegie Foundation for the Advancement of Teaching. *A Classification of Institutions of Higher Education.* (Rev. ed.) Princeton, N.J.: Carnegie Foundation for the Advancement of Teaching, 1987.

Carroll, G. R. "A Stochastic Model of Organizational Mortality: Review and Reanalysis." *Social Science Research,* 1983, *12* (4), 303–329.

Carroll, G. R. "Organizational Ecology." *Annual Review of Sociology,* 1984, *10,* 71–93.

Cowley, W. H., and Williams, D. *International and Historical Roots of American Higher Education.* New York: Garland Publishing, 1991.

Crowder, N. L., and Hodgkinson, V. A. *Academic Centers and Programs Focusing on the Study of Philanthropy, Voluntarism and Not-for-Profit Activity: A Progress Report.* (3rd ed.) Washington, D.C.: Independent Sector, 1993.

De Vita, C. J., and Salamon, L. M. "Commercial Activities in Human Service Organizations." In Spring Research Forum Working Papers, *The Constitution and the Independent Sector.* Washington, D.C.: Independent Sector, 1987.

Department of the Treasury. *Cumulative List of Organizations.* Washington, D.C.: U.S. Government Printing Office, 1992.

DiMaggio, P. J. *Nonprofit Enterprise in the Arts: Studies in Mission and Constraint.* New York: Oxford University Press, 1986.

Douglas, J. "Political Theories of Nonprofit Organization." In W. W. Powell (ed.), *The Nonprofit Sector: A Research Handbook.* New Haven, Conn.: Yale University Press, 1987.

Dun & Bradstreet. *Dun's Census of American Business.* New York: Dun & Bradstreet, 1991.

Edie, J. A. "Congress and Foundations: Historical Summary." In T. Odendahl (ed.), *America's Wealthy and the Future of Foundations.* New York: Foundation Center, 1987.

Ford Foundation. *Finances of the Performing Arts.* New York: Ford Foundation, 1974.

Ford Foundation. *Theater Reawakening: A Report on Ford Foundation Assistance to American Drama.* New York: Ford Foundation, 1977.

Ford Foundation. *Ford Foundation Support for the Arts in the United States.* New York: Ford Foundation, 1986.

Freedman, M. R. "The Elusive Promise of Management Cooperation in the Arts." In P. DiMaggio (ed.), *Nonprofit Enterprise in the Arts: Studies in Mission and Constraint.* N.Y.: Oxford University Press, 1986.

Furtaw, J. C. (ed.). *Hispanic Americans Information Directory.* (2nd ed.) Detroit: Gale Research, 1993.

Galaskiewicz, J. "A Community Institutional Response to a Crisis in Social Service Funding: The Twin Cities Case." In Spring Research Forum Working Papers, *The Constitution and the Independent Sector.* Washington, D.C.: Independent Sector, 1987.

Galaskiewicz, J., and Bielefeld, W. "Growth, Decline, and Organizational Strategies: A Panel Study of Nonprofit Organizations, 1980–1988." In Spring Research Forum Working Papers, *The Nonprofit Sector (NGO's) in the United States and Abroad: Cross-Cultural Perspectives.* Washington, D.C.: Independent Sector, 1990.

Garonzik, E. (ed.). *Guide to the Foundation Center's Grants Classification System.* New York: Foundation Center, 1991.

Gaul, G. M., and Borowski, N. A. "Warehouses of Wealth: The Tax-Free Economy." *Philadelphia Inquirer,* Apr. 18, 1993, p. 41.

Grønbjerg, K. A. "Developing a Universe of Nonprofit Organizations: Methodological Considerations." *Nonprofit and Voluntary Sector Quarterly,* 1989, *18* (1), 63–80.

Grønbjerg, K. A. "How Nonprofit Human Service Organizations Manage Their Funding Sources: Key Findings and Policy Implications." *Nonprofit Management & Leadership,* 1991, *2* (2), 159–175.

Grønbjerg, K. A. "The NTEE: Human Service and Regional Applications." Paper presented at the National Taxonomy of Exempt Entities Users Meeting, Washington, D.C., Oct. 22, 1992.

Grønbjerg, K. A. *Understanding Nonprofit Funding: Managing Revenues in Social Services and Community Development Organizations.* San Francisco, Calif.: Jossey-Bass, 1993.

Grossman, D. A., Salamon, L. M., and Altschuler, D. M. *The New York Nonprofit Sector in a Time of Government Retrenchment.* Washington, D.C.: Urban Institute Press, 1986.

Hall, P. D. "A Historical Overview of the Private Nonprofit Sector." In W. W. Powell (ed.), *The Nonprofit Sector: A Research Handbook.* New Haven, Conn.: Yale University Press, 1987.

Hannan, M. T., and Carroll, G. R. *Dynamics of Organizational Populations: Density Legitimation and Competition.* New York: Oxford University Press, 1992.

Hannan, M. T., and Freeman, J. "The Population Ecology of Organizations." *American Journal of Sociology*, 1977, *82* (5), 929–964.

Hannan, M. T., and Freeman, J. "The Ecology of Organizational Founding: American Labor Unions, 1836–1985." *American Journal of Sociology*, 1987, *92* (4), 910–943.

Hansmann, H. "The Role of the Nonprofit Enterprise." *Yale Law Journal*, 1980, *89* (5), 835–901.

Hansmann, H. "The Role of Nonprofit Enterprise." In S. Rose-Ackerman (ed.), *The Economics of Nonprofit Institutions: Studies in Structure and Policy.* New York: Oxford University Press, 1986.

Hansmann, H. "Economic Theories of Nonprofit Organization." In W. W. Powell (ed.), *The Nonprofit Sector: A Research Handbook.* New Haven, Conn.: Yale University Press, 1987.

Haycock, N. *The Nonprofit Sector in New York City.* New York: Nonprofit Coordinating Committee of New York, 1992.

Heilbrun, J., and Gray, C. M. *The Economics of Art and Culture.* Cambridge, England: Cambridge University Press, 1993.

Herrick, D., Leven, A. R., Remes, N. R., and Frey, N. E. *A Financial Survey of Nine Major Art Museums, 1991 Versus 1983.* Washington, D.C.: National Gallery of Art, 1992.

Hodgkinson, V. A., and Weitzman, M. S. *From Belief to Commitment: The Community Service Activities and Finances of Religious Congregations in the United States. 1993 Edition.* Washington, D.C.: Independent Sector, 1992.

Hodgkinson, V. A., Weitzman, M. S., Toppe, C. M., and Noga, S. M. *Nonprofit Almanac, 1992–93: Dimensions of the Independent Sector.* San Francisco, Calif.: Jossey-Bass, 1992.

Holland, B. "Survival of Symphonies: Radical Changes Urged." *New York Times,* June 19, 1993, pp. 11, 17.

Hopkins, B. R. *The Law of Tax-Exempt Organizations.* (5th ed.) New York: Wiley, 1987.

Internal Revenue Service. *Annual Report.* Publication 55. Washington, D.C.: Internal Revenue Service, 1991.

Karl, B. D., and Katz, S. N. "The American Private Philanthropic Foundation and the Public Sphere, 1890–1930." *Minerva*, 1981, *19* (2), 236–270.

Kendell, E. *Dancing: A Ford Foundation Report.* New York: Ford Foundation, 1983.

Kim, E. H. "Voluntary Liquidation." In P. Newman, M. Milgate, and J. Eatwell (eds.), *The New Palgrave Dictionary of Money and Finance.* Vol. 3. New York: Macmillan, 1992.

Kim, E. H., and Schatzberg, J. D. "Voluntary Corporate Liquidation." *Journal of Financial Economics*, 1987, *19* (2), 311–328.

Kimmelman, M. "A Museum Finds Its Time." *New York Times,* June 13, 1993a, Section 2, p. 1.

Kimmelman, M. "In Los Angeles, A Museum on a Roller Coaster." *New York Times,* Nov. 9, 1993b, pp. C17, C20.

Krashinsky, M. "Transaction Costs and a Theory of the Nonprofit Organization." In S. Rose-Ackerman (ed.), *The Economics of Nonprofit Institutions: Studies in Structure and Policy.* New York: Oxford University Press, 1986.

Levy, M. J., Jr. *Levy's Eleven Laws of the Disillusionment of the True Liberal.* Princeton, N.J.: M. J. Levy, Jr., 1981.

Liebschutz, S. F. "Coping by Nonprofit Organizations During the Reagan Years." *Nonprofit Management & Leadership,* 1992, *2* (4), 363–380.

Lifset, R. J. "Cash Cows and Sacred Cows: Commercial Activities in the Nonprofit Sector." In Spring Research Forum Working Papers, *Looking Forward to the Year 2000: Public Policy and Philanthropy.* Washington, D.C.: Independent Sector, 1988.

Lowry, W. M. (ed.). *The Performing Arts and American Society.* Englewood Cliffs, N.J.: Prentice-Hall, 1978.

McMurtry, S. L., Netting, F. E., and Kettner, P. M. "How Nonprofits Adapt to a Stringent Environment." *Nonprofit Management & Leadership,* 1991, *1* (3), 235–252.

McPherson, M. "An Ecology of Affiliation." *American Sociological Review,* 1983, *48* (4), 519–532.

Meeks, G. "Company Failure." In P. Newman, M. Milgate, and J. Eatwell (eds.), *The New Palgrave Dictionary of Money and Finance.* Vol. 1. New York: Macmillan, 1992.

Milofsky, C. "Neighborhood-Based Organizations: A Market Analogy." In W. W. Powell (ed.), *The Nonprofit Sector: A Research Handbook.* New Haven, Conn.: Yale University Press, 1987.

Moynihan, D. P. "Baumol's Disease." *New York State and the Federal Fisc,* 1993, *17,* entire volume.

Murphy, K., and Welch, F. "Wage Premiums for College Graduates: Recent Growth and Possible Explanations." *Educational Researcher,* 1989, *18* (4), 17–26.

National Endowment for the Arts. *The Arts in America.* Report to the President and to the Congress. Washington, D.C.: National Endowment for the Arts, 1988.

National Endowment for the Arts. *Annual Report.* Washington, D.C.: National Endowment for the Arts, 1992.

National Institute of Independent Colleges and Universities. *Openings, Closings, Mergers and Accreditation Status of Independent Colleges and Universities.* Washington, D.C.: National Institute of Independent Colleges and Universities, 1980, 1983, and 1984.

Nelson, R. L. "An Economic History of Large Foundations." In T. Odendahl (ed.), *America's Wealthy and the Future of Foundations.* New York: Foundation Center, 1987.

Odendahl, T. (ed.). *America's Wealthy and the Future of Foundations.* New York: Foundation Center, 1987a.

Odendahl, T. "Independent Foundations and Wealthy Donors: An Overview." In T. Odendahl (ed.), *America's Wealthy and the Future of Foundations.* New York: Foundation Center, 1987b.

Oleck, H. L. *Nonprofit Corporations, Organizations and Associations.* Englewood Cliffs, N.J.: Prentice-Hall, 1992.

O'Neill, J. P., and Barnett, S. *Colleges and Corporate Change: Merger, Bankruptcy, and Closure.* Princeton, N.J.: Conference-University Press, 1980.

O'Neill, M. *The Third America.* San Francisco, Calif.: Jossey-Bass, 1989.

Oster, S. M. "Nonprofit Organizations as Franchise Operations." *Nonprofit Management & Leadership,* 1992, *2* (3), 223–239.

Perry, M. (ed.). *Opera America Profile, 1991.* Washington, D.C.: Opera America, 1991.

Pfeffer, J. and Leong, A. "Resource Allocations in United Funds: Examination of Power and Dependence." *Social Forces,* 1977, *55* (3), 775–790.

Phillips, C., and Hogan, P. *A Culture at Risk: Who Cares for American Heritage?.* Nashville, Tenn.: American Association for State and Local History, 1984.

Provan, K. G., Beyer, J. M., and Kruytbosch, C. "Environmental Linkages and Power in Resource-Dependence Relations Between Organizations." *Administrative Science Quarterly,* 1980, *25* (2), 200–225.

Reiner, T. A. "Organizational Survival in an Environment of Austerity." *Nonprofit and Voluntary Sector Quarterly,* 1989, *18* (3), 211–221.

Renz, L. *Foundations Today: Current Facts & Figures on Private Foundations.* (7th ed.). New York: Foundation Center, 1990.

Renz, L. "Researching Foundations: What We Know and How We Find Out." *Nonprofit Management & Leadership,* 1991, *1* (3), 293–300.

Renz, L., and Lawrence, S. *Foundation Giving Yearbook of Facts and Figures on Private, Corporate and Community Foundations, 1992 Edition.* New York: Foundation Center, 1992.

Rockefeller Panel Report. *The Performing Arts: Problems and Prospects.* New York: McGraw-Hill, 1965.

Rodenhouse, M. P. (ed.). *The HEP 1992 Higher Education Directory.* Falls Church, Va.: Higher Education Publications, 1992.

Rudney, G. "Creation of Foundations and Their Wealth." In T. Odendahl (ed.), *America's Wealthy and the Future of Foundations.* New York: Foundation Center, 1987a.

Rudney, G. "The Scope and Dimensions of Nonprofit Activity." In W. W. Powell (ed.), *The Nonprofit Sector: A Research Handbook.* New Haven, Conn.: Yale University Press, 1987b.

Rudolph, F. *The American College and University: A History.* Athens: University of Georgia Press, 1990.

Salamon, L. M. "Partners in Public Service: The Scope and Theory of Government Nonprofit Relations." In W. W. Powell (ed.), *The Nonprofit Sector: A Research Handbook.* New Haven, Conn.: Yale University Press, 1987.

Salamon, L. M. *America's Nonprofit Sector: A Primer.* New York: Foundation Center, 1992.

Salamon, L. M., and Abramson, A. J.. *The Federal Budget and the Nonprofit Sector.* Washington, D.C.: Urban Institute Press, 1982.

Salamon, L., and Anheier, H. "In Search of the Nonprofit Sector II: The Problem of Classification." Unpublished paper, n.d.

Salamon, L. M., Musselwhite, J. C. and De Vita, C. J. "Partners in Public Service: Government and the Nonprofit Sector in the Welfare State." In Spring Research Forum Working Papers, *Philanthropy, Voluntary Action and the Public Good.* Washington, D.C.: Independent Sector, 1986.

Samuels, S. (ed.). *Theatre Profiles 10.* New York: Theatre Communications Group, 1992.

Samuelson, P. A. "The Pure Theory of Public Expenditure." *Review of Economics and Statistics,* Nov. 1954, pp. 387–389.

Sarnoff, A. T. (ed.). *Dance/USA Member Profiles, 1991–92.* Washington, D.C.: Dance/USA, 1991.

Schwarz, K. R. "The Crises of Tomorrow Are Here Today." *New York Times,* Oct. 31, 1993, pp. 31–32.

Shields, G. B., Dunn, K. C., and Stern, J. B. "The Dynamics of Leveraged Buy-Outs, Conversions and Corporate Reorganizations of Not-for-Profit Health Care Institutions." *Topics in Health Care Finance,* 1991, *8* (1), 5–20.

Simon, J. G. "The Tax Treatment of Nonprofit Organizations: A Review of Federal and State Policies." In W. W. Powell (ed.), *The Nonprofit Sector: A Research Handbook.* New Haven, Conn.: Yale University Press, 1987.

Simpson, S. D. *Tax-Exempt Organizations: Organization, Operation and Reporting Requirements.* Washington, D.C.: Tax Management, 1990.

Singer, M. I., and Yankey, J. A. "Organizational Metamorphosis: A Study of Eighteen Nonprofit Mergers, Acquisitions and Consolidations." *Nonprofit Management & Leadership,* 1991, *1* (4), 357–369.

Singh, J. V., Tucker, D. J., and House, R. J. "Organizational Legitimacy and the Liability of Newness." *Administrative Science Quarterly,* 1986, *31,* 171–193.

Smith, B. *The Use of Standard Industrial (SIC) Codes to Classify the Activities of Nonprofit, Tax-Exempt Organizations.* Working paper no. 19. San Francisco: Institute for Nonprofit Organization Management, University of San Francisco, Nov. 1992.

Soderlind. L. "Rapid Growth of Gay Groups Is Sign of Change." *New York Times,* Sept. 20, 1992, Section 13NJ, p. 1.

Stehle, V. "Symphonies Told to Change Ways or Run Risk of Financial Disaster." *Chronicle of Philanthropy,* June 29, 1993, p. 38.

Steinberg, R. "Nonprofit Organizations and the Market." In W. W. Powell (ed.), *The Nonprofit Sector: A Research Handbook.* New Haven, Conn.: Yale University Press, 1987.

Sterne, L. " 'Merger Mania' of Corporations Fails to Lure Tax-Exempt Groups." *Nonprofit Times,* Apr. 1989, pp. 1–18.

Stinchcombe, A. L. "Social Structure and Organizations." In J. G. March (ed.), *Handbook of Organizations.* Skokie, Ill.: Rand-McNally, 1965.

Sullivan, J., and Coleman, M. "Nonprofit Organizations, 1975–1978." In Statistics of Income Division, *Compendium of Studies of Tax-Exempt*

Organizations, 1974–87. Washington, D.C.: U.S. Government Printing Office, 1991.

Turner, S. E., Nygren, T. I., and Bowen, W. G. "The NTEE Classification System: Tests of Reliability/Validity in the Field of Higher Education." *Voluntas,* 1993, *4* (1), 73–94.

U.S. Bureau of the Census. *Statistical Abstract of the United States: 1992.* (112th ed.) Washington, D.C.: U.S. Government Printing Office, 1992.

U.S. Department of Education. *Digest of Education Statistics.* Washington, D.C.: U.S. Government Printing Office, 1991.

Veysey, L. R. *The Emergence of the American University.* Chicago: University of Chicago Press, 1965.

Weisbrod, B. A. *The Nonprofit Economy.* Cambridge, Mass.: Harvard University Press, 1988.

Wheeler, M. B. (ed.). *Directory of Historical Organizations in the United States and Canada.* (14th ed.) Nashville, Tenn.: American Association for State and Local History, 1990.

Whetten, D. A. "Organizational Growth and Decline Processes." *Annual Review of Sociology,* 1987, *13,* 335–358.

Winston, G. C. "The Capital Costs Conundrum: Why Are Capital Costs Ignored and What Are the Consequences?" *NACUBO Business Officer,* 1993, *26* (12), 22–27.

Wolf Organization, Inc. *The Financial Condition of Symphony Orchestras.* Parts I–III. Washington, D.C.: American Symphony Orchestra League, 1992.

Wolpert, J., and Reiner, T. "The Not-for-Profit Sector in Stable and Growing Metropolitan Regions." *Urban Affairs Quarterly,* 1985, *20* (4), 487–510.

Ylvisaker, P. N. "Foundations and Nonprofit Organizations." In W. W. Powell (ed.), *The Nonprofit Sector: A Research Handbook.* New Haven, Conn.: Yale University Press, 1987.

Young, D. R. "Local Autonomy in a Franchise Age: Structural Change in National Voluntary Associations." *Nonprofit and Voluntary Sector Quarterly,* 1989, *18* (2), 101–117.

INDEX